The Hollow Heart

Dublin-based ... turning to ... novels published since ... *... ...sen*, *Be Careful What You Wish For*, *Venus Reborn* and *Temptation*. More information is available on her website: www.martinadevlin.com.

The Hollow Heart

The true story of one woman's desire to give life and how it almost destroyed her own

MARTINA DEVLIN

PENGUIN
IRELAND

PENGUIN IRELAND

Published by the Penguin Group
Penguin Ireland, 25 St Stephen's Green, Dublin 2, Ireland
(a division of Penguin Books Ltd)
Penguin Books Ltd, 80 Strand, London WC2R ORL, England
Penguin Group (USA) Inc., 375 Hudson Street, New York, New York 10014, USA
Penguin Group (Australia), 250 Camberwell Road,
Camberwell, Victoria 3124, Australia (a division of Pearson Australia Group Pty Ltd)
Penguin Group (Canada), 90 Eglinton Avenue East, Suite 700, Toronto, Ontario, Canada M4P 2Y3
(a division of Pearson Penguin Canada Inc.)
Penguin Books India Pvt Ltd, 11 Community Centre,
Panchsheel Park, New Delhi – 110 017, India
Penguin Group (NZ), cnr Airborne and Rosedale Roads, Albany,
Auckland 1310, New Zealand (a division of Pearson New Zealand Ltd)
Penguin Books (South Africa) (Pty) Ltd, 24 Sturdee Avenue,
Rosebank, Johannesburg 2196, South Africa

Penguin Books Ltd, Registered Offices: 80 Strand, London WC2R ORL, England

www.penguin.com

First published 2005
1

Set in 12/14.75pt Monotype Bembo
Typeset by Palimpsest Book Production Limited, Polmont, Stirlingshire
Printed in Great Britain by Clays Ltd, St Ives plc

A CIP catalogue record for this book is available from the British Library

ISBN 1-844-88059-1

For my brothers: Frank, Niall, Cathal, Celsus and Conor Devlin. It was only as I wrote this that I grasped how lucky I am to have you all. You've stuck by me through thick and thin. A girl never had so many wonderful men in her life.

I have no child, I have nothing but a book.
  William Butler Yeats, 'Responsibilities'

Chapter 1

I waited for the thud of the front door closing on the floor below, my husband leaving for work. Now I was alone. Propped against pillows in bed, I bent my face towards my stomach and cupped my hands around it. I began to whisper.

'Stay with me . . . I need your help . . . you've got to cling to life, you have to want this too . . . just hold on there as tight as you can . . . I know it's hard, I know you're only tiny. But play your part now and we'll all have such a life together, I promise. A sunny, sunny life . . . I'll be the best mother in the world . . . I'll devote myself to you – day and night . . . you'll be everything in the world to me . . . But I can't do it without you . . . please, babies, please, stay with me . . . do it for me . . . Please.'

I was bargaining with my unborn children. Children who were no more than pinpricks of life, just a few cells – so rudimentary they were not even at the foetus stage yet. But who were real to me. They were my babies.

Three embryos had been returned to my body a few days previously, following a course of fertility treatment, and this was the crucial period during which they would seek to implant in my womb. I willed them to succeed, bathing them in love, pleading with them – as though it was a question of choice on their part whether to stay or go. Whether to opt for me as their mother. Or not.

Crouched within the nest of the duvet I stroked my stomach, convinced the rhythmic sweep of my palm would reassure the babies, imagining I was cradling their fragile heads. I crooned a lullaby to them I'd heard as a child, one my sister had sung to her son, too. A lullaby I believed I'd be humming to children wriggling and burping in my own arms soon.

> *Hush little baby, don't say a word,*
> *Papa's going to buy you a mocking bird,*
> *And if that mocking bird won't sing,*
> *Papa's going to buy you a diamond ring.*

As I murmured to my children I tried to envisage them growing inside me. I pictured them latching diminutive fingers and hooking minuscule toes onto the lining of my uterus. Limpets inside instead of outside the host hull of my body. I didn't see babies floating within amniotic fluid, tethered to an umbilical cord, as you do in ultrasound scans: I visualized them curling their bodies towards mine and fastening onto me. Hopelessly inaccurate biologically – giggles bubbled through me whenever I conjured up the image. Even now, I find myself smiling at my vision of Velcro babies.

It was five days after the embryo transfer stage of the *in vitro* fertilization procedure and I eased out of bed, moving tentatively to avoid jolting my body and dislodging the babies. I went to the window to stare at a tree we'd planted in our front garden the previous year. It was March and a suggestion of spring was visible on its branches. We'd chosen it to commemorate our unborn babies after the last failed attempt at *in vitro* fertilization, IVF. I'd lobbied for a cherry blossom tree – its ephemeral beauty mirroring, for me, the transient lives of those earlier embryos we had lost. Except they weren't embryos in my eyes, but babies waiting to be born. However my husband, Brendan, whose impulses were tidier than mine, had shuddered at the prospect of disorder from the blossom. 'One gust of wind and it's scattered everywhere,' he had protested.

We had settled on a miniature ornamental tree.

As I incubated this current cluster of embryos – the ones who were meant to survive – I wrapped a rug around my shoulders to study the stripling tree, its fingers waving in the breeze. It shored up my hopes. 'Life is meant to be perpetuated,' I told myself. 'Plant a tree in soil and it grows, never mind frost or wind or parasites. Human life is meant to survive too.' I watched the sapling, trance-like, until the cold prodded me back to bed.

When I'd warmed up I slid out from under the duvet again and sidled to the wardrobe, pulling out a bag tucked away at the back. It contained baby clothes I had bought clandestinely a few months earlier: an apricot sleep suit with a floppy-eared rabbit on the breast, a pair of embroidered dungarees, a mint green velour top with rainbow-striped sleeves. If I squeeze shut my eyes and concentrate, I can still feel the texture of the sleep suit between my fingers and hear the pop-pop-pop of its fastenings as they open.

Less frequently during those few days, a pleasure deferred, I had turned to a chest of drawers where, in the bottom one, mummified within layers of tissue paper and hidden beneath my T-shirts, was a damask satin christening robe edged with lace collar and cuffs. There was a matching ivory skull cap with a ribbon to draw under the chin and I visualized my child in it, sombre beneath the frill, like one of those ancient-eyed infants in a cracked oil painting. The petite perfection of this garment captivated me. I scarcely dared touch it: it was sufficient to gaze on its rippling folds and to imagine them filled with a flesh and blood baby. My baby.

Planning for our future as a family was a thrill; it generated an excitement I hadn't experienced since those years as a small girl on Christmas Eve, struggling to stay awake to catch Santa Claus in the act. I wanted to wrap my arms around my knees and draw them close to my diaphragm, hugging myself with joy. But I was loath to move an unnecessary muscle in case it harmed our embryos.

I whiled away hours musing over how the adjoining bedroom could be redecorated as a nursery. Anticipating a cot with at least one, maybe two, and even − did I tempt fate by hoping for such largesse? − three babies in it. I was unwilling to surrender even one of them. I debated the nursery's décor: a frieze of jungle animals around the dado rail, perhaps, and a rocking horse in the corner. I'd always had a fancy for a dappled grey wooden stallion, with a flyaway mane for dimpled fists to grip and a scarlet saddle for bouncing on. I had loved its twin during my first year at school, when it had waited for me on the fringes of the classroom until playtime was called.

So I lay there in our double bed, spinning my web, sketching a future crammed with children's birthday parties, trips to the pantomime, Irish dancing classes and bucket-and-spade holidays. Father, mother, babies. A family at last.

For fifteen days I fantasized as I rested in bed, trying to give my embryo-babies the best chance of life. The hospital had recommended two days, as a precaution, but I was determined to ease their path into the world by whichever means I could. If necessary, I'd gladly have spent nine months flat on my back memorizing every bump in the ceiling. Nothing seemed too steep a price to pay for motherhood. Put my life on hold? I had already been treading water for the past three years, another nine months would make no difference.

When Brendan would arrive home from work he'd perch beside me on the mattress and hold my hand. 'How are you feeling?' he'd ask, lantern-jawed with concern. I'd rally him, insisting everything was fine and we were going to be lucky this time. It was our turn to have a baby. Then he'd relax and we'd watch television, drinking tea and eating biscuits in an oasis of intimacy, the frustrations of the past months kept at bay. I was certain that our patience and perseverance would soon be rewarded – and Brendan's confidence was bolstered by mine. Soon our lives would be back on track.

I had already chosen three names for our babies. I had not discussed them with Brendan, not because I sought to exclude him, but because I knew he would be exasperated by such presumption. Certainly it was bold to the point of foolhardiness, naming children whose existence had not yet been confirmed by the thin blue stripe of a pregnancy test. But I could not afford to wait for them to push their way into the world. I named them right from conception, because names made real children of these three specks inside my body.

Finbarr, Rory and Molly.

Their sex had been determined, even at this early stage, and I guessed I was carrying two boys and a girl. Mother's intuition. There were extra names on standby – just in case mother's intuition proved wrong. I named my trio in the hope that my conviction would reinforce theirs. 'If you're named you must know you're wanted,' I reasoned, and no children could be wanted more than mine.

Names have always been important to me. As a child, I chose books where I liked the characters' names: tomboy Jo who resisted being a Josephine in *Little Women*; the exoticism of Pippi Longstocking; Just William's irritating neighbour Violet Elizabeth Bott, whom I always called Violent Elizabeth for the force of her tantrums. My three passengers would have to be introduced to Jo, Pippi and Violet Elizabeth.

I kept a book of children's names under my pillow, checking their connotations – the Fionn of Finbarr means blond, and I surmised that at least one of our boys would be fair since the colouring ran in my family. My father and two of my brothers were fair. Maybe Rory would have red hair and freckles like me. Perhaps Molly would be dark like her father – I hoped she'd have his smile too. I loved the way my husband's smile lit up his face. Sometimes I juggled the combinations in my parallel universe, beguiled by the permutations. Finbarr, Aidan and Molly, perhaps? But always I returned to Finbarr, Rory and Molly. Quite simply, those were the names that belonged to them.

I pressed my hands to my stomach and spoke to my passengers during those days while I waited for doctors to confirm their existence. For myself, I required no corroboration. I called my babies by name as I described to them how happy we would be together in this empty, echoing house that needed their scampering footsteps to awaken it.

This was a time of ripening contentment, despite the intensity of my craving. A period when I believed anything was possible. Daily life, stilled during these past three years when I had tried to become a mother, would thrum into activity again. I was convinced that the force of my longing for motherhood had finally surmounted every obstacle. Above all, it had prevailed over the most bewildering impediment: my infertility.

I wasn't nervous that I might miscarry, although in truth I should have been petrified. Already I had lost a total of seven embryos. But I locked away memory and its corollary, fear, and I concentrated – dear God, how fiercely I concentrated – on believing it would work this time. I was a seven-stone incubator of unequivocal certainty. In less than nine months I would be a mother. Every shred of willpower was trained on this result. I was suffused with blind faith, propelled by something I struggle to define. My absolute conviction was predicated on a visceral compulsion to reproduce – need, then, becoming the driving force.

Percolating through this tunnel vision was the Catholic ethos of my childhood, which promised recompense would follow suffering. Pain purified and prepared a person for reward, that's what I'd been taught. I seized on this theology, rationalizing that since I had withstood so much already, endured my purgatory, paradise must now be within my grasp. My babies would live because they had to live – because I had tolerated a barrage of disappointment to reach this stage. A positive result was as inevitable to me as the rising sun or the incoming tide.

As I lay in bed for a fortnight hatching my embryos, I refused to believe that fate could be so malevolent as to deny me even one of these babies from the ten I had carried. By this stage, my third IVF attempt in a year, I had driven my body to its limits. Perhaps even beyond. It wasn't just my body, subjected to a cocktail of drugs, that had been sacrificed. I had also forfeited control over my emotions, my mental health and my self-esteem to this yearning. To this baby hunger that burrowed into every cell of my body and wound its demands around every organ – my spleen, liver, kidneys. My hollow heart.

Our marriage, I knew, was becoming increasingly unstable, pummelled by the impact of successive IVF treatments – and by the demoralizing aftermath of failure. Assisted reproduction, as the medics refer to the *in vitro* fertilization process, is a cornucopia of possibilities. But it has a shadow side, too, and neither my husband nor I was prepared for it: for the blows to us as a couple, or to our perceptions of one another, which started to change, the further into this hopeful-fearful world we ventured.

As I rested in bed, however, our volatile arguments immediately prior to the treatment had receded from my memory. Stress had undermined the harmony between us, I told myself. I fooled myself that the children – for whom we had both been impatient from the start, and for whom we were by now desperate – would repair the frayed relationship. I believed this as fanatically as I believed I was born to be a mother. I believed because I wanted both to be true. Children would arrive and life would be restored to its pre-IVF harmony. Self-deception was an art I honed during these years.

I had been miserable for so long, awaiting the arrival of the children I craved, but during the incubator weeks, nurturing our embryos, I was happy again. I had forgotten what joy felt like, so enmeshed had I become in the mechanics of *in vitro* fertilization. The sense of relief at experiencing such an emotion again was rain on my parched soul. My body had betrayed me before, but I could forgive it now because it was finally about to fulfil its function.

Awash with hormones as a result of the fertility treatment, I even felt like an expectant mother. My breasts had swelled, the nipples darkened, and the area around my stomach was sensitive to the touch. I welcomed each twinge, every suggestion of nausea; I was impatient for morning sickness, for stretch marks, for back-ache.

I ate hardly anything during the day, apart from snacks Brendan left for me in the bedroom. I was wary of descending the two sets of stairs and tracking the length of the hallway to the kitchen at the back of our terraced house. I was even more hesitant to scale that Kilimanjaro of stairs again. I preferred to remain motionless. Who knew how the babies would react to being juggled around? It might dislodge their cautious hook-and-eye catch on my womb. Instead I used a kettle in the bedroom to make tea. Often the novel I was reading would slide from my hand, for my own fictional world, which I was busy refining, was more satisfying than any author's. 'Everybody well and happy? All my babies holding on tight?' I'd sing out, gently patting my stomach.

Molly would be the assertive one, keeping her unruly brothers in check. Finbarr would be the creative son and Rory the garrulous extrovert. Or maybe I had it totally wrong. It didn't matter – I was looking forward to making my children's acquaintance, whatever their traits.

I was never lonely – the babies were company enough.

Although I was contented within my cocoon, I suppose I was isolated. Perhaps that's why I wove my reverie in such detail. No family members lived nearby and, because I was recently returned to Ireland after more than a decade in England, I had few friends.

Sometimes my mother or sister would ring during the day for a chat, anxious that time might be passing slowly for me and causing me to mope. But there was never any drooping. I was growing more secure as each day passed, so confident that I'd plot dates with my sister Tonia, trying to guess the babies' star signs and their mannerisms. They'd be due towards the end of the year in November. 'Let's hope they're not Scorpio like me,' she'd joke. 'They'll have a sting in their tails. Try to have Libra children, even if they arrive a little early.' My mother was more prudent during her calls, or perhaps more superstitious, guarded against tempting fate. She'd check I was well and not too bored, and send her love.

★

Then came the evening when I walked to the bathroom, touching the landing walls for support. I was light-hearted, for as each day passed I had more reason to be optimistic. In another day I'd be returning to the fertility clinic to confirm what I already knew instinctively: I was pregnant. I wondered how long before they could detect the number of pulses beating inside me, still reluctant to surrender even one of our embryos. Two babies would be heavenly, but three would be more heavenly again. I dreamed extravagant dreams: three babies in my life.

Brendan was home from work and channel-hopping in the bedroom; the theme music from *Coronation Street* followed me along the landing. I set one cautious foot in front of the other, inching along, fearful of tripping. A circumspect shuffle had become second nature to me.

I reached the bathroom and sat down, distracted at realizing I'd missed a brother's birthday. I made a mental note to send him a belated card. Glancing casually into the porcelain below, I glimpsed a smear of blood in the bowl. I stared at it, willing it to be a trick of the light. The near-black blood gleamed against the white. Irrefutable. Yet I could not believe; I touched myself and held up my fingers to my eyes, so close they blurred. My fingertips were rosy.

After what seemed an eternity I stood, icy in my composure, although I needed to grip the wash-hand basin for support. I made certain to do it with my right hand. My left hand, the stained one, I extended at full-length from my body, its fingers splayed. Automatically I moved to pull the lever but could not bring myself to do it. I was not ready to flush away these almost-lives.

'Brendan,' I croaked, 'come quickly.'

His face appeared in the doorway, unsuspecting. I wondered at him that he did not realize, simply by looking at me, how our universe had tilted on its axis. But he seemed normal. I gazed at him helplessly and regretted the pain he was about to experience. Time seemed to come to a standstill, as I resisted seeing that untroubled expression crumple. As soon as I spoke Brendan would be overwhelmed by sorrow and I wanted to delay it – to allow him a few seconds more of our misplaced faith.

Then I stretched out my hand for him to see the smears of blood.

'I've lost them. Our babies are gone.'

Chapter 2

If anyone had asked me why I'd married Brendan I'd have answered simply, 'We fell in love, which was sensational, and then we realized we wanted to have children together, which was more sensational again.' So marriage seemed the natural course of action. In truth, however, I was preoccupied by the possibility of having children when I met Brendan. I had recently turned thirty and my sister, who lived nearby, had a baby I was besotted by. Justin had been born nine weeks prematurely and had spent his early life in special care in St Thomas's Hospital in London. Our terror that we might lose him made this small boy infinitely precious. He survived, we celebrated and my biological clock was ticking as loud as Big Ben when I met Brendan.

Part of my attraction to him had its origin in his candid admission, early on, that he wanted children. I wasn't accustomed to hearing this from men in the circles I moved among. None of my boyfriends had been marriageable. They were entertaining, winning, but decidedly not husband material at that stage in their lives. Subconsciously – or maybe not so subconsciously – I was looking for a husband and father for my children. I was a traditionalist at core, despite my career-girl pose, and aspired to the complete family package: mother, father, kids, dog, hamster, goldfish. Swing in the garden, bumble-bee wellies by the back door and tins of alphabet spaghetti in the kitchen cupboard. Children were the cornerstone on which we constructed our marriage.

★

I always believed in happy endings – they're facilitated by promising beginnings, of course, and I had one of those. A boy-meets-girl beginning. Ours was not such an unusual story. There was no thunderclap, at least not for me, but there was chemistry and liking that evolved into love. Brendan and I met in the early 1990s in London, where we both worked. I was a journalist with the Press Association, Britain's national news service, which also supplies Ireland. It bought a smaller company and moved the staff into our Fleet Street office. Brendan was one of those relocated employees.

We only spoke twice at work, the first time when he squeezed into the lift beside me just as it was closing and I asked him, 'Which floor?' He had one of those fresh-faced complexions you never notice living in Ireland, but which are conspicuous in London. Brendan heard my accent and inquired where I came from, as Irish people tend to do meeting one another in foreign countries.

'Omagh,' I replied. 'And you?'

'Belfast. Are you across from the Irish office for the day?'

'No, I work here.'

He looked confused and told me later he'd felt a shade foolish.

And that was nearly that. We didn't encounter one another again, working in different departments. Sometimes I saw him about the building and thought how solemn he looked. He seemed far from delirious to be working there, whereas I loved it at the Press Association; then again, I'd joined the company voluntarily, whereas he'd been shifted following a takeover.

A few months later he resigned to take up a new job. On his last day Brendan walked up to my computer terminal and invited me to his leaving do. That's when he spoke to me for the second time. I didn't even realize he knew my name, let alone where I sat. 'I'll show my face for half an hour,' I thought, 'just for some solidarity with another Irish person in London.' I knew hardly any Irish people in the city, for some strange reason, and wished it wasn't the case.

Nobody else from the newsroom was in the pub when I arrived, it was mainly friends of Brendan's from a previous job, and I didn't know why he'd asked me. I bought him a drink, made polite conversation and kept an eye on my watch for a moment when I could decently peel away. Brendan said he was going to Spain for a week's holiday – 'on my own', he added pointedly – before starting his new job. I finished my drink and, as I was scrolling through the 'good luck, hope it works out for you, must be going' spiel, he asked if he could ring me when he returned from Spain. 'Sure,' I shrugged, not bothered either way. 'You know the work number.'

He did ring a few days after he came back, and I remember thinking that was always the way of it. The girlie coterie and I agreed that men who didn't affect you were invariably the ones who called. We'd flutter our eyes heavenwards, imagining ourselves to be oh so urbane, and order another bottle of Chardonnay.

Brendan invited me to a friend's housewarming party the next Saturday night and, since I had nothing planned for the weekend, I agreed. We met in a pub first. He looked different in a bomber jacket instead of a suit. I registered quickly, with approval, that he seemed more relaxed – I felt there had always been an aura of tension about him in work. The date went well. Brendan was waiting near the door of the pub and spotted me as soon as I walked in. I appreciated that; I always felt awkward having to hunt through bars for the people you were supposed to meet.

We adjourned to the party and it was fun, crowded with

people laughing and dancing. They had filled the bath with ice and stacked the wine in it in an effort to keep the drinks cool. Easier said than done in London apartments in stifling summer heat. Brendan kissed me in the taxi on the way home. I giggled at that, because my mother had warned against the class of man who kisses a girl in the back of a cab. 'Times have changed,' I thought. I liked Brendan better than I had expected to: he was charming, interested in me and we had plenty to talk about. He made it abundantly clear that he found me absolutely gorgeous, which is irresistible to any woman (unless, I suppose, she knows she's gorgeous, in which case it doesn't flatter her the way it does the rest of us more ordinary souls).

'Pick a man and make it work,' my friends used to tell each other in London. We would sit in Covent Garden wine bars, all girls together, drinking Jacob's Creek back in the days when it was chic. 'You can't choose who to love but you can be selective about who to spend time with – on the off-chance you might fall in love,' we'd trill.

It sounds cynical – that's because it was cynical. But we believed we were being practical, not world-weary. We thought once you hit thirty, as we had or were about to, that a modicum of common sense should be deployed. Your twenties were for drunken pairings at parties, for unrequited passions and flaky relationships. All that should change on the cusp of the thirtysomething decade. Naturally we didn't heed our own advice. We continued to fall for pimpled youths without the price of a bottle of lager, let alone the champagne we aspired to cracking open; for Australian backpackers two days before they left for the Outback forever; for married men who told us they were separated from their Home Counties wives – without adding they were only separated during the week, but at weekends they caught the train to Mumbleby-under-the-Bridge, where their wives and offspring were parked.

I congratulated myself for missing those fates. I preened at my good fortune when I met Brendan: he was single, solvent and sane. The coterie's checklist – the Three S's – satisfied. It struck us that London wasn't over-endowed with such men. In addition, Brendan had recently emerged from a long-term relationship and I found that reassuring because it showed he could sustain one.

We single women in Covent Garden wine bars worried inordinately about 'men with baggage'. We accepted it was unrealistic not to have a man with some baggage, but we dreaded falling for one with excess stickers pasted all over him. The coterie spent hours debating baggage and its application to men. When we weren't deliberating over it we were reading magazine articles about it, or writing them ourselves, to put the fear of God in other women. We judged a man suspect without some history and its supplementary scar tissue. It meant either he had checked his past into a left luggage department temporarily, only to confront you with it as soon as you relaxed your guard. Or that there was something inherently suspect about him which had prevented him from committing to anyone before.

There we were, going on about men's baggage, when we had plenty of our own – mine was a previous marriage at a young age that had been annulled. It had ended amicably without undue trauma, but it meant that I didn't intend to exchange vows again without being absolutely certain I could keep them this time. I wanted marriage to be for ever.

Although I was still enjoying an independent life at this stage, when Brendan came along it was reassuring to have a steady boyfriend after some years on the London singles

scene – a take-no-prisoners landscape that could be enormous fun but was also daunting at times. You were always
encountering men, of all ages, professions and nationalities,
but how to separate the deserving few from the asylum
escapees, the dissemblers who'd hidden their wedding rings
and the criminals with a string of convictions? Meeting a
man from a place seventy miles away from where I grew up
seemed providential. Brendan represented a happy medium
between the metrosexual male and the mammy's boy, and
we discovered we had a certain amount in common. Fledgling
couples always seize on such factors, feeling reassured by their
common ground. Like when you were sixteen and thought
it must be love because you both loved Roxy Music. Or
Tutti Frutti ice cream. It's not so different, however many
years down the line you travel. So we ticked off our simi-
larities, Brendan and I, and interpreted them as validation
that we should be together. We had been through relationships of an equivalent length. Check. We each owned a flat
– or at least, were mortgaged to the hilt. Check. We had
comparable family background and sizes – I was one of seven,
Brendan was one of six. Check. His father came from the
same county as I did. Check. We had been in London for
an equivalent period. Bingo! The parallels hit critical mass.

I realized I'd fallen for Brendan shortly before our first
Christmas. We flew home to Ireland on the same flight and
then separated at the airport to spend the holidays with our
families. Frank, one of my brothers, was waiting to drive me
home to Omagh, while Brendan, who was going in the
opposite direction, went to a car hire desk to rent his trans-
port. My feet dragged as I walked away from him, and I kept
glancing back over my shoulder to where he queued. Much
as I was looking forward to seeing my family, I felt a pang
of loss. 'Look at me,' I willed Brendan, wretched at the idea

of parting from him. Just as I reached the exit Brendan turned and waved, breaking into that huge upturned smile of his, and I felt them for the first time in this relationship: butterflies in the pit of my stomach. I was in love.

He was on my mind constantly over the Christmas period and we spoke regularly on the phone. I missed Brendan so much that I didn't mind returning to London for New Year, as I usually would, because I knew he'd be there too. There was an added bonus to my feelings for Brendan. I felt fortunate to fall for a man with whom I shared common values; that's why we believed it could succeed between us. It's comforting to be with someone from an analogous background to yourself, after a decade or so away from home. It returned me to that sense of belonging I had lost, during those years in London, and that I now missed. Incrementally, I had become uneasy at how readily I was integrating into London life. Smoothing over my accent, banishing my colloquialisms, changing the subject if the North of Ireland was raised. Doing what I had to do to fit in. I recognized, with dismay, that I would be neither English nor Irish if I stayed, but a hybrid. In a few years it would reach the stage where I would be a tourist in my homeland. I had always intended to return to Ireland one day, but weeks had turned into months and then years and here I still was, making London and its concerns the hub of my universe.

I was aware of having a sense of dislocation in London. In my twenties I had revelled in its internationalism, its anonymity, its non-judgemental amorality, its willingness to welcome the stranger. Above all it represented freedom. But around this time I began to feel a chafing. I was heart-sore for greenery; not the cultivated restriction of a park, although I had a fondness for Kensington Gardens with its Peter Pan statue, but something altogether more untamed. I wanted to stare into the sky and absorb, not telegraph wires or the tops of vertiginous buildings, but blue stretching above and beyond me. I wanted pedestrians to meet my eye, to wonder, 'Do I know her? Did I go to school with her? Is she my cousin's friend?' as everyone does in Ireland – instead of looking through me. I thought it was high time I stopped looking through people too.

I wanted to stop sprinting for the Tube, squeezing my body into a rectangle of space too tiny and airless to accommodate it rather than wait a few minutes for the next train. To stop carrying a briefcase as though it were a shield. To stop dressing in a uniform of expensive, anodyne, Identikit clothes in the belief they lent me status. I wanted to connect with my environment again. Quite simply, I was homesick and longed to return to Ireland. In a novel I wrote that 'a man carries his homeland inside his heart'; but if he is able to live there too, so much the better for him. 'Dublin,' I thought, 'that's the place to live.'

The Celtic Tiger was rumbling up to a roar then, but I wasn't familiar with the Irish capital in that incarnation. My memories of Dublin were of a slightly seedy, charming Georgian city. I didn't know if I'd be able to find a job there, but I did believe I could locate a satisfying life.

I spoke about this to Brendan in the early days. Until then he had felt no urge to return to Ireland and was fulfilled by the London life that offered a kaleidoscope of temptations for single people. However he empathized with my need to be among my own again. And gradually he began to share my longing to go home – I infected him with the desire to be Irish again, not London-Irish as he described himself to me at that time, to my amazement. (If one good thing for Brendan came from our marriage, then I count it as that.)

Among our first dates in those early days of interviewing

one another, however discreetly, was a trip to Highgate Cemetery to see Karl Marx's tomb. Afterwards we had coffee and cake in one of those open-air cafes you find in English parks, where the tea ladies are wonderfully engaging Joyce Grenfell clones – they always made me wonder if I'd washed behind my ears – giving their services voluntarily to finance the upkeep of amenities. I meditated on how I liked having a boyfriend who was willing to humour me by taking me to a graveyard on a date. Someone who knew what I meant when I spoke of barm brack or a Sheela na Gig or the Stations of the Cross. Of shivering on Donegal beaches at the arc of the summer, Aran cardigan over your swimsuit but whipped off for the photographs. Of seeing boy-soldiers with rifles, their camouflage bizarre in a suburban street, walk edgily past your front garden.

I told him something I had never been able to tell an English person. A few years earlier, I said, I had been home for Christmas. On that overcast 25 December morning I stood at our kitchen window with a mirror in my hand, trying to borrow enough light to apply my lipstick, when a column of those glum boy-soldiers clutching their weapons to their chests passed by. They were wearing black paint on their faces and had twigs jutting at right angles from their helmets. I looked out over our low front hedge and caught the eye of a teenager from Hull or Liverpool or Sunderland, or whichever unemployment black spot they recruit these eighteen-year-olds from. Then I did something I'd never done to a British soldier before, child of the Troubles that I was. Instead of looking away, or looking through him, I saw a person there and smiled at him. Directly into his face. I mouthed the words 'Merry Christmas'. He didn't respond, except that he stumbled before regaining the momentum of his stride. Moments later my sister, Tonia, wandered into the kitchen. 'The strangest thing just happened,' she remarked. 'I was at the sitting room window and I saw a line of British soldiers. They all looked twitchy and uptight, the way they usually do. But one of them was grinning so hard you'd think his ears were going to drop off. I've never seen one of them do that before on patrol.'

People share episodes from their past to bond. To surreptitiously check, too, the listener's reaction to their story. Brendan's response was always exactly what I could have hoped: he grasped the nuances, the references, the emotions. We felt comfortable together. Comfort should never be underestimated in a relationship. It may not be gaudy enough to bring together a man and a woman, but it has the capacity to solder them into coupledom. I welcomed that feeling of ease with Brendan. It wasn't fireworks and shooting stars, it was a sense of cosiness with another human being.

Brendan fell in love with me more rapidly than I did with him: his eyes grew lambent when he saw me, his face relaxed into a smile. The more he loved me, the more I warmed to him. 'This is what I want,' I told myself. 'I want a man who's smitten by me.' I assumed it meant his love for me would always be as unconditional as it was then, in the first flush.

While it was fantastic having a boyfriend who cared about me and showed it – because boyfriends who did neither weren't as rare as you might hope – there was something more that I wanted from a relationship at this stage. It was a quality I perceived in Brendan and it was this, above all, that was persuasive: I believed that he would be a good father.

For some time I had been thinking about having children. I had always accepted that I wanted them in my life, but the time hadn't been right before. Furthermore, I needed to be certain that the man I had them with was the best possible father I could find for my children, not in material terms but in his capacity to reflect the loving environment I had been raised in. So I brought Brendan to Bromley, just outside London, where my sister lived with her husband, Tom, and son, Justin. It was my acid test, introducing boyfriends to my little nephew. Brendan hit it off with Justin immediately. Watching him play with my godson, I felt that I was right to love him – men who have a rapport with children are always beguiling. I imagined that interest in a girlfriend's nephew translated into a father's love for his own child, and was suffused with anticipation. Plus he was unfazed by meeting my family. English boyfriends always felt threatened by close family encounters, as if I was indicating a proposal of marriage should be immediately forthcoming. In Ireland, meeting relatives is quite natural and happens much sooner in a relationship.

Our courtship no longer had the meandering quality of our early months, for now we both realized intuitively that we were eager for more. Against that backdrop, we booked a trip to Prague during the week that wrapped itself around Valentine's Day 1994, less than a year after we had started going out.

I suspected that Brendan intended to propose to me in Prague. Women can generally sense when there's a proposal in the air and Brendan had dropped hints since Christmas. I'd had time to reflect on whether I was willing to marry him. I thought about it very carefully because I really wanted to get it right second time round. I loved him, but Brendan's affinity with children was the clincher, as was his open admission that he wanted to be a father. 'Yes,' I decided at Heathrow, boarding that plane for Prague, 'if he asks me to marry him, I'll say yes.' And this time I would understand the implications of what I was doing.

Brendan had an idiosyncrasy regarding holidays: he was always reluctant to reserve a place to stay in advance. It was too structured, he used to say. On the other hand I preferred to be sure of my bed before I ventured into foreign parts, at least for the first few days. I was invariably filled with trepidation that we wouldn't find anywhere to stay, and felt it was profligate to spend several hours of an all-too-brief holiday tramping unfamiliar streets in search of hotels with vacancies. It was to be the subject of friction between us later, but at that stage I was sensitive to the charge of lacking spontaneity. So when Brendan seemed insistent that we defer booking accommodation on our Valentine's break in Prague, I agreed.

It was a mistake. At the airport a babushka on commission persuaded us to rent a room plus bathroom in a private house, instead of checking into a hotel. While it was central, just off Wencelas Square, the room was cold and comfortless. There wasn't even a kettle, let alone a television set, and the bathroom was spartan. As for room service – we could forget about that. We had little option but to hit the streets as soon as we woke up, and in February those streets were arctic. Coffee shops in which to while away the time, as you do on weekend breaks, were rare, and we had to seek refuge in bars. We kept our coats on in some establishments, so frozen were we. It was a drunken break, in a fraught as opposed to a joyously raucous sense, not least because I was vegetarian and there were no meat-free meals to be found so I was permanently hungry.

We booked a Valentine's Day dinner in the city's smartest restaurant, decorated by the artist Gustav Klimt. Brendan took some trouble to make the reservation a day or two in advance intending it to be the scene of his proposal. Impulsively, however, he popped the question in a bleak Icelandic fish restaurant the night before Valentine's Day, as we drank cavity-rotting Georgian champagne and shivered in our coats and scarves. I remember I was only persuaded to take off my gloves when I realized I couldn't grip my glass wearing them. We had been trying to find a restaurant recommended in our guidebook but had abandoned the search, numbed by the weather conditions, and had stumbled into the nearest one. It was anything but romantic – harsh lighting, limited menu, surly waitress – but I think Brendan was too nervous to wait any longer. He was sitting opposite me in a booth when he asked me to become his wife, stumbling in his eagerness to get out the question ('There's something I've been meaning to ask you . . .'). I no longer noticed my surroundings: a wave of joy surged up inside me and I said yes without a moment's hesitation. I reached a hand across the table to link it with his and we grinned at each other, overwhelmed. Just then the waitress arrived to take our order for food but we sent her away, incapable of thinking about something so pedestrian when we had a glittering future to plan. We clinked glasses, toasting our dazzling prospects, and ordered a second bottle of champagne.

Waking the next morning, I was thrilled to realize we were really engaged and I hadn't dreamed it all. There was a tiny niggle that it had happened in such a bizarre setting – an Icelandic fish restaurant isn't a Mecca for romantics, and for good reason. To be honest I hankered after something a touch more romantic. A ring secreted among the after-dinner mints, say – that had happened to one of the Covent Garden friends – or musicians serenading us while Brendan sank onto one knee and embarrassed himself in public, as a colleague had described doing a few months earlier. But Brendan wasn't the type for elaborate amorous gestures, I scolded myself, and I loved him the way he was.

We dressed and went shopping, and my new fiancé bought me a magnificent present to celebrate our engagement. We found her in an antique shop: an art nouveau table centre-piece depicting a slender lady with one arm extended, Statue of Liberty-style. I have her still, although she broke soon after we returned home. She's in two pieces and I can't bring myself to part with her. Every once in a while I try to wheedle a jeweller into repairing her, but it seems she's beyond it. Now there's a symbol.

We got married just over six months later, at the beginning of September 1994. The setting was the seaside village of Mullaghmore in Sligo, where my family had been regular visitors for years. I had always thought it would make an idyllic setting for a wedding and I was right. The only hitch was down to me, for I was twenty minutes late arriving at the church, partly because we had been delayed by check-points crossing the border from the North of Ireland into the Republic. I felt guilty about the delay in case Brendan had been anxious. But he turned and smiled at me from the top of the aisle as I arrived on my father's arm, and he looked so proud and delighted that I felt a great whoosh of home-coming and thought, 'Everything is going to be fine.'

I carried a bouquet of lilies as I walked along the strand road to the little church, in a simple ivory silk dress made for me by a dressmaker in my home town of Omagh – there was only time for one fitting – with a coronet of flowers in my hair. My twin nieces, soon to celebrate their sixth birthday, were flower girls so sweet that people smiled instinctively when they saw them, while my sister Tonia was bridesmaid and Justin was ring-bearer. 'Tom Thumb,' one of the guests dubbed him, in his scaled-down morning suit. He toddled up the aisle of the Stella Maris church ahead of me, well-rehearsed by Tom, his father. Family and friends from England, Ireland and Germany congregated in Mullaghmore for our wedding day, but I only had eyes for Brendan. I floated on a ripple of happiness and wanted that day never to end.

We had not just organized a wedding in Ireland, we had devised a fabulous plan for a new life back home too. The Irish economy's tiger momentum meant that ours was the first generation of emigrants able to return. There were jobs to be found, at least in Dublin, and we thought it a gentler place to raise a family than London. We reasoned we'd be able to buy a house somewhere central in the Irish capital, whereas in England we'd need to commute to work. The new Mr and Mrs were ready to go home.

I'd picked a man, and now I'd make it work. Wasn't I ultra-modern? Wouldn't my Chardonnay-drinking girlfriends cheer? That's exactly what they did. They toasted my good fortune and we all laughed and hugged one another as we celebrated. To Life. To Love. To Babies.

Chapter 3

Almost as soon as we returned to London from our honey-moon in Venezuela and Ecuador at the end of September, Brendan prepared to move to Dublin. He had been job-hunting and was due to take up a new post in the New Year, which meant we could only see each other at weekends. I would join him in the summer when I'd finished an English Literature degree I was studying for in my spare time at Birkbeck College, part of the University of London. This was my final year and I had exams in June. Meanwhile, from our wedding night onwards, we were hoping for a baby. It couldn't happen too soon for me. And there was something wonder-fully liberating about no longer needing to bother with contraception. We started married life on a high note, despite the drawback that soon we would be separated during the week.

When we snuggled up and speculated about our hopes for the future, as couples like to do, children were always an integral part of it. We talked about them on honeymoon in South America, fantasizing about how perfect it would be if I became pregnant there; we talked about them during our few months together in London before Brendan started his new job; we talked about them when he joined me in our flat at weekends, after his working week in Dublin; or when I flew to Ireland to his eyrie at the top of a lanky Georgian house in Fitzwilliam Square. Babies were the focal point of this life together we were planning. We discussed them as if they were inevitable. We imagined you could no more hold at bay the seasons than you could defer the arrival of our first baby, now that we had abandoned contraception. It was only a matter of time.

It was a little lonely at times in London on my own – and Brendan was lonely too in Dublin, trying to settle into a new city and a new job. It was a time of protracted phone calls and quiet nights in on our own for both of us. I didn't want to return to the old Covent Garden haunts with my girlfriends; they had been part of my single life, and yet married life was in a vacuum because of our separation. But it was only temporary so we could manage. Brendan and I lived for the weekend when we could be together. I'd watch the clock on a Friday night for his arrival, sprinting to the hall when I heard his key in the lock. And he always looked so thrilled when he saw me step through the Arrivals door at Dublin Airport.

During my weekends in Dublin we house-hunted, poring over a map to crisscross the city as we searched for a permanent address. We didn't mind where we lived as long as it was a spacious home – one that we could fill with children.

Our babies were taking their time about joining us, however. Instinct whispered to me that something was wrong after six months and not so much as an excitingly late period – just a delay of a few days, at best. I made an appointment to see my GP in London. He told me that we'd have to wait a year before tests could be authorized. I fretted, feeling time drift away, but already in this first encounter with the medical profession there was a sense of inflexible rules.

I wasn't really worried, though. I understood a woman's fertility levels dwindled once she was no longer seventeen and fighting off her unbridled boyfriend in the back of a borrowed Ford Capri. My thirties still had a long way to run and there was plenty of time.

I reassured myself that Brendan and I had been through a testing interlude. We'd organized a wedding in Ireland, not the easiest of undertakings from a distance, then he'd moved to Dublin on his own. We were rushing around house-hunting, both of us working full time, and I was studying at night. We all have a habit of doing that, don't we? Imagining we've been oppressed by a multiplicity of burdens when we've had it relatively straightforward. So I reassured myself that our babies would make their entrance when there weren't so many demands on our time. Perhaps when I joined Brendan in Ireland.

Still, doubts started to niggle about our unscientific policy of trusting romance to conjure up an infant. I hunted the sitting room shelves for advice from my *Everywoman* book. A chapter titled 'The Infertile Marriage' leapt out at me. Author Derek Llewellyn-Jones noted the paradox whereby, in a world facing a population explosion – it's estimated there will be nine billion of us on the planet by 2050 – a group of 'quite desperate women' were seeking to become pregnant. I didn't like the sound of that. Surely I wasn't part of that band? The book advised that if a couple were normally fertile and had a reasonably regular sex life, pregnancy would occur within a year in nine cases out of ten. There! It had only been six months – I was over-anxious. Part of the imme-diate gratification generation.

So I waited a bit longer.

Nevertheless, as six months became seven, it puzzled us that our life wasn't slotting into the grooves we'd notched for it, drawing up our grand scheme for the future. Brendan and I were a healthy young couple who didn't appear able to have children as readily as we'd expected. We looked at one another and felt there had to be some mistake. Come on, we were tailor-made for parenthood. We'd done everything right, we'd even waited until we were married, for goodness' sake. It had to be time for Mother Nature to play her part now. Frankly, her dilatory approach was causing us undercurrents of concern. Mild, admittedly, but they trembled in the background. We talked it over and rationalized our lack of success as the result of stress brought on by the physical distance between us.

Seven months married and counting. Eight months married and counting. Surely we weren't going to be that one-in-ten couple Dr Llewellyn-Jones had referred to in his gynaecological guide? 'If we weren't husband and wife and watching through binoculars for the stork, there'd have been none of these delays,' we told each other, a fraction bitterly, but prepared to chalk it up to experience as soon as our hopes were fulfilled. But making love was starting to become 'trying for a baby'. How I loathe that phrase. As far as we were concerned we weren't trying, because that implied the possibility of failure. For us, this was parenthood postponed – not parenthood denied. It never occurred to either of us to feel fear. Impatience and occasional spasms of bewilderment summed up our attitude.

Back I went to *Everywoman*, where I was confronted by one of those ironies that life, just to be mischievous, lobs your way from time to time. Out from between its pages fluttered a couple of photocopied sheets about birth control. I must have been checking some alternatives to oral contraceptives at one stage, when I would not have welcomed pregnancy with open arms. What a difference a few years make. I rammed them back into the book and read up about ovulation. I was now paying scrupulous attention to information I had learned and discarded as a fourteen-year-old cramming for a biology test. For the first time I noted my period dates, marking them in my diary for reference – just to check I was as regular as

I'd always assumed. Periods you could set your clock by meant you were fertile, didn't they?

Other facets of our life vied for attention. By now we had isolated Ranelagh as the first-preference area in which we'd like to live. Close to the city centre, it reminded us of Islington with its cafés and somewhat bohemian aspect. It contained row upon row of large Victorian terraced redbricks, often with sizeable back gardens, and, although prices were creeping upwards, we hoped we might find a place in need of renovation at a price we could afford. There were still some down-at-heel houses, remnants of the student bedsit blight that had stripped Ranelagh of its cachet in preceding decades.

By July 1995 we managed to scrape together the money to buy a house that had been converted into flats. It conveyed the impression of a warren of bedsits rather than a home, with its four bathrooms, one for each bedroom – a maze of plumbing begging to be ripped out. The bedrooms were decorated with high-gloss vinyl bathroom wallpaper that had us howling with amusement. Other people's taste is always good for a laugh.

The property was sparse on period features, unfortunately, for they had been stripped away, but there were lofty ceilings, airy rooms and a fanlight above the front door. It had not been loved for years and had a neglected air. We even stumbled over a wasps' nest in the jungle of our back garden and had to track down a beekeeper in the Golden Pages to remove it. But Brendan and I believed we could nurse that redbrick terrace house back to life. Love could restore it. It had to be love because we had no money after agreeing to the purchase price.

After signing the papers, I rented out my flat to a Russian businessman and moved to Dublin to join Brendan. Despite my misgivings that I still wasn't pregnant, we had plenty to celebrate. Not only had we found a new home, I had been offered a place on a postgraduate degree course at Trinity College Dublin. The Master's degree in Anglo-Irish Literature lasted a year, starting in October, and I was keen to claw back that year from the workplace and pursue some full-time studying. Learning for its own sake: how decadent. Naturally we talked about whether we could afford to manage on one salary for a year. Fortunately I had savings that would pay for my university fees and cover my contribution to the house deposit, so taking a year out from the workplace wasn't going to stretch us too much.

Financially it would have been more sensible for me to stay in London on a salary until October, but we were newly-weds and had already spent six months apart. That wasn't going to help me get pregnant. In addition, by going to Dublin early I could make a start on my Trinity reading list. Just in case the swollen stomach I'd be hauling with me to classes in the later terms eroded my concentration.

'I'm only doing this to get a bust,' I joked with my sister on the phone. Though it was ten months on, I was still upbeat about my pregnancy chances. 'I want a cleavage for once in my life.'

'You get a belly to match the chest,' Tonia replied. 'Nature gives with one hand and takes with the other.'

'I'll risk it,' I laughed, wondering how I'd look when I was pregnant – short and squat, I decided. 'Save your maternity T-shirt for me, the one with Let Me Out doodled across it,' I told her, for Tonia was notorious for clear-outs. 'And the maternity nightdress with the lace collar that I bought you in America.'

My body was guaranteed to conceive, I was convinced of it – if not this month, then surely next. I used to scan articles on pregnancy, preparing myself for my own. Nausea, stretch marks, swollen ankles, insomnia. 'Ready when you are,' I thought. 'Can't scare me.' I'd digest the articles in bed, pillows piled against the headboard, imagining myself with a bump that needed pillows of its own. Every time I felt remotely queasy in the morning, hope flared. Morning sickness? It was a daft assumption for someone still getting periods. But I had heard stories about women unaware they were pregnant for months because they continued to bleed.

One day I found I couldn't face my customary mug of coffee for breakfast, and thundered upstairs for the magazine article beside my bed. 'Morning sickness causes aversion to certain foods,' I read, 'most commonly those containing toxins likely to harm the baby such as meat, fish, eggs and coffee.' Hurrah! I abandoned breakfast and raced off to buy yet another pregnancy tester kit. Its result was unambiguous: I wasn't pregnant, my body simply didn't fancy coffee that day. But I had semaphored that into a message from my womb. In less single-minded moments, my capacity for self-delusion astonished me.

As time wore on and still I hadn't conceived, I started to stare at pregnant women in the street; how I viewed them changed erratically from day to day. Sometimes they looked smug to me, preening themselves, their skin and hair sumptuous. 'See how our bodies are fulfilling their function?' their bloated bellies seemed to suggest. At other times they looked like members of an exclusive club to which I'd be admitted if I could only guess the password. On more optimistic days, they were a fecund sisterhood willing me to join them, showing me how easy it was. 'Come on, if we can manage it so can you.'

I noticed how they habitually connected with one another, pregnant woman nodding to pregnant woman on the bus, their eyes drifting downwards to assess the other's bulge. It struck me how self-contained these mothers-in-waiting were, as they focused on their bodies. Sometimes I fancied they had one ear permanently cocked towards their middles, communing with their unborn babies. I'd see them resting a hand on their stomachs and couldn't gauge the attitude. Proprietorial? Reassuring? Or was it simply an unconscious gesture, the bump transformed into a handy shelf? I missed stops on the bus, lost my place in queues, daydreamed time away watching pregnant women. I eavesdropped on them discussing their aches and pains, envious of every twinge.

'I don't know why they call it morning sickness, I feel nauseous all day long,' was a typical comment. Or 'I can't fit into any of my shoes, my ankles are so swollen.'

'Lucky you,' I'd think. 'You have nothing to complain about, nothing at all.'

Little by little I grew introverted, wary of sharing these feelings with my husband. I'd mentioned them once or twice but he'd told me to stop torturing myself watching pregnant women. Except I didn't want to call a halt. Even though it pained me, it was something I needed to do. Like jabbing at a wobbly tooth with your tongue, loosening it from its moorings.

The longer we waited, the more perplexed I grew. Brendan and I had successfully negotiated a number of hurdles in forging this new life together. Finding a decent job for him and a home for both of us in Dublin had appeared greater challenges but they had been handled with relative ease, and yet here was a snag we hadn't anticipated. Having a baby should be the easy part. But it wasn't happening. The possibility that I might have difficulties conceiving didn't confront us, not yet; it simply insinuated itself into our consciousness and wavered there – now you see me, now you don't – as a vague possibility.

Another month passed, another unwelcome period arrived to remind me of our thwarted plans, and I waxed covetous in the company of mothers – especially of babies. My response to babies was atavistic. Their little hands, in particular, unravelled me, starfish-like, dimpled and fleshy, waving in the air to a choreography uniquely their own. Encased in mittens, they still stirred me. Or even the mittens alone, because they conjured up an image of those fluttering, unco-ordinated hands.

During that first year there were so many false alarms – every time my period was overdue, hope whirred inside me. One day late and I was weighing up possible names. Two days late and I was ready to shop for maternity clothes. Three days late and I was testing prams and sizing up cots. Four days late and the godparents had been chosen. Five days late and I started wondering if our garden was child-safe.

But my period always arrived, bringing disappointment as well as cramps. And as I pressed a hot water bottle to my stomach, I pushed down my vexation that life was declining to follow the route we had plotted out for it.

I grew familiar with a bitter-sweet sensation of longing. But I also kicked against this craving that threatened to colonize my life. Most days, I hankered after a child nuzzling its face into the nook between my shoulder and neck. But a contradictory desire clutched at me, occasionally, towards the end of that first year: a yen so acute, it was akin to grief, for my single days. That carefree earlier time when men were temporary arrangements, not husbands who would shortly be home expecting cooking smells. And when babies were something to which the St Augustine approach applied: one day, but not yet. Motherhood was proving more difficult to achieve than I could possibly have imagined and I couldn't understand it. I couldn't control it. In truth, I could scarcely bear it.

I was shocked by how rapidly the yearning had infiltrated my life. But it couldn't be shrugged off; it was always on my mind. I should have negotiated a discount from Boots for the succession of pregnancy test kits I bought. All predicting the wrong result. You'd think they'd get it right eventually. Were they dense, or what? Come on, it couldn't be all that hard to show a thin blue line. I grew jaded at failing. It was a relatively novel experience for me and I disliked it.

Every period was a reminder of how my body was refusing to cooperate. I reflected on a decade of more or less permanent birth control in my twenties. Had it been unnecessary? I shuddered; this wasn't an issue I was ready to address.

Each month I trailed out to buy tampons, stockpiling none, convinced that pregnancy was a matter of a few weeks away. I resented handing over the money to pay for them; I wanted to buy anti-stretch mark cream instead for an expanding body.

I could hold off menstruation for a day or two, wishful thinking or sheer determination tricking my body into suspension, but sooner or later the blood trickled out. It left a stale smell, as though penned up too long in my body. God-oh-God-oh-God, how many more periods would I have to endure? Did some women refer euphemistically to a period as their friend? As far as I was concerned, periods were a nuisance at the best of times, but right now they were public enemy number one.

I would knead my hands against the slight mound of my stomach and wonder, every month, if a second heart was beating its metronome rhythm inside me. I thought intuition alone could alert me that this would be the month, but I never knew. Not until my body's discharges sent me the answer I didn't want.

Not this month.

★

I rang my doctor in London shortly after I moved to Dublin, just to check that I really needed to sit out that year. It was now ten months, after all. For a woman who expected to fall pregnant on her honeymoon, who had started to count months in dog years, this was akin to waiting decades. The doctor was placid. Exasperatingly so. 'Relax,' he advised. 'Let nature take its course.' If that was the best advice he could offer me, I was going to take his number off speed dial. I don't suppose he cared.

Everyone constantly tells you the failsafe way to conceive is to relax and stop thinking about it. Easy for them. Believe me, you can't think about anything else. Medics have a penchant for instructing patients to relax, especially if the unfortunate is naked from the waist down, or exposed and vulnerable in some equally ludicrous position. It's patronizing, this exhortation to relax. It may well be sound advice, but it's inherently impossible to comply with. Just hearing it is enough to make anyone uptight. Besides, it clearly needed more than relaxation to get me pregnant.

Any maturity I might have acquired melted away. As each month passed without the longed-for result, I descended into petulance. 'It's not fair,' I wailed. And neither was it.

I was lulled into a false complacency that life might be fair, because until then mine had been relatively untroubled. It had smiled on me, if I was honest with myself. So yes, some setbacks were inevitable. But there'd be a happy outcome after I'd survived adversity and shown myself worthy, wouldn't there? Wouldn't there . . . ?

Meanwhile there was an Everest of work needed on our new house – more than we'd bargained for signing on the dotted line, although even if we'd known, it probably wouldn't have daunted us. A queue of tradesmen, from electricians to roofers to carpenters, wended their way through our front door. Plus a charlatan who pocketed our payment for kitchen units that never materialized.

'You have it all ahead of you,' marvelled the woman from Bord Gais, selling us central heating. She gazed around at the cracked plasterwork, missing banisters, plastic door handles, unsanded floorboards and fifties fireplaces, and you could tell she was comparing the panorama – unfavourably – with the order in her own modern semi in the suburbs. All ahead of us? That was an understatement. But we never doubted that we could convert our ramshackle house into a dearly loved home, and that our children would rampage through it.

Right from the start we designed it as a family home. We had a ground floor toilet installed under the stairs, because toddlers wouldn't be able to tackle the cliff-face of our staircase. We spent the money on that at a time when other improvements were pressing their claims, but it seemed a false economy to postpone what would have to be done sooner or later. Sooner, as far as I was concerned. Brendan didn't think we needed to push ahead with downstairs lavatories for small children with quite the degree of urgency that I did, but I looked at him as though he was missing the point. 'Everyone knows children wouldn't be able to hold themselves in long enough to climb all those stairs, Brendan. When they say they want to go to the bathroom they mean right now, this very second. Otherwise they'll have an accident.' I spoke as though the toddlers had already taken possession of the house – and they had, in my imagination.

So we began to renovate our nest, intending to fill it with babies. We waited for them. And we waited.

Chapter 4

At month eleven I snapped. Enough was enough. I took myself off to Boots and purchased the most expensive thermometer in stock, to track ovulation. I began to chart my menstrual cycle with military precision: my fertile period wasn't going to sneak up on me and catch me unawares if I could help it. I kept the thermometer on my bedside table for regular – soon to be pathological – use. My life pivoted on the fertile days in the middle of each cycle. I was on tenterhooks for day fifteen, when my body would gear up for pregnancy, then I could take Brendan or leave him for the rest of the time until I was mid-cycle again. Making love began to strike me as a waste of time and effort unless it happened at that exact time when an egg would be rolling into place, ripe for fertilization. We were still newly-weds, less than a year into the lifetime of marital harmony we envisaged, yet there I was with a sneaking feeling that sex was a bit pointless when it occurred at the wrong end of the month.

Of course, I wasn't stupid enough to admit this to Brendan. Nor could I retreat from intercourse entirely outside of the ovulatory window – there was marriage maintenance and a husband I loved to consider – but in my heart I began to withdraw from lovemaking unless it was sanctioned by the rise of the thermometer needle. It wasn't a full-scale retreat but there was definitely a certain amount of repositioning in terms of my attitude.

I'd have compiled a wall chart and pinned it to the bedroom wall if I believed it would do any good. In fact,

I'm surprised I didn't think of it, I considered just about everything else. That would have looked alluring above our bed, wouldn't it? Days marked with green felt-tip pen – sex is mandatory; days marked in red – advisable; in yellow – discretionary. Never were a woman's secretions and body temperature noted and logged with such diligence. I was highly motivated, after all. I wanted a baby.

All the same, I was still fairly buoyant at this stage – I believed I could get pregnant in the traditional way. It was simply a case of creating the optimum conditions. A special dinner in a Ballsbridge restaurant. A bottle of wine and a video at home. A day trip to Malahide – 'which is Stephen Rea's house?' Quality time together. Quality time apart. Decorating a room together to help us bond. Calling a halt to the decorating because it wasn't conducive to bonding. Not after I kicked over a paint tin by accident.

Brendan was not impressed by my growing fixation, even though I concealed the extent of its hold on me. I convinced myself we were making love at the wrong time of the month, fretting that I had miscalculated ovulation. I was forever turning to my bible, *Everywoman*, in the hope of enlightenment. There was a pie chart on one of the pages that I used to pore over to confirm I was doing the sums right. Then I'd refer back to my state-of-the-art thermometer for constant temperature checks, monitoring rise and fall to establish when I'd be ovulating. I was on the look-out for that all-important increase of at least 0.4 degrees Fahrenheit for three consecutive days.

When my temperature climbed for three days a month, I expected Brendan to perform, irrespective of whether he was tired, or it was midweek, or it simply didn't appeal to him. If he suggested leaving it until the following day I was outraged. Tomorrow never came, as far as I was concerned.

It was the here and now that mattered: my thermometer had given us the green light. That's how we'd earn our thin blue line.

A succession of inked P's freckled my diary to indicate the start of each period, with O's spaced a couple of weeks further on to represent ovulation. So much for lunch dates and dental appointments. My diary was a portable fertility reference and I carried it everywhere with me.

I grew preoccupied by sperm, focusing on all those tiny spores inside my cervix after lovemaking, willing them to go for gold. 'Go for it, lads,' I'd whisper, giddy with the possibility that this month, finally, we'd score a bull's-eye. I wondered if I should build in two extra days for sex, one at each side of ovulation, for slothful sperm and sprinters. Just to give all of them an equal chance to impregnate me. All 400 million of them who'd be lining up at the starting gate.

On the increasingly rare day when a sense of humour managed to puncture my zealot's shell, I laughed at myself for this interest in sperm, with my fanciful provisions for the frail or downright idle ones and the fast-trackers. For my desire to take these little seed pods by the hand and lead them up the tortuous mountain tracks of my fallopian tubes to the ovum, saving them the bother of wriggling unaided to their destination.

Invariably I'd remember the sperm vignette from Woody Allen's *Everything You Always Wanted to Know About Sex (But Were Afraid to Ask)*, with a phalanx of the lads lined up for action. I trusted the throng inside my body were equally dedicated.

I hadn't been obliged to pay so much attention to sperm since Form II biology, sniggering over text book illustrations of turbo-charged tadpoles. In my more lucid moments I'd shake myself, but such intervals were increasingly atypical.

When I first considered sperm in those early days, I was reading Aldous Huxley's poem 'The Fifth Philosopher's Song' – I was a student, I had time on my hands – and I noticed how Huxley rhymed spermatozoa with Noah. Which always struck me as singularly pertinent, since the morality tale that is Noah's Ark deals with the survival of species. Some were selected and some failed to make the final cut. I began to feel like something substandard that wasn't chosen initially. Some bizarre-looking genus, an ant-eater, perhaps, that had stowed away as one of Noah's sons shouted 'Anchors aweigh'.

All this mental energy devoted to sperm! At first I felt fastidious about it; let's face it, which woman really wants to acquire an expertise about sperm? I hardly fancied offering it as my specialist subject on *Mastermind*. Your starter for ten: in which part of the male reproductive cells known as spermatozoa is the nucleus contained? But I overcame my delicacy, especially after reading up on what they had to endure to reach the Promised Land. Crossing the Red Sea of my inner tubes and organs was only the half of it. If cheering them on helped the lads home in on their target, my egg rolled into place and waiting for that hole in one, squeamishness wasn't going to stop me. This was a team effort.

When you learn how sperm must first complete the obstacle course of a woman's internal plumbing, you'd wonder how anyone manages to get pregnant. It's the equivalent of attempting to swim a crocodile-infested river, arms and legs bound, with sharks imported to patrol the finishing line. The sperm have to be ejaculated into the vagina, wriggle through the cervix and use their whip-like tails to swim up the mucus stretching down from the cells lining the cervical canal. Then they have to negotiate the cavity of the uterus. By the time they've achieved this, it's hardly a revelation that of the millions swished forth on their biological quest, only hundreds remain active. The also-rans have all peeled off to hyperventilate over a glucose drink.

Now the hundreds still on active service have to squeeze through the narrow entrance joining the cavity of the uterus and the hollow tube of the oviduct (the route by which the egg escapes from the ovary) – only a few dozen prime specimens accomplish this. Then the A-team swims along the oviduct, against the current, to reach the outer portion. If this occurs just at the time when the egg has been expelled from the ovary, and if the egg has been taken up by finger-like fronds at the end of the oviduct, conception may occur. May occur. It's exhausting just reading about it. Dodging shark patrols seems a safer bet.

But we're not finished yet. The fertilized egg has to pass down the oviduct again, spending three days in the process, during which time it has divided and the one original cell is now a collection of cells. The fertilized egg reaches the cavity of the uterus and implants itself in the lining. A result!

When I worked out exactly what the sperm had to accomplish to impregnate an egg, I felt ashamed of myself for my faintly supercilious attitude towards them in the past. Sperm were have-a-go heroes.

But there were no sperm to have a go at my eggs without Brendan. Bit of a biological blunder by Mother Nature there, I thought, as – once or twice mutinous – he refused to act as my own personal semen production line. I was aghast, for I could not understand how he might be willing to allow any opportunity for conception to leak away.

'There's always tomorrow,' he shrugged.

'Tomorrow?' I gasped. Tomorrow might as well have been next year to me.

'Stop treating me like a sperm bank,' he complained.

'Anything you say. Can you just hop up there and impregnate me first, though?'

He was absolutely right. I did treat him like a semen conveyor belt to be switched on and off at will. I never considered whether he might feel demeaned by this – I believed I was entitled to behave as imperiously as I chose if it meant we ended up with a baby. I was doing it for us, I reasoned. He was supposed to want a child too, after all. I didn't care how half-hearted he might be about performing on cue as long as he kept his side of the bargain. I wasn't interested in passion, foreplay or even technique, all I concentrated on was a result.

The pressure on Brendan to perform to order was immense. If he wouldn't oblige I'd sulk. 'Fine, he needn't think he can have sex when it suits him ever again if he won't do it when I need him to.' I don't blame my husband now for protesting, I'm sure I was as alluring as yesterday's coffee grounds, waggling my thermometer at him. But at the time I was devastated, believing him cruel beyond belief; also, crucially, less committed to the baby venture than I was.

I don't think this is fair; he simply didn't share my tunnel vision. I was driven, even in those relatively early days – and he wasn't. If I'd had any sense I'd have treated it as a game, lightening it with a suggestion of naughty fantasy, but I was a basilisk-faced martinet. Pay attention! At 22.00 hours you must present yourself in the bedroom, stripped and prepared to service me. Romance? Foreplay? For pity's sake stop prevaricating and just crack on with it. You want to give me a back rub? Would you ever just give me a baby. A man would truly, truly need to love a woman to be party to that.

At some stage I began to miss sex for its own sake – spontaneous lovemaking with the man I loved and had married, for nothing more demanding than mutual pleasure, instead of a coupling dictated by the confluence of calendar and thermometer. Good God, did I once have a brain and use it? Did I pay attention to subjects other than sperm and eggs and computing when they should be united? I was indistinctly aware that we'd lost something joyous that might be irretrievable.

Then I stopped caring because my sole consideration was getting pregnant.

Our sex life could always be sorted out at a later date when we were parents. We could leave the baby with its grandparents and have a weekend away together – check into a hotel and let good old quality time come charging to the rescue. But that wasn't important now, it was a distraction from the baby-making mission.

When we did make love, I couldn't concentrate on cuddling afterwards until I'd shoved a pillow under my bottom to give the sperm a leg-up, so to speak. Just in case the prospect of their epic journey was discouraging. At least by pointing them downhill there'd be no confusion about which direction to swim in.

There were days when I could laugh about my preoccupation with sperm – even then – but much of the time I ached. This year of trying and failing was taking its toll on me. My mind despaired of my childlessness and my body throbbed in empathy, my womb, breasts, arms all empty. My baby's absence was a physical pain.

As our first wedding anniversary neared and still no baby, I took to phoning my sister in England to ask her advice. After I'd offloaded my store of grievances, naturally. She was a midwife, she should know the theory. I could read it in *Everywoman* but I wanted to hear it from someone who had pulled off this Olympian feat of getting pregnant.

'Count fourteen days from the start of your period if you

have a twenty-eight-day cycle,' Tonia would advise patiently. 'Add an extra day for every day you go over twenty-eight days.'

Maths was never my strong suit and I fussed about my calculations. Sometimes my cycle was thirty-one days, or even thirty-two or thirty-three. I might be misjudging the dates. Imagine if my ovulation had been and gone when I wasn't paying attention! My stress levels escalated.

'You could always do a cervical mucus check as well, for belt and braces, to show if ovulation is occurring,' she recommended.

'Yuck!' I responded, still enjoying the luxury of delicacy.

By now, baby hunger had me (by the throat, it sometimes felt) at the stage where I was reluctant to have sex until after I'd consulted my diary. At which stage it's a mechanical act. Impulsive, unprompted, natural intercourse? Spur-of-the moment coupling? 'Don't be ridiculous, Brendan, we have to save your sperm for when they can be most efficient.'

I'm amazed he tolerated me for as long as he did.

I was illogical, loath to squander a precious consignment of sperm that might contain The One to impregnate me. I didn't think of sperm as plentiful and easily replaced, as men tend to – I fell into the habit of regarding them as precious commodities that had to be rationed out.

There was one silver lining, however. In the aftermath of lovemaking – at the right time of the month, naturally – I'd lie in bed with Brendan imagining the moment of conception approaching, a meteorite collision that would produce a hail of firefly sparks. Our baby. No sensation could match the tantalizing possibility that the two of us had created life.

'Do you think it worked this time?' Brendan or I would ask.

'Absolutely,' one would reassure the other. 'Piece of cake.'

And everything seemed possible.

Chapter 5

Our first wedding anniversary was approaching but to me it did not have the usual romantic significance. Obviously I wanted to celebrate the first milestone in our lifetime together, of course I did, but I was also thinking how it meant I'd be able to return to the doctors. And they'd have to take me seriously. Meanwhile I rang my sister for a therapeutic rant. She was sympathetic, allowing me to fulminate, then suggested the mucus test again. I had nothing to lose so I relented. 'Tell me how you do it,' I acceded. 'What? Stretchy mucus that feels slippery to the touch? Gross! No, don't hang up, I do want to know.' Then I used it as a back-up method. Calendar, thermometer, mucus. My three talismans.

There was nothing I'd have ruled out as an aid to conception. Walking barefoot through a dandelion patch when the moon was full? No problem. Should that be clothed or unclothed? Could I do it on my own or should I yank my husband along with me? All right, I admit I didn't try that, but I copied out the instructions from some Wiccan Fertility Tips tome or other and slid them into a drawer.

Breezily prepared to merge the Catholic with the pagan, I hoarded more medals and prayer cards to Our Lady than a Lourdes souvenir shop. I was always nipping into churches to light a candle. 'Come on, Blessed Virgin, intercede to let me have a baby. You had one yourself, you must know how irresistible they are. Mine needn't be an immaculate conception, a normal one will do. Sorry, don't mean to be impious, it's just this perpetual waiting and hoping is wearing me down.

I know I only pray when I want something but please forgive me and organize this one favour, I'll never ask for another. I'll do the Lough Derg pilgrimage if you hear my prayer. I'll make sure the baby is brought up a Catholic. I'll keep all the commandments, even the really tough ones nobody bothers with any more. I'll volunteer for charity work, Meals on Wheels, Oxfam shop, just point me in the right direction.' Then I had a brainwave. 'Publication promised,' I bartered, remembering the formula I'd read in small ads placed in newspapers after prayers were answered. 'Any paper you like.'

I did novenas, chanted rosaries, carried a miraculous medal in my purse, promised everything short of renouncing the world and entering a convent if I could have a child. I couldn't ·pass a church without detouring to plead at the altar rails. 'Why won't you hear my prayer? Why not? Why not?' I stormed the gates of heaven with my increasingly shrill demands. A relative was going to Rome and I gave her money to light a candle at St Peter's Basilica for my special intentions. There was only one intention.

I was inconsistent and impervious to my inconsistency, unconcerned with what did the trick – totem or prayer – so long as I had a baby to show for it. On a piece of paper I wrote my heart's desire, that which I wanted most in the world, and burned the plea in the flame of a red candle. Watching it catch fire and crumble to ash, I didn't care if it was heathen superstition. I'd chance anything. And there was always St Peter's to fall back on.

I went about muttering to myself. 'Green's meant to be a fertile colour – I'll wear it every day. Slow down, better read up on it in case I'm confusing my colours. No, here we go: *Green symbolizes fruitfulness and growth; it was associated with fertility ceremonies in the days of the druids, that's why the early Christian Church banned it and it's still regarded as an unlucky colour today*. Excellent, let's have some of that fruitfulness and growth in my life.'

I made sure I always sported something green, if only a pair of socks.

But surely there must be something else I could be doing. Would St Jude, patron of hopeless cases, be a persuasive advocate for my case or should I try St Anne, the Virgin's mother? How about St Elizabeth, John the Baptist's mother? She'd been barren until apparently past childbearing age, she'd be receptive to my prayers. I had an aunt who swore by St Gerard Majella for answering mothers' prayers, should I give him a try? I believed in all of them and none of them. It's no wonder I wasn't heard.

I checked out herbs as a possible fertility boost and came across black cohosh, which has an oestrogenic action and stimulates the ovaries. I didn't suppose I'd be able to buy that in Superquinn. Sensible diet was also helpful, I read – hmm, must introduce some vitamin supplements into my daily regime. How about green tea? That's healthy and the right colour as well, two for the price of one.

I cudgelled my brains trying to second-guess the root of the problem. Smoking and drinking were factors in fertility problems. Couldn't be that, I was a moderate drinker and had never smoked. Taking no chances, I decided to turn teetotal for a while. And a desultory attempt it was. Let's face it, when life sends you up one blind alley after another, you find you really do need a drink after all. There might not be any answers in the bottom of a glass but at least its contents numb the question. Stress was also cited as a negative factor in an article I came across. I knew my emotions were like bolting horses but there didn't appear to be much I could do to rein them in; it was a vicious circle, because this stress taking possession of my life was caused by childlessness.

You store up more data than you really need when you start researching infertility. For instance, I chanced upon something called hostile mucus. Truly. It conjures up an image of marauding braves on the warpath as terrified settlers circle the wagons. Apparently some doctors believe the mucus secreted by the cervical glands can be unreceptive to sperm. This was something new to worry about. I considered my mucus and Brendan's sperm: could there be antipathy between them? Even my obsessive hungering for a child couldn't persuade me to investigate that any further. I did consider sending the article to Woody Allen, however, in case he fancied using hostile mucus for a sequel to *Everything You Always Wanted to Know About Sex*.

My need for a child sometimes overwhelmed me. Even if I'd wanted to park the issue to give us a breathing space, I was incapable of it. It began staking a claim on my every waking moment. I couldn't stroll along the seafront at Sandymount without thinking that it would be a bracing place to wheel a pram. I couldn't buy an ice-cream without imagining the day when I'd break off the bottom of my cone and feed it to our son or daughter. Every time I happened across a name I liked – during the Fair City soap credits, listening to the news – I filed it away in my mental folder of potential baby names.

And I brooded about why this was happening to us. Couples formulate plans all the time, we were no different. In our innocence, in our arrogance, we had imagined it was simply a case of deciding what we wanted and then pursuing it. But our desires weren't excessive, I entreated the contradictory voice in my skull – the one that whispered I might never have a baby.

Even before I realized my limitations; even before I fell to regarding myself as flawed; even before we seized on medical intervention as the answer to our problem; even before all those stages, suspicions prickled inside me. Long before the testing started, instinct hinted that I was the source of the stasis. As month after month passed and still I needed to go to a chemist's for tampons instead of disposable nappies or teething rings, I guessed I had a defect. I knew it as you intuit something, then bury that knowledge because it has the potential to detonate your dream.

I had lost interest in my career by this stage and wanted – demanded – that which, at eighteen, would have seemed anathema to me. 'Women spend their thirties pulling down what they build up in their twenties,' one of the coterie had commented, topping up the glasses in our Covent Garden haunt. I didn't believe it then – I regarded it as one of those superficially clever remarks that didn't bear scrutiny – but the observation stayed with me and I was starting to think there might be some truth in it. I'm not sure I would have taken a pickaxe to my career, exactly, but I no longer valued it. My wants were reduced to just one: to have a baby.

I would return to work, of course, as soon as I had my MPhil, because most families needed a dual income. But I hoped it could be a part-time position, at least while the children were small. In terms of a woman's career that's often the death knell. I knew this and I didn't care – biology had swallowed me whole. Brendan appeared to be more or less in agreement. He worried about cash flow more than I did, but we were in accord over the broad strokes of the plan. We longed to be a family.

Our first wedding anniversary arrived and we spent the weekend at Tinakilly House in Wicklow. It was the home of a former ship's captain, famous for its kitchen and for a recent visit from Julia Roberts, bolting from her wedding to Kiefer Sutherland. Although it was borderline, timing-wise, on the ovulation front, I whispered to myself it might still work here. My hope glands were always ready to believe. Tinakilly could perform its magic on us, with its four-poster beds and country house charm.

We laid aside the differences growing between us, as obsession threatened to devour me and Brendan – although he never said anything – missed the partner he'd married. We became friends again at Tinakilly. We decided we'd like to return there every wedding anniversary. I had some fanciful notion about a huge family get-together at the hotel for our silver wedding anniversary. Bounding ahead, as usual. I hadn't even produced a baby yet and already I was a mater familias, surrounded by children and their partners, maybe even their babies too.

We wandered around the wooded grounds, relaxed into the genteel hospitality, and I thought, 'If there's any justice, it will all meld together here. I'll get pregnant this weekend.'

But soon after we checked out, I felt the dull ache in the pit of my stomach that signalled the onset of a period. I pressed a hot water bottle to where the cramp marked the spot, Feminax at the ready, and conceded defeat: we couldn't manage this on our own, even with thermometers and ovulatory windows. Or country house hotels and four-poster beds. Or miraculous medals and wishes consumed by the flame of a red candle.

We had waited out the year, although waiting does not come easily to the inhabitants of this corner of the world. In Africa I observed stately, impassive people who would wait all day every day, if that's what they were required to do. Neither their bodies nor their faces expressed a single particle of impatience, for all their lives they had waited in line. It was a state at which experience had taught them to excel. But we're not adept at waiting, we have no practice.

As for Brendan and me, our imperfect version of stoic endurance had achieved nothing. I was consulting a doctor again and I wouldn't be fobbed off.

Until recently a GP wouldn't even consider referring a patient for fertility tests until a couple had been trying for a year. It makes sense, because some couples take longer than others to conceive. Many, like us, covet a baby too greatly. I was beginning to suspect the number one way to get pregnant was not to want a baby. Simple as that. So when a couple start trying, naturally Nature, with her Puck's humour, keeps them waiting a while.

Age is also a factor. In her thirties, a woman's fertility levels are declining; she's more stressed, less healthy. It's not time to send out a Mayday signal yet, particularly in her early thirties, as I was, but neither is it ideal. These days, some doctors will consider fertility tests after six months if the woman is thirty-five or over, but most still believe a year is a fair unit of time to allow. And do you know, I can actually see their point, even though a year seemed interminable to me (twelve missed opportunities to conceive!) when I was waiting for something to happen. Women often say, 'I just know in my heart there's something not right' – then proceed to have a healthy baby without medical intervention. So doctors are understandably wary. But the reason I think it's probably sensible to wait a year is because fertility tests are invasive. Why subject a patient to them if it might prove unnecessary with a little patience? They are humiliating, undignified and degrading – and you're still at the positive stage. You haven't started down the treatment trail.

That autumn, after a year of trying and failing, I made a

doctor's appointment to explain my predicament. I had just enrolled at Trinity, so I signed up with the college doctor. As other students milled around swapping lecture notes and making friends, one of my first ports of call was to arrange a doctor's appointment.

A few days later I was directed into a room to consult with a middle-aged woman, dark hair in a bob, wearing glasses that reflected back twin shrunken images of me. I was startled by a sense of impotence as I noticed them: my two scaled-down selves were insignificant.

Throughout my adult life I'd believed I could have it all. It was an unparalleled time to be a woman, the coterie and I had agreed back in London. You could have a toy-boy to play with. You could have an older lover who'd worship you. You could hold down a challenging career, take out a mortgage on your own – unthinkable a few decades earlier – and defer motherhood until you were good and ready for it. Until it suited you. Until you were prepared to make space for a child in your life. Until the checklist had been ticked off. Graduated from college, had a succession of exotic holidays, tried out a variety of lovers, been promoted at work, met a suitable mate, bought property. *All right, eggs, I'll let you get fertilized now. Don't keep me waiting too long, I have a busy schedule.*

But my eggs weren't prepared to be hectored into reproduction, and I was at a loss to know what to do about it – other than turn myself over to the medics. Perhaps this one might offer a quick-fix solution.

The doctor didn't see a married woman in her early thirties – I'm small-boned and have always looked younger than my age – she saw a typical student with books under her arm, bicycle clips in her jeans. So she was bemused by my approach. Desperate though I felt, I laughed at the dubious expression on the doctor's face when I said, 'Please help me, I can't get pregnant.' She thought it was an elaborate hoax. Her eyes kept flickering over my shoulders for the camera crew. I had to explain my predicament several times before she digested it. Finally I convinced her that I was really keen to have a child, that I wanted her help in the matter. This was the first time, she admitted, a student had ever approached her to complain about *not* being pregnant.

She asked about any operations or illnesses I may have had – nothing, apart from pneumonia as a toddler. Then she inquired about my menstrual history, which was regular. Questions about menstruation were probing: when did the menarche start, how long did a period last, how long between periods, were they painful?

'Do you and your husband have sex regularly?'

'Yes,' I said.

'More than once a month?'

'Certainly. It wouldn't count as regular if we only had it once a month.'

'At least once a week?' she pressed.

I nodded, thinking guiltily about the thermometer whose fluctuations had a direct impact on my levels of desire. I was eager to provide any information that might be relevant, but it's difficult to discuss your sex life with a stranger.

She smiled, to set me at ease. 'Sometimes couples have sex infrequently and still imagine they'll get pregnant at the drop of a hat. I'm just establishing that you fall within the parameters of normal.'

The doctor took a blood sample to test if I was ovulating and the consultation was over. I went outside, feeling deflated, and decided to go to the library. The other students who crossed my path seemed so light-hearted – all they had to worry about was whether to meet their friends for a drink tonight in Keogh's or Grogan's. I marvelled at their carefree attitude. Had life been like that for me once? But at least I felt I had accomplished something. I had brought in the medics.

The blood test showed I was ovulating – another hurdle surmounted. What next? The upshot was that we needed tests. In around 25 per cent of cases, I was told, the woman is the reason why a couple don't have a baby; in an equivalent percentile it's down to the man; and in the remaining 50 per cent there are factors present that affect both of them.

Splendid, I was ready to be investigated, eager for it, in fact, because tests would show if there was anything wrong with Brendan or me.

Then it could be fixed and – about time too – we could get on with our lives.

Chapter 6

Now a division was created between Brendan and me, for each of us had to be tested and passed or failed. We weren't a self-contained unit any more, we were two components in a unit that might or might not be able to gel.

The test involving a man is always the most straightforward so Brendan was despatched for a sperm count. That idea always makes me snigger like a schoolgirl. I can't shake off this vision of a laboratory assistant in a white coat going 'one million, ninety thousand, two hundred and fifty-six, one million, ninety thousand, two hundred and fifty-seven . . .' Of course it's not just quantity the doctors are checking, but motility as they term it: that the lads are pelting along with the required amount of vim and a good sense of direction, as opposed to being under-motivated and a bit dense in terms of route-finding.

Brendan dreaded the sperm count, I think – he admitted he was nervous setting off to have it – and his relief when he was pronounced normal was almost infectious. He had not been able to disguise the frailty of the male ego, masculinity at stake at the prospect of inactive or even simply sluggish sperm. Still, I was glad for Brendan when the result came through, for his fear had been understandable, instinctual.

I wondered, later, whether he'd have agreed to us using donor sperm if he had been the one with the fertility problem. Or did testosterone combined with territorialism mean that any baby he might raise had to be his child biologically? There's no way of knowing, for we didn't discuss it, but I've never forgotten his anxiety about that sperm count and his aura of being a man reprieved from the gallows.

Brendan's all-clear bounced the spotlight back onto me: I was the one who couldn't have children, I was the faulty batch, just as I'd suspected when doubt had started assailing me months earlier. And the female reproductive organs, like female modes of reasoning, are more convoluted than the male's.

The procedures began piling up thick and fast now, after that year of stagnation. Action cheered us, however; action produced results, we inferred.

I was sent for a laparoscopy, a rather more complicated undertaking than the sperm count, during which a camera would be inserted through my navel to plumb the inadequacies of my reproductive organs. I still have the scars — they were followed by others. I survey them sometimes, charting the map of my attempts to become a mother through the marks of the surgeon's knife on my body. I used to despise them, for they represented failure to me, but now I've grown attached to those narrow squiggles indenting my flesh because they remind me that I tried. Trying and failing isn't as satisfactory as trying and succeeding — but it has a currency of its own.

I've looped ahead, however. The laparoscopy is a surgical show-and-tell exercise carried out under general anaesthetic. Its name derives from laparoscope, a tiny telescope. Basically it allows a surgeon to inspect a woman's reproductive engine using a telescope. Pressurized carbon dioxide gas forces her stomach wall away from her organs to provide a clear view of the field of play. The doctor can see if the tubes are swollen, deformed or trapped by adhesions and scar tissue. He or she can check for fibroids, or for endometriosis — where the womb lining grows outside the womb.

'How odd,' I thought, when I learned what a laparoscopy entailed. 'This is the first time anyone has gone on a sight-seeing tour around my ovaries.' Followed by: 'God, there's any number of potential problems.'

The laparoscopy was being provided gratis on the state's health service, which meant a delay of some months. (I haven't a clue why we didn't avail ourselves of Brendan's occupational private health scheme to queue-jump; presumably I still had a few socialist tendencies that militated against it. In the face of baby hunger they didn't last much longer.) We seemed to have grown accustomed to waiting and so we prepared to sit out those additional months until it was our turn for investigation.

In the meantime we carried on 'trying', with me using that trinity of talismans: calendar, thermometer, mucus. I was bound now by a ritual of obsessive counting, logging and checking for signs that intercourse was permissible. I started to forget that lovemaking was predicated on a mutual pleasure principle – convinced, by now, that pleasure no longer signified.

It was time for the laparoscopy. Brendan and I were in this together. A team. He drove me to the Holles Street Hospital – it was my first time there and I remember noticing how close it was to the house where Oscar Wilde grew up. On the pavement outside the hospital we passed twitchy expectant dads congregating for gasping inhalations of nicotine before tumbling back to the labour ward. In the corridors inside, a herd of fledgling fathers clutched helium balloons and expanses of rainbow flora, grinning as though a lifetime's happiness had converged on this single instant. 'That will be Brendan soon,' I thought, aping confidence.

I had spent no time in hospital since pneumonia at the

age of fourteen months. Like most people, I sidled into one occasionally to visit a friend or relative, covertly clock-watching until I could escape. Hospitals have a stifling quality, perhaps because they are repositories for pain and death as well as for cure and birth. However this was a hospital visit I welcomed. At least it would supply answers – we'd know the nature of the problem and how to resolve it. I still believed there was a solution to every problem.

We were nervous, all the same, in Holles Street that morning. I had missed my morning mug of coffee because I was required to present myself in a fasting state before the anaesthetic, and not having it left me even more jittery. There was a queue of women ahead of me, all waiting to have laparoscopies. Waiting, like me, for a tube to be fed through our navels and for our insides to be pumped full of gas. That's scar number one. Scar number two follows hot on its heels: another puncture, this one just above the pubic bone, to insert a probe. Then that tiny telescope with a camera attached would ease in through another incision. Scar number three.

I was exhausted afterwards and extremely sore, with pains from the gas bubbles under my diaphragm and in my shoulders. All I wanted to do was sleep. The laparoscopy was supposed to be a straightforward procedure, women whipped in and out of the ward in a matter of hours. But my adverse reaction – debilitated, floppy, having trouble being roused – persuaded the ward sister to detain me overnight for observation. Relief flooded through me as I closed my eyes and was allowed to drift back towards oblivion. The prospect of trekking from the ward to the car outside seemed an ordeal that her kindness had spared me.

The next morning I was wobbly, but well enough not to trespass on a bed someone else needed. A freckled, fair-haired Scottish girl was waiting for a taxi as I stood in the foyer watching for Brendan to arrive and drive me home. She'd had her laparoscopy a couple of hours earlier and was on her way to work as a childminder.

'I can't afford to take the day off,' she explained chirpily.

Still feeble from my operation twenty-four hours earlier, I felt diminished in the presence of her sunny insouciance. 'Are you sure you should? Wouldn't you at least like a lift?' I asked. 'My husband ought to be here soon.'

'Ah no, hen, there's my taxi now. Hope I see you in here again when we both have stomachs that wobble like jelly,' she laughed, and bounced off.

I crossed my fingers behind my back and hoped so too.

I didn't know that renovation work had been carried out on my fallopian tubes – I thought the laparoscopy was simply a reconnoitre. But improvements to my tubes were effected and they may have been the reason why I was floored by the laparoscopy. Of course it made sense to press ahead with anything that could be done while I was on the operating table, instead of bringing me back a second time. But some basic information would have helped. A few possibilities outlined. Or even someone to explain why a procedure everyone kept describing as very minor, usually performed on an out-patient basis, should knock me sideways.

Later, submerged in more invasive treatment, I wondered if that first hiccup when I had to be detained in hospital after a supposedly routine procedure was an omen. Until then I had been reasonably indifferent to my body. It was naturally slim, for which I was nonchalantly grateful, but other than that I didn't think much about it one way or the other. Here, however, at the first hint of investigation, was evidence that it might not perform as it should. That it might prove . . . recalcitrant. In time I grew to feel contemptuous of my body, betrayed by it.

But that's hindsight at work again, spotting auguries when you have the leisure to search them out. Waiting in the foyer of Holles Street hospital for Brendan to collect me, I was jaunty. A surge of optimism warmed me, despite the physical discomfort.

I kept thinking, 'They'll have discovered what's wrong with me now and they can cure it.'

Some time later, I think it was about a month, we were recalled for a diagnosis of the test results with the surgeon who had been the day-tripper around my reproductive organs. I sat there with Brendan, confident that this doctor would fill the cavity at the centre of my life.

The medical man was businesslike, terse, and looked at his notes rather than at us. He told us the laparoscopy showed I had kinked and warped fallopian tubes, the result of an undiagnosed bug. I was dumbfounded. The surgeon was still studying his notes but he seemed to sense my disorientation. He said I'd contracted it a minimum of a decade earlier and probably longer. He knew this from the lesions on my fallopian tubes, where damage was at an advanced stage – meaning I was unlikely to conceive a child naturally.

I was jolted. No, I was devastated. There was something wrong with my body and it had been like that all along – all through that year and a half of trying and failing to have a baby. I stole a glance at my husband and he looked equally shell-shocked. 'God,' I thought, 'what's Brendan thinking?'

The surgeon described the deficiencies of my fallopian tubes with the clinical distance that often defines the profession. Whoever had trained him in detachment had taught him well. As he spoke, I felt a wave of shock and then resentment at his objectivity: I wished for some sign that he was human and understood this was a blow for us. A simple, 'I'm sorry, I know this must be difficult' would have helped in the middle of the diagnosis. I badly wanted an acknowledgement that I was a human rather than a case. But there was nothing. I looked at Brendan again – his stunned expression hadn't changed.

As I listened to what the surgeon was saying, I tried to read his eyes behind his glasses. But I felt there was a barrier between us and I couldn't connect with him. So I concentrated on his words instead, and as I did I registered a sense of helplessness. For the first time I became conscious of the past's capacity to shape the present. Something had happened a decade or more previously – something I wasn't even aware of – and instead of being safely consigned to history, here it was doing a demolition job on my life.

The surgeon noted there were adhesions so thick and numerous around my fallopian tubes that the tubes could scarcely be seen. 'Like Rapunzel's Castle,' I thought.

He gave the impression of being busy and distracted as he spoke. 'Any questions?' he asked.

We were so dumbstruck we hardly knew how to manage a sigh, let alone a question.

If only people could be given a chance to adapt to news they may find shocking, then have a follow-up meeting once they've assimilated it and questions can be framed. It's too confusing on the spot. We weren't offered that option, however – there was a teeming waiting room at our backs. I don't know if we'd have been treated with more consideration as private patients, but afterwards I did feel I had been handled somewhat dismissively.

So many emotions were churning around in my mind that day, in the place where birth was a prosaic miracle. Where one-in-twelve Irish citizens began life. Where, but for the intervention of a bug, I should have been attending clinics for my pre-natal check-ups. I had been mesmerized, as the surgeon had explained in his impersonal manner that my tubes were in an appalling state. He hadn't used the term but I remembered thinking, 'He's explaining they're banjaxed.'

Afterwards I tested the word on my lips, so compellingly did it resonate in my head that day. 'What was that medical expression for my problem again? That's right: banjaxed. I was told my fallopian tubes were well and truly banjaxed.'

As I sat in his consulting room, my brain was in seizure. Having a baby seems to be the easiest, most natural thing in the world. Until you can't. And when you can't, the desire to be a mother – controllable until this point – becomes overwhelming. I was engulfed by the unexpected, unreasonable, undue severity of my sentence. I was in the dock before a hanging judge and he'd just donned the black cap. 'This is a miscarriage of justice,' I wanted to howl. 'Someone's made a mistake.'

Then another emotion rose to the surface. It was distaste – with its corollary, indignation – at discovering I had been mangled by a bug inside me all these years. (Sometimes I wonder if it's still there, rummaging away. Will I bring it to the grave with me? Is it part of my fibre now? I haven't tried to find out if I still have it; maybe it's because I'm afraid of the answer.)

Later I recollected visiting a GP when I was living in London because I was ill in a low-grade, listless way. The doctor, a brisk man in his fifties with scrupulously parted hair, said that if he could prescribe a cruise for me he would. Since it was beyond his powers I'd simply have to knuckle down and go back to work. 'It's just one of those pains a young woman gets from time to time,' he pronounced.

Yet that was when the infection must have been attacking me. Stealing my fertility. Altering the course of my life.

All these memories came later: peeling away the layers of the past in an attempt to assimilate the how, if not the why, of my quandary. For now I was sitting, nauseous, in a surgeon's consulting rooms, too dazed even to feel affronted that some bug had stolen my future.

In fact, I was so confounded I never thought of how Brendan must be feeling, hearing that something in my body, something that hadn't been treated, was interfering with our dream of having a family. Of course, it wasn't my fault: I couldn't get treatment for something I knew nothing about. But I wish I had reached out, squeezed Brendan's hand and said, 'I'm sorry this should have happened to us because of something I had.' But we sat there silently, side by side. Isolated. Neither of us said a word. If you listened intently, however, you could hear it – the first hairline crack in our marriage.

Chapter 7

Immediately after our hospital visit, the future seemed a desert. Looping repeatedly in my mind's eye was an image of myself as a small girl playing with my dolls. I would feed them, change them, bath them, cuddle them, marry them off to each other. It's how all little girls play, copying their mothers. I had smaller brothers to practise on, too – Tonia and I were determined junior madonnas, taking it in turns to wheel the younger ones about in the pram.

There's an old black-and-white photograph of me hugging my first doll, Joan, by the neck in a stranglehold grip. I always believed one day I'd be a mother for real. For me, mother-hood was as inevitable as the white wedding and the happily ever after that also lay in wait. How to explain to this small girl, squinting against the sunlight in the photograph, that she can't be a Mammy? That her game is the only reality? How to explain to her older self, also squinting, now, in an unforgiving beam of light?

There were days when I'd study myself in the bathroom mirror, astounded by how normal I appeared. Yet I couldn't have children. I imagined this catastrophe should be visible in the altered planes of my face. But there was no change in my features, I looked much as ever. Not at all how an infertile woman should look: singled out for punishment.

I may have looked the same – I didn't feel the same, though. Some days I was self-pitying, others, disbelieving. I'll never forget the sense of failure that dogged me in those initial days after the blocked tubes diagnosis. The bewilderment. The sense of injustice. The taste of it, a sour residue on the cave of my mouth that curled the lips into a misshapen moue. I held grief at bay for an age, this misery that would eventually saturate me; for now I sensed it would inhibit my determination to pursue a remedy. Grief was the enemy and I needed to raise my drawbridge against it.

Yet I grew engrossed in brooding about my fallopian tubes, which took over from sperm as the focus of my introspection. If sperm had barely impinged on my consciousness, until I charted their epic journey through a woman's body and marvelled at their tenacity, fallopian tubes had not figured at all. Quite simply, I had never thought about them before. Frankly, now that my attention had been drawn to them, I felt it was ungracious of my fallopian tubes to decline to cooperate: after all, they'd been housed in perfect comfort for thirty-odd years somewhere south of my stomach – I was hazy on the precise location of most of my internal organs. Finally invited to earn their keep, they'd defaulted with all the loyalty of reneging tenants doing a moonlit flit with the landlord's television set and three months' rent arrears. It wasn't as if I'd worked them hard, they'd had it easier than most of my other body parts. Really, I felt extraordinarily betrayed by them, as I fretted over these tubes taking up space in my body. A cul-de-sac for sperm, instead of the dual carriageway I needed.

I studied a biology book diagram. Complicated-looking things, fallopian tubes resembled an underground irrigation system on Mars – and that was in peak condition. I shuddered to think what mine looked like, mutated into a malfunctioning body part. I checked to see what I could learn about the problems that attacked them; it did not make pleasant reading. 'Tubal malfunction is the leading cause and accounts for nearly half of female infertility, according to US research.'

Nobody warns you when you're a very young woman, glowing with conviction that the universe is yours and you can shape your destiny – including taking control of your fertility – that just one rogue piece in the jigsaw can subvert your hopes. That, through no fault of your own, you can be caught in an indiscriminate withdrawal of privileges. The reproductive ones.

I understood that, trapped in adhesions and scar tissue, my once active organs could no longer move to retrieve the egg and nudge it towards the uterus. No rendezvous with sperm could take place as a result. And there was precious little chance of pregnancy if sperm and egg didn't become acquainted.

Around this time I grew brittle, starting to think in terms of fault – specifically mine. I felt profoundly, intrinsically, forlornly defective. I wondered if Brendan viewed me as defective too but lacked the nerve to ask him for reassurance that he didn't. That I was still the woman he'd married. But of course I wasn't.

Brendan and I made a conscious effort to set aside the shock and deal with this together. We decided to be positive and pro-active, not squander energy brooding. And yet, how could either of us avoid thinking about what had brought us to this, at least furtively?

The diagnosis wasn't an eclipse of our hopes, not totally. Creeping past the alarm and distress, overtaking the difficulty of being confronted with reverberations from one partner's medical history, came a reassuring thought. At least we knew what exactly was wrong and why we hadn't produced a baby. At least we knew there was something medically wrong, which had been defined for us, as opposed to dealing with inexplicable infertility – to my mind the most merciless cut of all. At least we could try to rectify the problem. Modern medicine could cure me.

Couldn't it?

I decided not to think of myself as an infertile woman, but as a fertile one suffering from a slight touch of infertility. There! That was more bearable. But only for a short time. Positive spinning doesn't work indefinitely.

If our sex life had been framed by calendar and thermometer and had lost its spontaneity, that period ranked as the good old days compared with what happened next. I found my attitude to lovemaking changed profoundly after I realized it wasn't a means to having a baby – that even when I was ovulating, there was no way for the egg to be fertilized. From my perspective, there was a futility to the act if it couldn't produce a child. I would watch us in bed, sometimes, with an unhealthy detachment, and marvel at us for going through the motions. Sex seemed ridiculous, stripped of its ultimate purpose. Pleasure alone struck me as a woefully inadequate end. I didn't know it, but we had entered barbed-wire territory. Brendan probably still cared about lovemaking as an expression of intimacy, but I didn't pause to consider that. Or I registered it, but only in a hazy way. It was a detail. My focus was motherhood, not checking whether my partner was happy or the relationship sound.

During this time, there seemed to be a pregnancy epidemic. All my friends and relatives were getting pregnant – even the ones who'd say, 'I don't know how we managed it, we weren't even trying.' The phone would ring, an excited voice would burble, 'Guess what?' and a giant fist would slowly squeeze my heart.

I tried hard not to spoil their moments. I hope I didn't. I did my best to say all the congratulatory things – then I locked myself in the bathroom and howled. I particularly hated it when couples spoke in the plural – 'We are pregnant, we are expecting a baby,' because I felt so singular. There was only me, not me plus my child, and less and less was it a case of me plus my husband. I felt isolated; I, not we.

There was an antidote to this slight touch of infertility. IVF. During the consultation after my laparoscopy, the one where I walked in as a normal woman and walked out branded, my traumatized brain had kicked in with one useful contribution.

'Could IVF help us?'

The laparoscopy doctor had agreed that we might well be suitable for IVF treatment.

Unfortunately the brain cells had been exhausted and had needed to regroup, so I hadn't asked any more questions. Nor had the doctor volunteered any information about the treatment. I think he must have been one of those medics who likes to operate with a certain aloofness, like the senior clerics of a previous generation.

We knew about the availability of IVF, *in vitro* fertilization, because my sister had undergone two cycles of it and we had recently heard that she was pregnant. Which meant it worked! It was modern medicine's fairy godmother gift. Tonia had been able to have her son, Justin, naturally, but complications after his birth meant she couldn't have a brother or sister for him. She and her husband Tom had tried IVF and, because they had been successful, I was certain it could be the answer to our problem too. However my sister lived in England, so we weren't familiar with what precisely IVF entailed. I'm not sure we even cared, so long as it supplied results. All I knew was that it bypassed a woman's fallopian tubes, so I assumed it would circumvent my problem. We had been assured that I was ovulating, while Brendan's sperm had stood up and been counted, so we decided to make inquiries about IVF.

Even before we investigated it properly, however, Brendan and I latched onto the treatment with a tenacity that degenerated into desperation. We didn't regard it as a grace, a reprieve to be snatched from the maw of infertility. We perceived it as doctrine. We would have IVF treatment and it would lead to a baby. Elementary.

Except. Except the boon is not available to one and all. IVF chooses who to reward and who to withhold its bounty from – and it does so in random fashion. The average woman is estimated to have a one in five success rate. And that's per cycle. You don't have a 100 per cent chance of bringing home a baby if you have five cycles, as I convinced myself. The gamble applies each time you embark on treatment – your chances are no better by cycle number six than they are at cycle number one. Statistically, the chances of success are illstarred, but try telling that to a childless woman's hope muscle. Arbitrary luck, that's what we trusted in. We had no choice.

IVF was not well-known in Ireland. It was still occasionally described as 'test-tube babies' when I started researching it, although it was nearly twenty years since it had been pioneered successfully in Britain with the birth of Louise Brown in 1978. I wondered about the '*in vitro*' aspect and discovered it was Latin for 'in glass', which is where the test tube misnomer comes from. In fact, fertilization occurs in a dish.

'A laboratory conditions merger,' I thought, allowing myself a wry smile. So much for a night of passion after a bottle of wine and a meal in our favourite restaurant. Or my pipe dreams about conceiving our child in a four-poster bed in Tinakilly House. But a laboratory conditions merger was better than none.

I opted to think of IVF as an arranged marriage as opposed

to a love match; made matches sometimes panned out better than those predicated on romance, I reminded myself. Based on absolutely no evidence other than what I wanted to hear.

IVF suppresses a woman's menstrual cycle with a barrage of drugs, further drugs then stimulate her ovaries into over-drive and multiple eggs are produced instead of the usual one. These eggs are gathered from the woman's ovaries, mixed with the man's sperm and at least some of the eggs hope-fully fertilize. After two or three days, several embryos are returned to the woman, and if they implant on the uterine lining she's pregnant.

Her partner's role in the treatment cycle is a cameo – crucial but brief. The ghost in *Hamlet*, say, or Alec Guinness in *Star Wars*. The man provides a sperm sample on the day the eggs are extracted. That's it. However hand-holding, fears-allaying and a thoroughly partisan approach, reassuring the woman she's brilliant, beautiful and brave, aren't to be under-valued. In fact, I recommend classes should be offered in that supporting part because it underpins the entire exercise.

We threw ourselves whole-heartedly into chasing our fairytale solution, Brendan and I, but we never surveyed the root of the problem. I can't help wondering, all these years later, after the mistakes are beyond expiation, if the outcome might have been different had we reviewed the reason for my infertility. I believe I became damaged goods for my husband in that moment in the specialist's consulting rooms. I doubt if he ever admitted it to himself, but I trace the arc of altered feeling between us to that day.

IVF was to be the panacea.

I hadn't met Tonia during her courses of treatment, so I hadn't seen its impact on her. And, of course, IVF affects some women differently from others, depending on everything from temperament to life experience. When I telephoned Tonia for advice, I inquired about the theory behind it – but not how it made her feel. As someone with medical training (she was a nurse), she was able to regard it as a 'procedure'. I knew no better. To me it was also a procedure: one that would give me a baby, as it was in the process of doing for my pregnant sister.

I understood and failed to understand her explanation simultaneously. To someone of my non-scientific background, a lot of what I heard was gobbledegook. I filtered out anything technical but I did learn that a cycle lasted four to six weeks, that you inhaled drugs continuously through a sniffer to send you into a fake menopause, then other drugs were injected (or taken orally) to make more follicle-stimulating hormones and coax the ovaries into producing anything up to twenty eggs.

'I'll be turned into a battery hen, in other words,' I inter-rupted, with a glimmering of apprehension.

But I was speaking to a woman who was pregnant by IVF; did I need any more potent inducement?

So, I'd be awash with eggs thanks to drugs – and, by moni-toring my blood hormone levels, doctors could tell when my eggs were mature. An ultrasound would confirm when they were ready for harvesting, as the medical term had it.

'How lush,' I thought, reassured now. 'My body will be harvested and there'll be a crop of babies.'

I could have been repelled by the harvesting analogy – I know some women are – but exigency kept revulsion at arm's length.

What I didn't know was how the drugs would affect me, beyond galvanizing the engine of my reproductive system into GTi mode. Nor did I have the sense to ask my sister, or indeed, the professionals – I just assumed I'd be able to cope with whatever the treatment required of me.

★

Brendan and I believed ourselves ready for IVF, but was it ready for us? A shuttlecock interlude followed, as we ricocheted about trying to discover where to go next. I wasn't even certain I could receive IVF treatment in Ireland. It was hardly written about, to the best of my knowledge, and it wasn't discussed. I thought I might be obliged to travel to England, an added expense, plus I wouldn't be in my home environment and would feel less relaxed. I was flailing about and realized, with a sinking heart, that our difficulties were exacerbated by our recent return to Ireland: we didn't yet know how the procedures worked.

Through this period I tried to contain my emotions. I needed to be pragmatic if I was to pursue a solution. Yet I had been crushed and shocked – humiliated too – to be told I couldn't have a child. All the time I was ploughing through abstruse medical terminology, trying to grasp procedures phrased in language I couldn't fathom, struggling to make sense of what might be on offer. For while I may not have fully comprehended the nuts and bolts of IVF, I recognized it as hope. And hope was something I clung to instinctively: it was the flotsam in the shipwreck of my life.

Finally I learned about Human Assisted Reproduction Ireland at the Rotunda Hospital. The HARI unit. Groundbreaking work was carried out in this fertility clinic at a time when there was no significant general support for it. Indeed, I suspect it took me so long to discover its existence because people who knew about it kept their heads down and their tongues still in case the Catholic Church tried to halt its activities. Back then it was tacitly condoned rather than actively encouraged in a state only incrementally coming to terms with a more permissive society.

When we contacted the unit we were told we needed a letter of referral from a specialist. That seemed straightforward enough. I was relieved that treatment didn't take place in Holles Street Hospital, for I had developed an illogical aversion to the building based on that brief consultation. (I still turn my head aside if I drive past it, seized by a 'shoot the messenger' reaction. I always think of it as Dublin's equivalent to Paradise after the forbidden apple is eaten, when the scales fall from Eve's eyes and she realizes she's naked. I felt naked there too.)

I made an appointment with a specialist. I picked the specialist for no other reason than the consulting rooms were within easy reach and a neighbour had just given birth to a baby in the clinic where the specialist was based and recommended it. I explained my predicament and asked for a letter of referral but the specialist refused.

'Why not?' I was bewildered.

The specialist wouldn't give me an answer and just looked at me, impassive, then studied the notepad on the desk, pointedly waiting for me to leave. I found myself snuffling back tears and pleading.

'Please,' I begged. 'I can't have babies any other way. The fertility clinic won't accept me without your referral.'

'No,' the specialist said. 'I can't give it to you.'

I was a menace on the road as I drove home, mystification, hurt and rejection liquefying into salt water and blinding me.

I still can't understand why the specialist didn't spell out whether it was a case of disapproving of IVF for religious, ethical or even medical reasons, or on what grounds it was not possible to help me. (I understood later it was religious – in my ignorance I blundered into the consulting rooms of someone – a parent, it so happened – whose virulent brand of Catholicism censured IVF.) Particularly puzzling to me about the encounter was that I had explained my purpose to the secretary when making the appointment. As I stumbled from the consulting room I felt somehow at fault. In the absence of an explanation from this specialist, for all I knew there wasn't a consultant in Dublin who would supply me with that letter of referral. I was deemed undesirable. At the time I felt inclined to accept that evaluation because I had already been judged infertile. Unsuitable, too, seemed par for the course. An impasse of several months followed, during which I felt frustrated and checkmated.

The deadlock was broken by a lovely girl called Barbara Barry, at that time my brother's girlfriend, who heard of my dilemma through him and asked her gynaecologist sister to see me. That's the unstructured way things work in Ireland, and lucky for me that it happened. My brother, Celsus, could as easily have said nothing, or his girlfriend could have decided not to intervene. And what were the chances she'd have an older sister who was a consultant specializing in fertility problems? But Barbara spoke to her sister about me, and I'll always be grateful. This empathic, compassionate woman – Doctor Carole Barry-Kinsella – interviewed me without delay, and after a consultation she wrote that gold-dust letter of referral. She didn't even present me with a bill.

It was so simple and straightforward, I could hardly believe it.

'Professor Harrison's the man you need to see,' she said, and her letter made it happen.

A burden was lifted from my shoulders. I danced out of her room to the bus stop, grinning at passers-by. Of course I had to be vetted before being accepted onto the IVF programme, but I was sure that was just a formality. The hard part was over, I reassured myself; now I was on the bend for home.

Chapter 8

We were hopeful that parenthood was finally within our grasp, that day in September 1996, as we made our way to the HARI unit in the Rotunda Hospital, just north of O'Connell Street. We had already been married for two years and it had taken a year of investigations to reach this stage. But we felt we could make real progress now. The HARI unit was the main assisted reproduction technology centre in Ireland. Others have developed since then but it was a trail-blazer. There was a sense of relief when we walked in: relax, you're in the hands of professionals.

At the unit we met a charismatic man in his fifties who inspired immediate trust in us. Professor Robbie Harrison was neatly formed, English, sandy-haired and a whirlwind of energy. He had founded modern infertility services in Ireland in 1985, was director of the HARI unit and had more letters after his name than anyone I've met before or since.

I was relieved by how unassuming he was; how he used no jargon, unlike many of the other doctors I'd encountered; how he offered us hope. 'You have a one in three chance of success,' estimated Professor Harrison.

I didn't hear the word 'chance' – I heard the word 'success'.

His statistics seemed slightly higher than others I've heard subsequently but maybe because I was relatively young and healthy he was more optimistic. Or perhaps clinics have grown pessimistic about success rates. Anyway, you could not fail to be impressed by the man – by his vision and drive, by his devotion to his work.

'I wish I could send home every couple who comes to see me with a baby,' he told us, sincerity radiating from him.

When Professor Harrison said he'd try to help us I could have genuflected. 'Give me your ring to kiss, professor, even the toe of your shoe will do.' Just as well he wasn't a mind-reader.

'There are no guarantees,' warned the professor.

We were wildly positive, however, and could hardly wait to start the treatment. I'd have begun it that very day, given half a chance. Break out the drugs, doc, and let's get stuck in.

We had to attend a group information meeting first, where HARI staff would highlight the pitfalls of IVF treatment and a roomful of prospective parents from around the country would nod and pretend to be prepared for the setbacks. But like us they'd be thinking, 'That only applies to other people – we'll be among the lucky ones.' These sessions were held every three months; we'd just missed one so we had to wait until December for the next.

As Professor Harrison spoke to us in his northern English accent, trying to contain our expectations, no doubt, I remember reflecting how overwhelming is news of infertility. It's akin to discovering that while you were sleeping an arm has been amputated, so you can no longer manage the simplest combinations – carrying something and opening a door at the same time, for example. Something you take for granted is snatched away from you. There's a sense of injustice, of course, for infertility is unjust. As well as that, there's a sense of recognition. Remember how, when you were a child, you were beset sporadically by a formless, name-less fear? A prickle on the back of the neck signalling fore-boding, terror of a bogeyman? The moment a doctor reveals your infertility, the bogeyman is unmasked. Now it has an identity. A sense of *déjà-vu* grips: the bogeyman is every iota as hideous as you imagined.

Perhaps it's odd that these feelings didn't seize me during the laparoscopy consultation – that was, after all, when I first had my infertility laid bare before me. Yet they seemed to have been placed on ice until my encounter with Professor Harrison. When you're having a consultation with an authority on infertility, that's when you truly understand you can't have a child without major intervention. The heavy-hitters have been called in.

It was now, sitting in Professor Harrison's office, that I fully accepted my laparoscopy result wasn't a mistake and the night terrors couldn't be contained by daylight. IVF was the only chance Brendan and I had of resurrecting the blueprint for our life together. So we were propelled forward towards another, heightened level of medical support.

We were also interviewed by a clinician and a counsellor before being accepted onto the programme. But I don't remember the interviews being difficult or fearing that we'd be turned away. The impression was of a clinic that wanted to help as many childless couples as possible, not for the money but because the people there genuinely cared about their work. 'Assisted reproduction' was how they referred to it, presumably so would-be parents didn't feel quite so inadequate. They were only lending some help, not doing the entire job for them. I always had a cartoon image of couples having marital relations in a room, with someone in a white coat banging on the door calling, 'Need a hand in there?'

I asked why older women's eggs were not regarded as being as desirable as younger women's. After all, older men's sperm could still perform, given half a chance. (Rich, male celebrities of a certain vintage were always sloping about reproducing, as far as I could gauge.) I was told there was an increased chance of chromosomal deficiencies in an older woman's eggs – that's why it was harder for her to get pregnant too. Survival of the fittest means survival of the youngest, in the female's case. Fertility rates drop after thirty-five and especially after thirty-eight.

'Nature is merciless,' I thought.

Someone should jog career girls' memories – not to panic them but to alert them. A timely reminder wouldn't have gone amiss with me.

I also wondered – but didn't ask – why it was always called IVF. I decided I knew the answer already. Men pioneered IVF and men have a weakness for acronyms and initials. A woman would have named it something more accessible, 'fairy godmother babies', perhaps; I persisted in regarding IVF as a fairy godmother treatment. Gift babies would be a good name too, it could even be an acronym.

We were accepted onto the programme and I was grateful, but unsurprised. As someone born for motherhood, naturally I'd be accepted. But we had still to attend that open meeting in three months' time as a condition of treatment. So we waited for that. Waiting was becoming a habit with us.

IVF costs around €3,700 a try. Allowing for inflation, and the change in currency from Irish pounds to euro in the meantime, the price was about equivalent back then. That was just for the hospital procedure. When I started it, couples were advised to budget for three attempts, so we were prepared to spend a minimum of €10,400 in today's terms. Most people have probably spent a few thousand more on doctors' bills, referrals and drugs before reaching that stage (though it is possible to offset the cost of the drugs against tax). As far as we were concerned, we would have to find the money. There was no question of further postponement, our plans had been in cold storage for long enough. We could tighten our belts, or borrow from the bank, or try to earn more money, or all three. Come what may, the bailiffs if necessary, we'd be having IVF treatment.

Desperate though I was, I realized it was non-essential treatment. Of course it was of vital importance to me, but I wasn't going to shrivel up and die if I was denied it. IVF treatment might improve the quality of my life immeasurably, but I didn't believe other taxpayers needed to shoulder that responsibility. In 1990s Ireland the hospital waiting lists stretched interminably. I thought of cancer patients waiting for radiotherapy, senior citizens hoping for hip replacements, maternity services shut down in one hospital after another around the country in 'rationalization' exercises. I couldn't justify condemning a dying man to wait an extra month for treatment so that I might have a free IVF cycle; I couldn't even defend an old woman waiting an extra month for a cataracts operation on my account.

Brendan and I could afford it, just about, so it was appropriate for us to pay. People spend more money on a holiday, on a wedding, on items of furniture. I'm constantly surprised, even with its cumulative cost, by how relatively inexpensive IVF is. I never begrudged a penny we sank into it. (I know Britain has recently introduced one free IVF cycle for women under forty, but Britain is richer than Ireland, with a larger tax base to generate revenue. Perhaps in time Ireland will follow its example.)

Finding the cash was tough but not impossible. We had an occasionally unreliable old car that we wouldn't replace as soon as intended, and anything I could earn would go on IVF bills. As a postgraduate student at Trinity, I was eligible to invigilate exams. I remember cycling to the Coombe

Hospital to supervise a medical students' exam and not being able to keep a straight face as a couple smooched at the back of the hall after handing in their papers. They couldn't wait to get outside. 'The bedside manner will be no problem to that pair,' I thought, tickled.

But it reminded me that Brendan and I didn't kiss each other as much as we used to, any more. Not passionate kisses. We seemed to make do with duty pecks. I felt unhappy about that as I collected exam papers. But I didn't do anything about it – I didn't have the energy to spare.

I also started to freelance at the *Irish Independent* and banked those cheques towards the baby fund as I waited for a place on the IVF programme.

Except something happened to interrupt the wait.

I woke one Friday morning in November complaining of cramps in my lower stomach. When I tried to stand up I felt faint. The cramps were so debilitating I decided to spend the day in bed. Since neither of us thought it was anything critical, Brendan went off to work as usual. By the time he came home that evening, the spasms of pain had moved to my upper stomach and midriff area. Dull aches were transformed into piercing darts.

I asked Brendan to buy me some painkillers from the chemist on the main road. I wasn't sure what the problem was because the pain wasn't like menstrual twinges or anything I had felt before; for starters it was concentrated on the right side of my body and was gradually moving up through it. Still, I took a couple of the tablets he brought me and they eased the pain.

We had been invited to a dinner party at a friend's house a few doors away that evening but my limbs were stiffening and I had difficulty getting out of bed. I realized I couldn't attend but encouraged Brendan to go on without me, feeling it would be unfair on the hosts if both of us pulled out at this late stage. Brendan dropped home between two of the courses to make sure I was all right and I was in reasonable spirits, having ignored the instructions on the box of pills and guzzled the lot. But when he returned at the end of the evening I was crippled with pain and screaming – with no more painkillers I was frantic for some relief.

Panicked, I attacked him for leaving me alone for so long, which was unfair since it wasn't long after midnight – he hadn't exactly stayed out till dawn. And he had come home to check on me, when I assured him I was fine. But the pain had grown almost unbearable and I was lashing out.

As the night progressed I grew steadily more distressed but, in my weakened state, I was unable to rouse Brendan. The pain had progressed to my chest and was squeezing it in an iron grip, threatening to suffocate me. I was so terrified I could feel beads of sweat spring up along my hairline.

'Wake up, Brendan,' I whispered.

No response.

By 3 a.m. the pain had mounted to my shoulders, with shooting stabs of pain in my neck too, and I was experiencing breathing difficulties. In a moment of insight between the tremors, I understood that I urgently needed to reach a hospital.

'Please, Brendan. For God's sake, wake up.'

He didn't hear me.

I tried to climb out of bed to reach the phone. It seemed impossible. I was now in a state of near-paralysis – even moving my head was becoming tricky. Finally, the survival instinct enabled me to shimmy by degrees towards the edge of the bed where I rolled out, pulling down the bedside lamp as I fell. I lost consciousness.

The almighty clatter woke my husband, who saw the state I was in and rang for an ambulance. Fortunately there was one passing nearby. Two ambulance men came into the bedroom, took one look at me and went into emergency mode. There was no time to dress, they wrapped me in my dressing gown and carried me downstairs on a stretcher. I heard them tell each other that I was waxen and had obviously lost a lot of blood. I was loaded into the ambulance and Brendan followed in the car.

The journey seemed to last seconds. As they raced through the streets I heard the voices of the ambulance crew, but their words slid away from me. Now and again a man with a reddish moustache, the one who wasn't driving, turned and smiled reassurance, but all I could think of was that my head was attached to my body via a singularly unstable glass neck. One more bump on this road, I fancied, and my neck will snap and my head plop off. And then wouldn't the man with the moustache get a fright. I felt eerily calm about the possibility. Next I was being carried through deliciously cold air and into the bustle of the Meath Hospital, where I noticed, with surprise, that staff seemed to be expecting us.

A young junior doctor asked me my blood type and I said I was fairly sure I was A positive, but he took a quick sample anyway.

'Could you be pregnant?' he asked.

It suddenly dawned on me I had missed my last period.

A call was made to wake the duty surgeon and staff prepared to move me into the operating theatre, but there was a slight delay while a porter was found to wheel the trolley. Meanwhile Brendan arrived at my side and said he'd just vomited up his dinner. My earlier terror had been alleviated by the arrival of the ambulance men, with their cheery efficiency, but now I was starting to feel very, very frightened:

I could sense the medical staff were extremely concerned. They appeared anxious for me to reach the operating theatre but still a porter hadn't arrived.

'I'll push her,' volunteered Brendan, but he was told this wasn't possible. Absorbing the expressions of urgency on the faces of the nurses and junior doctor who'd checked my blood type, my distress levels ratcheted up. Just then a porter hurried over and I was sent spinning along cool corridors towards masks, gowns and merciful anaesthesia.

Something didn't feel right. I concentrated, frowning, although my eyes remained screwed shut. There was something amiss but it eluded me. I struggled to prise open my eyelids and finally managed one, then the other. They stung. At first I couldn't distinguish anything but the blur steadied and I saw I was in an unfamiliar room. My eyes travelled along the walls. Pistachio – a chilly colour. The lampshade was alien too.

I tried to move my head to the side to seek for clues about my whereabouts but the same adhesive that clung to my eyelashes appeared to have been applied to my neck. All I could direct were my eyes in their sockets. I saw a shut door, another that was ajar – it seemed to lead to a bathroom – and a cupboard. Finally I managed to swivel my head to the left, where I could discern the emaciated limb of a tree. I did this cautiously, for even the slightest movement was agonizing.

Suddenly I remembered the ambulance ride and realized some disaster had befallen me, but the details were sketchy. A nurse pushed open one of the doors.

'Where am I?' I asked. It took a few stabs to force out the question, and I noted, with some detachment, that it didn't sound like my voice, for it croaked.

'The Meath Hospital.' She checked my drip. 'You were

operated on in the middle of the night. The surgeon will be along to see you shortly. He'll explain everything then.'

I felt exhausted by the exchange. It required a Herculean effort to continue so I allowed my eyes to flutter downwards. I must have slept. When I opened them again Brendan was there, looking ashen. I felt a surge of relief at seeing him, for I was finding hospital a bewildering experience. I still couldn't fathom what I was doing there. He was solemn as he told me about the medical emergency: I had had a ruptured ectopic pregnancy requiring surgery. The baby had attached itself to one of my fallopian tubes instead of making it as far as my uterus, the tube had burst under the pressure and I had started bleeding internally. A blood transfusion had saved my life. I snivelled a little as I heard about my baby setting out on a journey through my body and getting trapped halfway, but even this required energy I lacked.

Nurses called in while Brendan was there and I heard their tones mingle with his, but I drifted through layers of consciousness and could not decipher the words. Nor did I want to. Their voices were part of a reality I was in no way anxious to regain.

I was awakened when the surgeon who'd operated on me arrived, raincoat flapping open, dark circles under his eyes from his disturbed night's rest. 'It's still only Saturday,' I marvelled to myself, as the nurses bustled around him. The surgeon joked about how he'd been shaken out of a lovely sleep to attend to me. He was boyish and lively, only recently qualified, and younger, even, than either Brendan or me. He said I'd needed a massive blood transfusion, as much as they could give me.

'You were haemorrhaging blood,' he explained. 'The blood was rising through your body and when it reached your throat you'd have suffocated to death.'

'What would have happened,' I asked, 'if I'd left it until the morning to call out the doctor?'

His reply was stark. 'You'd have been dead. You'd have bled to death.'

Chapter 9

The dead baby preoccupied me, and lying there in hospital I had all the time in the world to dwell on its loss. Imagine, there had been a child inside me and I hadn't known. For a while I had been an expectant mother, one of that elite club I envied. I could have had a baby! I almost had a baby!

But my baby was dead.

Trapped in bed, alone for long periods and bullied by the restless pacing of my mind, came another realization: I might not be able to embark on IVF treatment for some time. My body would need a chance to heal. Oh God, what if the HARI unit rescinded its permission for me to join the programme? There seemed to be so many hurdles strewn across my path to motherhood.

Even though Brendan was attentive in his hospital visits, I became prey to doubt. *Maybe Brendan doesn't love me any more . . . maybe he's sorry he married me . . . but he has to love me . . . how can we have babies if he doesn't? . . . Don't be silly, he can't have stopped loving you already . . . but he might have . . . for heavens' sake!* I didn't have the strength to dwell on these meanderings, however.

My mind gave me no respite, and I allowed it to flit around tangential issues as a distraction from babies. I spent one afternoon wondering who had donated the blood for my transfusion – whether it had all emanated from a single source or if several people's blood coursed through my veins. I wished blood came labelled, not just with its type, A positive in my case, but with the name and address of its donor. I would have liked to send a thank-you card and a bottle of champagne. (Donating blood yourself is the best expression of gratitude, so I tried that later but was turned away for being underweight.)

'It wasn't a viable pregnancy,' said another junior doctor, fair-haired and striving for gravitas as he conducted his rounds. I felt a spurt of rancour towards him in that moment. My baby may not have been a viable pregnancy but it was still my baby. His words lacerated me. I invented a girl-friend for him called Winifred, who nagged mercilessly and rationed their intimacies, and a stomach disorder that reacted against spiced foods although he was addicted to them.

'How big was my baby?' I asked the junior doctor later, stifling my antagonism because I needed information.

He held up his smallest finger and indicated as far the first joint. 'About so big. It was only six to eight weeks old.' His pink face was still a boy's, I noticed, and looked kinder than it had initially.

Tiny, I thought. My child was quite, quite tiny. But it would have had a gender. Features would have been budding. Its height was already decided, whether it would have a sweet tooth, a sense of humour, a bent for mathematics; 30,000 chromosomes were already crammed into its minute body, defining its uniqueness. I stared at the ceiling.

The young doctor waited but I had no further questions for him. Still he didn't leave. I was aware of him, fidgeting beside me, and wished he would go on about his business so I could mourn my missing baby in peace. Then he began to talk about the loss of his mother a year previously. How, watching her pain in the death throes of cancer, witnessing her stoicism, he had learned more about being a doctor than five or six years of medical school had taught him. He said he had intended to go to the US after qualifying, but following the funeral had decided to stay with his father.

'We only have each other now,' he explained.

A ragged pause intervened.

I moved gingerly as I navigated the pain in my lower abdomen to look at him while he spoke.

'Do you know what I regret above all else?' he continued. 'It sounds ridiculous but I can't get it out of my mind. I hadn't started earning real money before Mam died. I never sent her on a holiday or bought her anything of value – a piece of good jewellery or an expensive handbag. I always intended to do something for her and I never had the chance.' The tips of his ears were branded with colour.

I met his eyes, which were gooseberry pale, and I recognized the ache of loss in them.

'She'd have been proud of you for becoming a doctor,' I said. 'That probably meant more to her than a gold bracelet.'

'You're right,' he agreed. 'But we lost her too soon all the same.'

I nodded and we rested in silence for a time.

A dear little nun, eighty if she was a day, came to see me on her hospital rounds a few days after my emergency surgery. Standing 4 feet 8 inches high, at a push, she tottered into the room and asked if I objected to a visitor. I did mind, I wanted to be left alone to wallow, but she looked so wholesome, so expectant, with her wrinkled-apple face and her candid smile, that I couldn't turn her away. She sat in a chair at the foot of my bed.

I studied her covertly while she spoke: integrity and sincerity radiated from her eyes. She had a silver wedding band on her gnarled finger, as befitted a bride of Christ, and she hunched forward in the chair to speak to me. She was in black and wearing a veil – nuns hardly ever wear veils any more – and a diadem of silver hair at the top of her forehead was visible.

As she spoke earnestly about God's will and how he moved in mysterious ways, I had the strongest impulse to slap her. It horrified me, but there it was, prickling at my hands. The urge was so pronounced that I had to knead my fingers to control them. I studied them, lying on the counterpane in that ice-green room, and they seemed to be independent entities. They might fly across the room and cuff that sweet old nun if I didn't keep them under restraint. I braided finger through finger and gripped for dear life.

The nun's eyes twinkled, convinced she was offering consolation, feeling useful. I nodded when she looked directly at me and wrung my hands together. Please go soon, I begged silently.

'There's a reason for everything, even if we can't yet see it,' chimed my visitor.

'Indeed there is, sister,' I agreed dully, although I didn't believe it for a second. There could be no reason for this loss. No reason could be trotted out to justify it. It was a double debit – the loss both of my baby and my one functional fallopian tube. I wasn't about to accept it as part of a benign power's master plan. An underhand pass from that arch-joker, chance, more like.

I urgently wanted my visitor to leave, but fourteen years of convent education are no preparation for evicting elderly nuns from your hospital room. Fortunately the nun stood up. Good, she was going, No, false alarm, she was rooting in her handbag, a vast black Gladstone, for a holy picture. She presented it to me with a smile that would melt polar ice caps. And the final ignominy: it showed the Madonna and

Child. *Holy Mary, Mother of God, pray for us sinners*, read the invocation along the bottom.

'Even the Virgin Mary has a child,' I thought sourly.

The nun settled herself back into her seat and recommended trusting to the healing powers of the Holy Spirit. 'He impregnated the Virgin Mary,' I thought, 'I wish he'd turn his attention to me.' Drained, limp and disposed towards gloom as I was, I still found the energy for a flash of cheekiness. A convent education is never wasted.

Nurses sometimes have a sixth sense about when a patient needs them. One of them popped her head around the door and detected something – desperation, probably – in my expression. Her eyes flickered to my visitor.

'It's time we gave you a drop of tea, sister, we'll have you worn out from all the visits you're paying,' she said.

'A cup of something would be pleasant,' agreed the nun as she allowed herself to be levered to her feet. She hobbled past my bed, pausing to pat my hand, not noticing the bone gleaming white through clenched knuckles.

'I hope I've helped you, dear, it's good of you to let me talk to you. You'd be surprised how many people don't want to be bothered these days. They tell me they've lost their faith. As though you could misplace it like a spool of thread.' She shook her head in bewilderment, then lingered for my response.

'Thank you for your trouble, sister,' I mumbled, despising myself for my hypocrisy.

After she left I tore the holy picture into shreds. It didn't make me feel any better.

'She wouldn't have known what you're in hospital for.' The chestnut-haired nurse who had rescued me assessed my slumped demeanour later. 'You're not our usual type of patient. The ambulance brought you to us because we were the nearest hospital but we mainly deal with geriatric cases.'

'She didn't know,' I agreed, 'she meant no harm.'
I turned my face to the wall.

At some stage during the night I woke up with the sudden, rather unwelcome realization that I was now an adult. I had never really felt like a proper grown-up before: it was as though I had been only playing at it. But a woman knows she's an adult after, not marriages and mortgages, but miscarriages. Yes, a lost baby was my admission to the grown-up world. It struck me as a forbidding place.

My room was a bower but I wasn't interested in flowers, considerate though people had been to send them. We were running out of space to display them — I gave the chestnut-haired nurse her choice of the bouquets and another to the tea lady. There was a window to my left and through it I could watch the tree branch that had first attracted my notice. I could only discern the branch, nothing more, because of the angle. It was skeletal, in keeping with the season. Nevertheless I studied its contortions, the angular twists of its digits, as though they had to be mapped in my memory. I grew attached to that tree branch: each morning when I opened my eyes I rotated my neck, seeking it out. For some reason I needed it. And it comforted me. It represented order in the midst of uncertainty: it was not a tidy piece of creation, with its contorted limbs veering and careering tangentially, but it pleased me more than — I counted idly — the eight floral bouquets I'd been sent by relatives and well-wishers. There was beauty in its simplicity and an adherence to natural rhythms. It was winter, it was right that it should be bare, but within a few months blossoms would bud on its outcrops. To everything there is a season.

On several occasions a plump robin alighted on my branch,

beady eyes glittering, neat head jerking left and right as he assessed the lie of the land. I called him Mr Pickwick and wished I could tempt him into my room, for his impudent colour and poise reassured me. I fancied I might borrow some of his self-assurance, for my own was leeching into the starched white hospital sheets. I was reduced to a crepe paper cut-out of myself. Not only had a bug robbed my fertility, its aftermath had hacked away my baby and one of my fallopian tubes. I felt I was being eroded, not by progressive degrees but in clamorous swathes and chunks.

The tree appeased me, not only because it obeyed the rules of the seasons, but because I associated trees with children. It was a link with the baby I'd just lost. The baby I thought of as my son. Little boys are drawn to trees, they want to climb them, build dens in them, scratch their initials on their trunks. I imagined my son in such a tree. I believed I had lost a son, although it was too early to determine the baby's sex. I moved my hand, the one without a drip attached, along my body until it reached the place where my son was cut from me. It hovered for a moment and then I touched my flesh through the hospital gown. My hand jerked away as though it had received an electric shock. The wound was excruciating.

The highlight of the week was when my brother Niall, his wife Fiona and my mother drove down from Omagh to see me at the Meath. My mother, Bridie, cried when she saw me, shrunken in stature, my pallor blending with the hospital bedding. 'Poor angel,' she kept repeating, stroking my hand.

We spoke about the traffic they'd encountered, whether they'd had trouble finding their way through the city, if they had stopped for a break en route. The usual desultory chit-chat between patient and visitors. Every so often, mantra-like, they'd repeat 'God, you're as white as a sheet,' marvelling. I did what all hospital patients find themselves doing sooner or later, I boasted about how close my brush with death had been. 'I had to have a massive blood transfusion – three litres,' I bragged. How quickly we become institutionalized.

My brother, Niall, brought two bottles of wine as a gift because he predicted I'd have enough flowers. You don't expect such practicalities from brothers. Even when they grow up to buy houses and run businesses, you still see them ridding the Wild West of cattle rustlers in their cowboy outfits with cap guns, or asking your advice about whether to write SWALK on their first Valentine card. He was right about the wine, though. There was no prospect of drinking it but the gesture pleased me.

The tea lady arrived with refreshments for my visitors, in view of their long journey, although she wasn't supposed to cater for them. Later she'd tell me she'd been diagnosed with cancer. There was resignation in her whispered confidence.

Another morning Brendan's brother drove from Belfast with flowers. I was touched, for he had a busy job that involved an excess of travelling, as well as a wife and young daughter. I thought it decent of him to take time out from his schedule and make the trip. But I worried about him having a meal before the return journey and he and Brendan went out to a nearby café.

Hospitals are a microcosm of society and you become interested in other people's lives, despite your preoccupation with the unsatisfactory nature of your own. Or perhaps as an escape from it. The kind chestnut-haired nurse was a single mother saving up to buy a car. One of the cleaners had just become a grandmother ('A little boy – he's the spit of my father'). The surgeon who saved my life arrived, beaming, and announced it was his thirtieth birthday. He had a wife

and young family and so wouldn't be going out to dinner.
Maybe at the weekend if they could drum up a babysitter.
Anyway money was in short supply, since he was only starting
off. I edged out of bed and shambled towards the wardrobe
where my brother's wine was stashed. 'Happy birthday.' I tried
to rustle up a smile.

The surgeon's face was transformed by a grin as he checked
the label; Niall always chose his wine well. He'd drink it that
night to celebrate his birthday, he promised. Meanwhile I
toasted myself with tea, rather smug at having a brother who
brought wine to a hospital instead of flowers.

I used to lie in my bandages, afraid to look at the scar beneath
the dressing. It was a constant source of pain, not just physical but mental, for it was through this livid slash in my body
that my finger-joint baby had been yanked. It hurt more on
the right side: that's where my baby had clung fleetingly to
life. 'Poor little mite,' I wanted to console it, 'you didn't stand
a chance.'

I know the baby would have killed me if it had been left
in place but that didn't minimize the loss of having it whipped
out. During that week in hospital, I thought how I'd have
preferred my baby left inside me, irrespective of the consequences: it was part of me, after all. But nobody had asked
me what I wanted – they couldn't have let me keep it,
anyway.

I'd have liked to have seen something, even if it was so
small I couldn't recognize it as anything other than a blob
of matter. Sometimes it still perturbs me that it was probably deposited in a petri dish and then sluiced down a disposal
unit. I understand why it happens but I also grieve that it
should be so.

So I pined for the baby, scarcely formed though it was,

and I despised the weakness of my body – the ineptitude of its workings.

It took me almost a week before I plucked up the courage to peek at the scar and what I saw horrified me, for it seemed to encompass my entire body. I could not imagine it ever healing. I could not anticipate how this six-inch laceration, a violent gouge of black and crimson running in a straight line along the top of my pubic bone, would ever be subsumed into the white of my flesh, as previous scars had been. It seemed animate, hostile, too brazen for my body to reclaim itself.

The surgeon arrived to examine his handiwork. 'It's a good scar,' he whistled appreciatively.

The junior doctor who had cancelled his American plans took a look too. 'It's a very good scar,' he agreed.

I scowled at both of them but they were too busy being congratulatory to notice.

'I had very little time to do it. But it turned out well,' continued the surgeon.

I frowned all the harder. This man had maimed me for life, how could he call it a good scar? Unexpectedly, their admiring faces made me laugh – except I had to stop because it hurt too much.

Since my scar wouldn't let me laugh, I lay there sulking after they'd left. I thought about checking on it myself, in case I'd missed any extraordinary features. But the truth was I didn't care to look at the slash, unlike the surgeon, who seemed frankly enamoured of it. I learned later that it was his first ectopic scar. Perhaps surgeons always remember their first scars, the way I recall my first assignment as a junior reporter. I sometimes wonder if my scar is immortalized in the surgeon's memory, just as I recollect the unexceptional pun I used in writing about a youth volunteer group redecorating a home for senior citizens. (Something embarrassingly obvious about a splash of colour in their lives.)

'My scar doesn't look like that any more,' I want to tell him now. 'You were right, it was a good scar: a clean line that faded.' But he knew it would.

I didn't believe it then, though, and because I wept – poor, overworked tear ducts pressed into service yet again – if I thought of my trapped baby and my sacrificed fallopian tube, with a hunk sliced out of it, I obsessed about the scar instead. It was an overbearing trespasser on my body. Offensive enough that it should be there, but it had no humility – it advertised its presence via spasms of pain if I moved, and sometimes even if I didn't. And it provided the dull throb that accompanied my morbid introspections. Looking at the scar hadn't contained the genie of my imagination. Quite the reverse. The scar wasn't reduced to manageable proportions but became ever-larger – so much for confronting your fears.

I stumbled across this information quite recently and it shocked me, even all these years later. The period of greatest fertility follows first surgery on fallopian tubes. So my chances of getting pregnant were relatively high after the laparoscopy. But nobody told me. The surgeon who performed the laparoscopy had mentioned that he'd managed partly to 'clean up' one of the tubes – the other was kinked and beyond repair. He didn't advise that there was a possibility I could become pregnant.

But I did. Instead of two obstructed tubes I now had one with a path partially cleared through – meaning egg and sperm could meet, after all. However if there's even a partial blockage, sperm and egg may connect but the developing embryo is trapped inside a tube, causing a painful and possibly life-threatening pregnancy. An ectopic pregnancy – literally one that is 'out of place'. In short, pregnancy can be dangerous following a spot of laparoscopy repairs.

Nobody warned me there was a chance of any kind of a pregnancy, let alone an ectopic one. If they had, I might have been warier when I started suffering with those stomach pains – concomitant with internal bleeding – that progressed up my chest. I wouldn't have been a sitting duck, waiting to bleed to death. 'Once the tubal problem is corrected there is a 50 to 65 per cent chance of getting pregnant,' I read much later. It might have been useful if someone had drawn our attention to that. 'After tubal surgery, implanting in the fallopian happens in ten to fifteen per cent of cases.' Nobody mentioned that either.

I was starting to feel a little better by the sixth day, leaping at the suggestion from my chestnut-haired nurse that she shower me and wash my lank hair.

'There's nothing like greasy hair for making you feel low,' she said. 'Having your hair washed is as good as medicine.'

The last time someone had soaped me I was still sharing a bath with my sister, and our idea of a treat had been to stay up watching *Ironside*, with chocolate biscuits on a plate between us. We weren't mad about the detective series but we preferred it to bedtime.

The nurse donned a plastic apron and hosed me down in the shower, while all the time I had to protect the ogre above my pubic bone in its welter of dressing. 'Keep the scar dry,' was the constant refrain. I was so relieved to be clean that any hesitation to do with loss of modesty was suppressed. I had a flicker of insight into what it must be like as a geriatric patient. 'Not so bad,' I allowed. Although it's degrading to sit naked on a plastic chair while someone directs jets of water at you, if the alternative is that sticky, unwashed feeling, you weigh the options and realize dignity is expendable.

I was an old crone half a century ahead of my time as I shuffled towards the bathroom for that shower, bent forward as though nursing a basket of eggs, white opaque surgical stockings on my legs. They were to prevent varicose veins, I think the nurse said, although afterwards I doubted the evidence of my ears. I never liked to quiz her about them, I simply continued wearing them because I'd been instructed to do it.

The nurse carried in a plastic chair for me to sit on, while I demurred, for I was sure I'd be able to stand up. I wasn't. She chatted while she shampooed my hair, talking about her teenage son. As a single mother, she worried at the lack of a strong male influence in his life. I was always fascinated by how much of their private lives these nurses were prepared to share – by the end of my week's stay they felt like friends who just happened to be able to change my dressing.

The following day I was allowed to go home. Obviously having my hair washed was a restorative. Another nurse, a curvy, dark one, sat with me while a senior doctor checked me over before discharging me. He was booming and jovial, and had been lavish with the aftershave: Ronald McDonald in civvies, clown suit at the drycleaner's. I shrank from this noisy, bustling individual, straining back into my pillows, and the nurse reached across unobtrusively to take my hand. She was one of the team I thought of as my clique, partly because of the details I knew about their lives. Her contribution was that she doubted whether her boyfriend, with whom she lived, had any interest in marriage.

'Now, now,' roared the doctor, a vast grin cracking his florid jowls, 'no pining. This is only a temporary setback, there'll be plenty more babies.'

I winced and the nurse sensed it, squeezing my hand.

'You'll be pregnant again in no time,' he bellowed.

'Doesn't he realize I only have one fallopian tube left? And it's banjaxed?' I thought.

The nurse increased her pressure on my hand. I was amazed at how needily I clung to the life-raft of her fingers.

A few checks and the doctor was on his way. 'Home you go. I'll see you in the maternity ward one of these days,' he roared from the doorway.

The nurse and I looked at one another wordlessly.

Brendan brought in something loose for me to wear for the short drive home, because touching the dressing sent a warning flash of pain. It felt liberating to shed my night-gown. All of the nurses on duty left the office to say goodbye, some teasing me about looking different with my clothes on. They hugged me and one of them hugged Brendan too. They waved as I walked slowly along the corridor, an arthritic 90-year-old trying to become a mother, and unexpectedly I felt a stab of loss. I knew how one was planning to emigrate to Australia – 'I'm going to take up with a surfer because they have great bodies on them, those fellows' – and that another despaired of ever paying off her credit card debts. They had been so kind, so open – I was on familiar terms with the quotidian of their lives and cared about them.

We never addressed this ectopic episode properly, Brendan and I. I tried talking about it later, to clear the air, but he became upset. I decided there should be a memorial to honour this boy-baby who had clung provisionally to life. I pondered on it, wanting to choose something that was exactly right, and plumped for stained glass window panels on either side of the front door. But what design should decorate them? At first I considered commissioning a motif of daisies – I'd loved them as a small girl, braiding daisy chains to wear as a fairy princess's tiara. Then I remembered reading how children are attracted to bright colours and I fancied our son would prefer something more vibrant. I thought of the sunburst orange and yellow nasturtiums that had bloomed in our garden that summer. They had sunk back into the earth now and the representative from the stained glass firm had no template of nasturtiums to copy. So I drew an uncomplicated picture of clambering flowers for him to use, twin bean stalks to the left and to the right of the door.

The stained glass was as beautiful as our unborn child and every time I turned my key in the lock I remembered him. On mornings after Brendan had left for work, I used to slip down and crouch on the bottom tread of the staircase where I could best admire the tentative fingers of wintry sunlight lighting up the flowers. It spilled through the glass and puddled into saffron shoals on the floorboards. I was celebrating my ephemeral days of motherhood as I shivered there, hugging my knees: that interregnum when my body had nurtured life, even though I'd been unconscious of it.

Then I hurled myself into fertility treatment with an emotion akin to despair.

Chapter 10

The Christmas season was gearing up when I was discharged from hospital but I did not see how I could bear to celebrate: to decorate the house with holly, listen to carols, wrap presents in gaudy paper and celebrate the birth of someone else's baby. Even if he was the Christ Child. But I struggled to do it because life goes on, in its impervious way, and because I had a husband who was looking forward to the break – who worked hard and deserved a proper Christmas. All the holiday season meant to me was the passage of time until I'd be well enough to try IVF treatment.

Something corrosive had happened as a result of that medical emergency, however: there was a scratchiness between us, a brittle quality introduced into the relationship; our love struck me as porous.

Now, here's the insane part, the point in the horror film where you're cowering behind the sofa, begging the girl not to venture into the room with all the strange noises. Instead of looking at these fissures in our relationship we forged ahead with IVF, pelted headlong into it, in fact. We thought it would ease all our tensions, for we were bickering constantly now – and about the most trivial of matters, from whether to buy low-fat or full-cream milk, to which route to drive through the city. We sniped about anything and everything – except the real issues. And while we knew these petty arguments were unhealthy, we convinced ourselves they were caused by our childlessness. As soon as we were parents the strain between us would be eased.

★

And indeed we were excited, a couple again, when the day came to attend an open meeting at the Rotunda about IVF. I was still having trouble walking, inclined to hunch over my scar, which registered its vexation if my body attempted any exertion. But I wouldn't have dreamed of waiting for the next meeting another three months down the line. We had to get cracking!

The quantity of couples in the room startled me. It was a large space but every corner of it seemed crowded. Was infertility really so widespread? We spoke to a number of couples who'd travelled from around Ireland, north and south. An evangelical atmosphere permeated that room, everyone intent on miracles. People spoke of borrowing from banks, ostensibly to buy cars and undertake home improvements, but in reality to finance their fertility treatment. One couple told us they were cashing in an endowment policy, another woman was sacrificing her pension. They admitted to delays of a decade or more in their quest for parenthood and our handful of years seemed meagre by comparison.

A woman from Derry with rimless spectacles told me she'd tried IVF in Belfast and was now planning on giving Dublin a whirl.

'Change of scene, change of luck,' she sang out, crackling with energy, although desperation crawled from behind her eyes and clumped at the lines around her mouth.

'Where will you stay?' I asked.

'We'll probably drive up and down,' she shrugged, minimizing the round trip of almost 300 miles.

Her partner was silent, hunched into his matching Aran jumper, listening to our conversation but not participating.

I wondered how many attempts they'd made in Belfast before switching to Dublin but thought it intrusive to ask.

She'd have told me, though, that woman – she was frantic to connect with someone.

I hunted out Professor Harrison after the formal element of the evening ended and told him about my ruptured ectopic. Did it preclude me from IVF? This possibility had gnawed at me. He reassured me I could still have the treatment but advised a minimum wait of three months for my body to heal. I'd been secretly hoping he'd say I could start immediately but even I realized my body was in poor shape. That evening I had been obliged to lean on Brendan's arm to walk from the car to the hall. I fainted if tried to vacuum the stairs, I grew dizzy if I carried shopping. My physical strength was at a low ebb, although my determination to have a child was undimmed. Quite the reverse. This setback made me more steadfast than ever.

There was free treatment for medical cardholders on the backs of the other patients' fees, we were told at the meeting. Obviously we could afford to pay, however, and it was right that we should. But it was a bit of a struggle to find the money and we had to budget carefully. An economy drive was soon under way in the household. Brendan brought sandwiches into work and I tried to make all my phone calls at cheap rate, switched to supermarket own-brand labels, borrowed library books rather than bought them, didn't turn on the central heating until the evening, hunted for clothes in charity shops. I didn't need perfume or nail polish, lipstick or expensive face creams, magazines or haircuts, I decided – extravagances I had taken for granted in London. What constituted a necessity was reassessed rigorously.

I used to cycle to save bus and taxi fares, but Dublin is notorious for bicycle thieves and after two were stolen in less than a year I decided to cut my losses and start walking instead. We ate out rarely, socialized hardly at all; it was a far cry from our single days when we both had substantial disposable incomes. Life wasn't a great deal of fun, to be honest, but personally I wasn't bothered; I believed I had more important matters than entertainment on my mind. I didn't trouble myself to check whether Brendan cared about us forgetting to have fun together.

Life steadily became a grind, as we put everything else on hold and concentrated exclusively on preparing for IVF treatment. Having a baby was proving to be a Gordian knot and our stabs at unpicking it sapped all our energy and enthusiasm. At least with most chores, if you plod away at them, eventually they'll be completed. But no matter how hard we worked at having a baby, it was a mountain that seemed beyond our abilities to scale. Unhappiness became a habit with us.

I hustled into fertility treatment too quickly, not allowing myself enough time to recover. I probably needed longer than the three-month bare minimum suggested by doctors, but that was all I permitted myself. Even if I was physically fit for treatment – which I presume I must have been or they wouldn't have accepted me – I certainly wasn't up to it psychologically, my emotions chaotic. But I couldn't delay: I was starting to grow increasingly panicky, imagining my biological clock ticking inexorably, time dwindling away. I was still relatively young. Not even one of those elderly primigravidas, as medics – cruelly, but accurately, I suppose – refer to first-time mothers in the second half of their thirties and beyond. I felt there was no time to lose, however.

The first tranche of the IVF money was due and, serendipitously, I had just been handed a cheque for £1,000 as prize money for a short story competition. I had been named best newcomer in the Hennessy Literary Awards a few weeks before my ruptured ectopic. Even in fiction I was consumed by my desire for a baby: the story centred on a pregnant woman. Asked at the prize-giving what I intended to spend the money on, I knew it would go towards my treatment but didn't like to confide this, so I was vague. Still, that award could not have arrived at a more opportune moment.

The story had arisen out of that well-known phenomenon, Student Laziness Syndrome, to which I had naturally succumbed when I was a student at Trinity. During the Hilary term, a creative writing class under the stewardship of writer-in-residence Sebastian Barry was on offer. Any interest I had in writing fiction was so latent it was practically comatose. But presented with a choice of drumming up a short story for Sebastian, or presenting an essay on nationalist allegory in nineteenth-century Irish literature, I had no hesitation.

I thanked my lucky stars that it would provide the cash to start us off on an IVF cycle. As far as I knew, the short story had appeared out of nowhere and there were no successors on the horizon to keep it company. By this stage – MPhil finished and faltering efforts to ignite a freelance journalism career under way – I had no imagination to spare. I needed it all for castles in the air about the day when I'd hold a baby in my arms.

And so the year wound down. Soon it would be a new year, 1997, and I believed this would be the one when I'd become a mother at last.

Chapter 11

It was spring and time to embark on our first IVF attempt. I was positive it would work, convinced we'd go home with a baby in our arms. By the end of 1997 our empty house – with its three unoccupied bedrooms and its downstairs lavatory for small legs too short, as yet, to manage the stairs leading up to the bathroom – would reverberate to the sound of a baby's gurgle. Those statistics about either a one in three or one in five chance only applied to other people, couples who wouldn't be as fortunate as ourselves. I felt sorry for them, but was glad to be among the elect.

I looked around our house, assessing whether it was ready for children yet. There was no nursery prepared – even I realized that would be tempting fate – but I had it modelled in my head. I knew which bedroom would be converted for the purpose: not the one on the half-return, it was too far from the others; not the one at the back of the house, you could hear the plumbing babble there as the cistern filled up, it might disturb the baby. At the front of the house were two interconnecting bedrooms and I decided that we would sleep in one and our infant in the other. I could be with it in an instant if it stirred.

The nursery would be mint green, with daffodil yellow door and window frames. Pride of place would go to that dappled grey rocking horse I aspired to, crimson saddle and harness on a sturdy wooden body. Twin to the one I remembered from my first year at school. The children in *Mary Poppins* had just such a horse.

There'd be a rainbow mural painted on one wall, and under it a cot with Tigger bedding – I even had a Winnie the Pooh video all ready to play for our baby, featuring Tigger embroiled in one of his trademark scrapes. There'd be a gargantuan honey-coloured teddy bear, a musical toy that played 'London Bridge Is Falling Down' and a squashy armchair in which to nurse the baby. Or better still, babies. My optimism knew no bounds.

A toy box decorated with alphabet letters would stand in one corner, and a painted bookshelf would hold pop-up books, foam books for the bath, illustrated fairytales, nursery rhymes and Oscar Wilde's children's stories. I also intended tracking down a book I used to read to my youngest brother, Conor. He'd been word-perfect on *Have You Seen My Puppy?* Cathal – another brother – had loved it too. I used to read it to a hypnotized audience.

There'd be a second shelf supporting a musical box, a painted wooden nutcracker standing to attention, a CD player with music that would soothe the baby, and photo frames showing his or her grandparents and other relatives. So our child would grow up familiar with the faces of those who loved it. A chest of drawers would have a changing mat on top, while each drawer would contain thumbnail vests and sleep suits. A dragonfly rug would cover the wooden floorboards and the nightlight would be a toadstool. Or it could be a pelican. But it definitely wouldn't be Our Lady appearing to St Bernadette at the grotto in Lourdes, the one I'd had as a child, brought back by my granny from a pilgrimage to the shrine. I'd adored it then, of course, but times had changed.

Best of all, the nursery would smell of babies – that powdered, silken fragrance that clings to them alone and can never be duplicated. The room would be saturated with that kissable warmth of baby scent, an aroma that makes you gather an infant closer and rest your cheek against it, craving its touch. But it wasn't a nursery yet, it was a spare room waiting for an identity. Still, I had an infinite capacity to imagine it settled and claimed.

Brendan and I presented ourselves at the fertility clinic to begin this treatment that would restore our damaged lives to us. A logo on the glass door as we walked into the purpose-built clinic entranced me. It was a heart-shaped symbol, each side representing a face, with a baby sketched in the middle. Mum, Dad, Junior. That was a promising start: they were stating their credentials, advertised at the entrance for all to see.

Immediately I felt a sense of purpose in the atmosphere. I had an impression of a low-key, clean space in its gardened enclave, at a remove from the bustle of the Rotunda Hospital and the even more urgent thrum from Parnell Square. Of experts in green scrubs moving decisively from one room to another. Of the murmur of subdued consultations.

We gave our names to the receptionist who asked us to take a seat. Two other couples were ahead of us. Nobody smiled or spoke; everyone was a bit tense. I looked at the other would-be parents in the cool detachment of the waiting room and our eyes skittered away from one another. Silence reigned. If a couple had to communicate they whispered. I could not decipher if it was shame or an attempt to maintain privacy. I had the distinct impression many people there would have been horrified to encounter someone they knew socially or from work. Maybe couples felt cowed by the environment: it was infinitely more pleasant than any of the waiting rooms I'd sat in before starting down the baby road, but there is a sterility to any medical establishment.

When my turn came a nurse carried out some medical checks on me, then I was given a prescription and sent into the hospital pharmacy for a course of drugs. These would override my menstrual cycle. The chemist read the scribble, sized me up and handed across the medication that would send me into a fake menopause. 'Keep these refrigerated,' he instructed, as I wrote out a cheque. He winked when I paid up. 'Himself will have to drink his beer warm if there isn't enough room in the fridge.'

The parcel of drugs always struck me as incongruous when I went to the fridge for milk. I'd open the door and the bulb would light up: fruit juice, butter, cheese, eggs, hormone suppressants. Hundreds of euro worth of drugs to be shot up my nose.

I grew light-headed, with a constant pounding headache, from pumping hormone suppressant into each nostril. I always overdid it, propelling too much in case I accidentally under-dosed. I inhaled every six hours and watched the clock avidly for my next snort. I'd set the alarm clock to take my sniffer at night, for the rule about inhalation every six hours was rigid according to my interpretation. I suppose a few minutes either way wouldn't have mattered, but I believed I couldn't afford to take that chance. Often I failed to return to sleep and lay watching the street-light outside. Dark semi-circles formed under my eyes and my pallor was pronounced. I grew distracted, my concentration levels were impaired, and crossing the road began to resemble a game of Russian roulette.

When I returned to the clinic for the next phase of treat-ment, they said my hormones weren't yet suppressed and to come back next week. Next week? That was light years away. I was determined it wasn't going to happen again. If my hormones had to be suppressed I wanted them annihilated. There wouldn't be a hormone left in my body, which was the general idea. Instead of one snort per nostril I increased it to two, eyes streaming and a steel band practising in each of my temples. My head was on the brink of exploding, but still I pressed my finger against one nostril, inhaled extravagantly, gave an extra blast for luck and turned my attention to the other nostril. I started having hot flushes – I was menopausal now, by God.

I decided to give up alcohol properly this time, instead of my half-hearted previous effort, in the hopes it would leave me more receptive to the drugs. Three-quarters of the children walking around the city were probably conceived on a few belts of gin, but that didn't dissuade me from my self-imposed abstinence. Besides, their mothers were probably so fertile that a steamy kiss would leave them three months gone. I needed the heavy artillery – sobriety plus drugs. While I wasn't a serious drinker, I enjoyed splitting a bottle of wine with my husband in the evening occasionally, especially at the weekend. It was what passed for a social life for a couple recently arrived in Dublin who didn't have a wide circle of friends. To be honest we couldn't afford much of a social life anyway, with a steep mortgage and only one regular income – what I had started to earn freelancing had tended to go on repairs as we attempted to upgrade the house, and was subsequently diverted to pay for IVF treatment.

It wasn't difficult renouncing wine because the sniffer suppressing my hormones left me with a permanent headache, and that, allied to the hot flushes, meant I was disinclined to drink anyway. Then my moods began swinging indiscriminately, fluctuating between joy and fear, exhilaration and depression. I felt guilty about these extremes of emotion, which Brendan found a trial, but I didn't seem able to control them – and I hadn't the sense to attribute them to the drugs. If I had understood them properly it would have made me feel less of a jangling bag of emotions coming unstitched at the seams. I thought that life, that disappointment, was making me tense; and that my husband's corresponding tautness of manner meant he was beginning to suspect he had made a poor bargain, landed with me for a wife. I didn't take account of the hormonal pinball games playing inside me, and nobody warned me about them. I presume Brendan was similarly ignorant and that he was wondering how on earth he'd wound up married to such a volatile loser.

As I continued sniffing and suppressing, waiting for phase two of the cycle, I realized there had never been a stage in my life when I hadn't wanted children at some point – when I'd thought that I'd prefer a higher income, or promotion at work, or a spare room to house my books and clothes instead of a nursery. Sure, I'd deferred motherhood, but that had been because I believed I could pick and choose when to enjoy the dual-income lifestyle and when to make space and time for children. It was always a case of when, never if. Now I wanted to turn back the clock and warn that carefree young woman, 'Do it now, don't procrastinate!' But you needed the right convergence of circumstances to have a baby and I never believed I had found them until I met Brendan.

After the sniffer came a different drug onslaught to rouse my ovaries into hyper-production. It was a hormone for stimulating egg-follicles, introduced into the body by needle, and I had to be taught how to inject myself daily. I've always had a phobia about needles but I couldn't allow myself to capitulate to it now. If injections were needed, then I'd learn how to do them.

'You have to inject the upper outer quadrant.' A nurse demonstrated the theory.

'Sorry? Do I have an upper outer quadrant? How will I recognize it?'

'Divide the buttock into four quarters and inject the upper outer one,' she explained.

Right. Not quite my bottom, not quite my hip.

A warm, supportive neighbour who had previously worked as a nurse came to the house to supervise my first injection and I soon came to terms with it. Still, if I worried about sniffing the wrong way with the nasal spray, I fretted twice as much in case I was doing the injection ineptly too. I knew I had to hold the needle, pencil-fashion, at a 90-degree angle and dart it in, but I was never convinced I'd managed it according to specifications. What if I dawdled instead of darting, would that affect the outcome? And how about the angle, did I need specialist equipment? I turned my haunches into a pin cushion in the process but I felt inordinately proud of learning to inject myself.

And, more to the point, I managed to stimulate egg production. Just what the doctor ordered. By the end of the treatment my ovaries felt heavy and swollen, a pair of over-ripe plums that were painful to the incautious touch, like budding teenage breasts. My body was puffy from this augmented egg production and I thought I was going to spontaneously combust when staff at the clinic scanned me and decided I needed a few more days for the eggs to mature. I felt as though I was hatching ostrich eggs – any bigger and they'd swallow me up.

Yet looking at my eggs on the scanner – well, at dark patches that the staff assured me were eggs – they didn't seem all that gargantuan. In fact, some of them were down-right minuscule. It was the oddest sensation watching the HARI people manipulate the equipment to measure my eggs, frowning with concentration. The eggs had to reach certain dimensions or they were no use to me. So size *was* everything, after all.

Towards the end of the cycle it seemed I was trailing in and out to the Rotunda daily, although it wasn't that often. Still, I wouldn't have been surprised to look down at the pavement and see a channel gouged into it from Ranelagh to Parnell Square. While I could handle the ovaries' stimulation stage of the treatment at home, I had to attend the clinic regularly to be monitored for hormone levels and follicle size and number.

Also for blood to be taken. For me, the hardest part of the egg production aspect of the treatment was the blood letting. The needle I used for ovary boosting was a tiddler compared with the horse needles staff brandished. The whole business of needles and veins terrifies me, I'd willingly donate a pound of my flesh before a pint of my blood. But I had to grow accustomed to an inexorable succession of needles, enlarged, by my cringing eyes, to enormous spikes. *Come on, ladies, you're not seriously considering shoving that javelin in my arm? It will drain me dry in five seconds flat.*

'Ready, Martina?'

'OK – but I'm not looking.'

I used to stand outside the clinic bolting my courage into place before keeping an appointment, wondering if I could plead a cold and be let off the hook this time.

'Why do you need so much blood?' I bleated to a nurse, buying myself a minute's grace.

'It's for storing your eggs,' she replied.

That answer comforted me. If I was providing a safe haven for the eggs after they were taken from my body, I could spare the blood. Just about. I never stopped scrunching up my face and tensing, all the same. I never lost the desire to cut and run when I saw the needle approaching. Giving blood was a misnomer: they prised it out of my reluctant veins, syringing it from me at every opportunity, it appeared to me.

'Sorry to be such a coward,' I apologized, even as I shrank from a blonde nurse approaching me with a needle. Not just any old needle but the Eiffel Tower in kit form. I bet they were saving it up especially for me.

She paused, amazed. 'None of you women who have IVF treatment are cowards,' the nurse replied quietly. 'Quite the reverse.'

We are, though, I contradicted her mentally; we just find the idea of childlessness more frightening again.

Having a baby was my alpha and my omega and I could not develop a sense of proportion about it. I was incapable of saying, 'All right, it's a shame, but at least Brendan and I have each other.' You might just as well have told someone whose house was burning to the ground that at least they didn't have to worry about buying new curtains. As far as I was concerned our present life was meaningless without children. And without them I felt excluded from the future as well, disbarred by childlessness from participating in it. To me, having babies was a way of investing in society's prospects and without children I could stake no claim.

During that first attempt we spoke tentatively about the possibility of adoption. We agreed we might consider it further down the line – the unspoken thought being that if IVF didn't work, it was a fall-back position. But of course the IVF was going to be successful so really there was no point in dwelling on adoption. In addition, the two-year time-frame for adopting a baby was a deterrent, as was the prospect of intensive vetting. Checks are only right and proper – better for the child, better for the parents in most cases. However these stipulations pitched couples such as us back onto the fertility treatment conveyor belt. It seemed the fastest, easiest, most certain chance of parenthood. Adoption, bizarrely, appeared more of a long shot. Except IVF wasn't the easy option we had mistaken it for, and I wasn't far enmeshed in the treatment before I realized that. Realized it and yet had no choice but to continue, since opting out meant acceding to infertility.

Sometimes, in that warren of rooms in the HARI unit, it felt as though I had ceded my sovereignty to IVF. There were always undercurrents of submission for me because it is a supremely invasive treatment. Once the medics laid their hands on me, scanned me with their instruments, plumbed the depths of my inadequacy with their microscopic cameras, I felt dehumanized. I was caught in a pincer movement: trapped between the biological imperative of my hunger and the bells and whistles of science, which regarded me as matter. Not as a woman.

At times I wanted to explain this to the people who treated me. I wanted to say, 'I have emotions but I'm not allowed to show them, in case they interfere with the smooth running of medical procedures.' I was always afraid to succumb to the outburst, however, in case they dismissed me as unstable and postponed the treatment. Baby hunger had made a captive of me, yet I was also a victim of Stockholm Syndrome for I was in thrall to my jailer.

You leave your dignity at home when you enter a fertility clinic. It takes no time at all for you to feel diminished as a woman: you're something under a microscope for medics to prod and consult one another about. I used to wonder where I was in all of this — I felt I was shrinking, that I'd drunk from the same bottle as Alice in Wonderland. The erosion of one dogma — that I would become a mother — seemed to have induced a decomposition process in all my orthodoxies. I was worthless; my self-esteem was the first casualty.

It's not that staff at the clinic handle you with disrespect; quite the reverse, the staff are what makes this process bearable, with their compassionate professionalism. I remember the kind faces of every nurse and doctor who treated me. But taking the fertility treatment route strips you of pride and self-reliance. You are already shaken, as you walk through the door, because the certainty of parenthood has been compromised. You have undergone invasive tests, you know you and your partner can't handle this alone any more, and the notion of self-determination is ashes. These factors conspire to leave you feeling demeaned – arriving at the fertility clinic in a humbled state.

You're hopeful too, however. Optimistic that the techniques of medical science – state-of-the-art drugs and revolutionary treatments replacing eye of newt and toe of frog – can set everything to rights. Humankind can achieve anything, after all. We can send a man to the moon, we can transplant hearts, we can clone living creatures. Helping a man and woman to get pregnant should be child's play.

My favourite part of the week was Saturday morning, when I'd buy a copy of the *Irish Times* and climb back under the duvet with it, while the central heating fired up to the unequal task of warming the house and Brendan napped beside me. I'd turn immediately to Births, Marriages and Deaths near the back – I was only interested in Births. I'd linger over the announcements of children born to people I didn't know and never expected to meet.

DRUMMOND – Ross and Sarah are thrilled to announce the birth of Leo on March 2. A second grandchild for Timothy and Paula Drummond and a first grandchild for Liam and Miriam

Boyle. Many thanks to Dr Patrick Foy and all the wonderful staff at the National Maternity Hospital.

KINSELLA and O'TOOLE – To Daragh and Heather, a beautiful baby daughter, Rose, on March 3. A little sister for Aidan. Buíochas le Dia.

How I loved these columns. How I savoured their names. A little girl called Rose. Now, would she be Rose Kinsella or Rose O'Toole? Or maybe she'd have both names? I wanted our children to have both our names. I'd have liked Devlin as their surname, for I was attached to my name and felt the automatic patriarchal selection was unfair, but I accepted that Brendan might not be happy if I suggested this. Our children would have Devlin as a middle name though.

Sometimes Brendan would indulge me in my game, listening as I read aloud the names and hooting at some of the concoctions children were saddled with. I liked it when he'd do this, I felt close to him. Other times he'd cavil that it was thumbing our noses at fate and we shouldn't risk it. I preferred it when he humoured me so I could have a partner in my make-believe. He'd splutter at one entry with half a dozen Christian names topped off with a double-barrelled surname.

'Who do they think they are, royalty?'

'Maybe they couldn't decide and left in all the names they liked,' I suggested. 'Or maybe they're trying to appeal to every wealthy relative in the family.'

'A wealthy relative can be the only excuse for a name like Petronella,' he'd say. 'Even then, I'm not convinced it's excuse enough.'

I never tired of reading about grandparents in heaven watching over them, or trying to decipher personal messages ('welcome to the convent, Daddy' – now what on earth could that mean?). Or remarking how people named their children one way, but intended calling them another.

To Eugene and Megan, a perfect daughter, Alexandra (Alex).

Or noticing how foreign-born parents also wanted to announce their children's births in the *Irish Times*.

SCHMELTER. To Heinrich and Sheila, a son, Owen Heinrich, a first grandchild for Friedrich and Gaby in Berlin and a second for John and Noreen in Naas. Sincere thanks to Dr Valerie Moloney and the caring staff at The Coombe.

I lingered over one in which the parents announced they were 'overjoyed and somewhat surprised at the arrival of Orla Ellen, a little sister for Jack and Sam'. Had they given up hope of a daughter? Had she been premature? Or had she been a tummy ache transformed into a baby? Oh, I could pass the day with no trouble, weaving elaborate stories from the birth announcements.

As time passed Brendan wanted to ban me from drooling over them, for I surrendered myself to those columns. He was trying to insulate me against disappointment, or maybe he feared I was becoming fanatical – which I was. So then I read them in secret, although I missed our shared chortles at the names we'd encounter, and our joint speculation about the lives of these families. I missed saying to him, 'Here's a name we haven't put on our list. How about Declan? I can see us with a son called Declan.' And him considering, weighing the name in his mind and trying it out against his own surname. Or producing some anecdote from his past to endorse or invalidate the selection. 'Every boy at school I knew called Declan was good at football.' Or 'Every Declan I knew had a runny nose.' I regretted losing the closeness, the sensation of moving towards a shared goal that we had when we had read them together.

But we did make progress towards this target all the same,

snort by snort and pricked vein by pricked vein. Moving steadily towards extraction day, when my eggs would be 'harvested' by the medics. I wasn't one of those women who read about IVF every chance that came her way, at that stage. I didn't want to hear about others who'd had seven attempts and still failed. Or about women who'd succeeded on their ninth try. I think I knew, at some level, I wouldn't be able to keep trying indefinitely. My courage would dry up. Three attempts was reasonable, my husband and I decided at the outset – the doctors had recommended three tries, not four or seven or nine.

Meanwhile, the cocktail of drugs flooding my system continued to make a whirligig of my emotions. But it would all be worth it soon because we were nearing egg-extraction day, the day for which the battery of drugs had been preparing us. It was time to gather the harvest. Trepidation was replaced by excitement.

Chapter 12

I was too keyed up to sleep on the night before my eggs were due for collection. I hadn't slept the previous night either, because I had to stay alert until midnight when I went to a neighbour's house, clutching my little kit supplied by the HARI unit. This was for a special hormone injection, hCG, to help release the eggs. It had to be absorbed into the bloodstream thirty-four to thirty-six hours before harvesting – mimicking the menstrual cycle again – and would facilitate egg retrieval. It was too important an injection to risk tackling myself. This neighbour, the same former nurse who had shown me how to navigate my upper outer quadrant – now there's a skill – had kindly volunteered. Goodness knows what I'd have done without her; learned to do this injection too, I guess, or made a midnight dash to the HARI unit.

Brendan and I held hands walking into the clinic on egg-collection day. It was early – hospitals always want you at the crack of dawn – but not too early for me to be whisked away and instructed to don another of those nighties flashing my bare backside.

At least I didn't have to travel or stay in a hotel or with relatives, unlike couples from the country who attended the HARI unit. I shuddered at the thought of that extra burden, remembering the woman from Derry with the hopeful, desperate eyes. But the women I encountered in these situations were universally uncomplaining – they were simply grateful to have this chance of motherhood.

The theatre was akin to a topsy-turvy dentist's, with four women up for extractions that morning. I was the first to be wheeled in, my legs hooked into stirrups by one of the green-gowned acolytes who surrounded Professor Harrison. He was in the theatre and it looked as though he'd be performing the operation. Good, I was in safe hands. My eggs would be removed using a fine, hollow needle, with an ultrasound to help the doctor locate them, I had been told. 'Hope I don't have to see the needle,' I thought, just before the anaesthetic shut down my powers of observation.

After the extraction Brendan was waiting for me near the operating theatre, outside a bank of curtained cubicles. I was woozy but Brendan seemed animated. Approving, too. 'They extracted fourteen eggs, Martina, that's four more than average. The medics seem very pleased with you.'

But he hadn't been too impressed with the amenities where he was invited to make his sperm contribution while I was under the anaesthetic. 'It's just a little room with no facilities. They offered me a magazine for "stimulation" but I said no, it didn't seem right. It was grim in there, I can tell you.' Later it struck me that though the man's role in the IVF procedure is painless and relatively straightforward, it must be tough for men being left more or less on the sidelines, their role reduced to a brief walk-on part, while the medical focus is on their partners.

The nurse's head materialized through the curtains. 'You can go home as soon as you've finished your tea. Take it easy for the next two days and we'll see you on Thursday for the egg transfer. Ring tomorrow to check fertilization has taken place.'

'You mean it might not?' I was shocked at the prospect. Nobody had warned us of the possibility.

'It probably will,' she soothed, 'just ring to be on the safe side.' Brendan and I looked at each other, petrified. A new source of worry.

He removed the teacup from my hand. 'Let's get you home to bed.'

We were given progesterone – the female sex hormone – pessaries for me to take daily for the next couple of weeks. After egg transfer, these would be boosted by oestrogen tablets.

I was nauseous on the drive home after the anaesthetic but I kept thinking, 'This is it, we're about to become parents.'

Brendan put me to bed and brought me more tea. You drink a lot of it, whether you want it or not, in these situations. It felt odd being separated from these eggs I had been growing so assiduously, having them measured and scanned, waiting for them to grow some more before they were harvested. It was weird to think of them in a laboratory four miles or so across the city. I was conscious of a surge of protectiveness towards them and spent the next few days concentrating on those fourteen specks marked with our names. (Later my sister told me that was her favourite part of the procedure – when the eggs were in the laboratory. 'They were somebody else's responsibility and I didn't have to worry about them for a few days,' she said.)

The next day we heard that seven of our eggs had fertilized. The clinic only intended to replace three, to give them the best chance of taking. I worried about what would happen to the other four and meant to raise it with the HARI unit. When it was time to return my fertilized eggs to me two days later, however, I was so caught up in the excitement that, I'm ashamed to admit, I forgot.

It wasn't Professor Harrison but a different doctor replacing the eggs, only this time they had subdivided and were four-cell life-forms. No longer eggs but embryos.

I had to have a full bladder and assume the position – naked from the waist down and bend your legs like a frog's. Brendan waited outside with his newspaper during the insertion. It was something of an anti-climax. No anaesthetic, no theatre trolley, no hoopla. I had expected some procedure requiring a tad more scientific ingenuity than an instruction to spread my legs. Surely it couldn't be this straightforward? I craned down, trying to see what was happening, but it was impossible due to the angle. All I could discern was a doctor at the foot of the bed, intent on what she was doing. It hurt a bit, but nothing compared to previous prodding.

'They're good quality embryos, all grade As,' remarked the nurse, making conversation.

I was relieved, until I thought, 'Hold your horses, do they grade them like fruit and vegetables?'

The doctor didn't speak, sitting between my wide open legs and concentrating with admirable attention on my vagina. There was no distracting her as she used a fine catheter to transfer the embryos into my uterus through my cervix. No more than three can be returned legally – some clinics only return two, in view of the risks associated with multiple births.

'There,' said the doctor. She was the clinician who had interviewed us after Professor Harrison when we'd been applying for admission to the programme. 'Lie quietly for twenty minutes and then you can go home.'

'Is that it?' I was astounded. No fanfare, just a bit of poking about in my nether regions.

'It only takes a few minutes,' smiled the doctor, unpeeling her surgical gloves.

'I'll send Brendan in to you,' interjected the nurse.

They always made a point of remembering couples' names, a practice that lent an air of intimacy to proceedings that were unconventional, at the very least. The use of first names set us at ease, and I wondered if it was a directive from Professor Harrison.

Brendan arrived. 'Three good quality embryos,' the nurse told him. 'Grade As.'

His expression showed he was just as taken aback as I had been.

'Tell me when twenty minutes is up,' I suggested, to lend him something to do. He nodded and consulted his watch.

'So you're pregnant now,' said Brendan, when we were alone.

'We won't know for certain for a few weeks but . . . fingers and toes crossed.' I beamed, unable to rein in my optimism. Of course I was pregnant, the only question was whether I'd have one baby – or three. 'I hope it's at least two,' I thought, 'so I never have to go through this again.' Once was quite enough.

Brendan was so protective, he virtually carried me to the car and clipped me into my seatbelt, driving home in third gear, to the fury of every vehicle behind us. I felt caressed by his solicitude and relaxed into the comfort of optimism.

'I've moved the television set up to the bedroom for the next couple of weeks, to keep you company,' he said, pulling the handbrake on outside our house.

We smiled at one another, in love with life. In love with the lives I was carrying. Then I walked upstairs carefully, gripping the banister in case I tripped and jeopardized everything.

The days passed in a blur of soaps, crossword puzzles and phone calls with my family. I watched the sky turn from slate grey to powder blue from the nest in my bed, and was grateful for a window on the world, even if the telegraph wires I'd intended to leave behind in London scythed through my vista. I thought about spring waking up the patch of green behind the house, and about the lilies transposed from my grandparents' garden in County Limerick stirring into life. One of the babies should be called Lily, I decided, making a mental note to check Brendan's response to the name. Lily would be an auspicious omen: a connection with my long-dead grandmother who had lavished so much devotion on her lilies – although it was my grandfather who had dug in manure and spent hours pruning them – and this product of the next generation she had not lived to see.

It was a little lonely there, spending all day in bed, but if it helped the babies I had no complaints. The warm, considerate neighbour who had given me some of my injections called one day to keep me company, bringing her quilting with her. It was therapeutic to watch her industrious fingers while I was a study in indolence. She was making the quilt for her daughter, and I adored the idea of this small girl having a reminder of her mother's love in future years to come, thanks to the patchwork blanket growing before me.

My main terror was of accidentally rolling onto my front and somehow damaging the babies. Squashing them or something. I knew the chances of a pregnancy going awry were at their highest during the first trimester and felt vulnerable. Any time I developed a twinge I could hardly breathe for fear it heralded some more ominous development. So I lay serenely on my back, day after day, a brace of pillows propped behind my head, and simply incubated. I thought I should be working my way through that year's Booker Prize shortlist or the complete canon of Dickens, but I lacked the concentration. Newspapers were as much as I could manage.

Each evening Brendan would come home, kick off his shoes, stretch out alongside me on the bed and I'd feel a soporific buzz of contentment. The sort that's redolent of a languid summer's day when the sun's warmth strokes your face. Brendan and I were on our way, at last, to the place we were meant to inhabit.

'Everything all right?' he'd ask as soon as he came home, anxiety crisscrossing his forehead. I'd nod, beaming. Everything was waxing more positive by the day. For as each one passed, my optimism swelled. By day six I was calling the babies by their names, by day nine I was checking their star signs in the newspaper, by day fourteen I was trying to decide whether I should use caterers for a christening party at home or book a restaurant, by day fifteen I knew with every fibre of my soul that I was a mother-to-be. On day sixteen we were due to return to the clinic for a pregnancy test, a foregone conclusion as far as I was concerned, although I wanted to participate in the ritual. I was eager to experience all the rites associated with motherhood. Brendan was caught up in my excitement and certainty, part of it all now, at last, no longer marginalized as he had been during the medical procedures.

'Can you feel anything?' He stared at my uncovered stomach.

'No, it's like a late period except you definitely know you're growing a baby.'

'You're growing a baby,' he grinned.

'We're growing a baby,' I beamed back.

'Let me massage your neck for you, I saw you rubbing it earlier. You're probably stiff from lying propped up in bed.'

'That would be great. I'll just go to the bathroom and then you can do it.'

I sat on the toilet seat for aeons. I had glanced down into the bowl and been confronted by traces of pink mixed in with the urine, the early warning signal of a period. It's a mistake, I told myself, mesmerized by the shoal of pottery fish on the bathroom wall that we'd brought back from our honeymoon in Ecuador. I knew that when I looked a second time there would be no sign of pink — it had been a trick of the light. I gazed into the bowl again, willing myself to see clear water, but there they were. Pink streaks. I touched my fingers to my body and they were rosy-tipped when I drew them away.

I dragged my drooping body to my feet and tottered along the landing in search of Brendan. Poor, unsuspecting Brendan, flicking through television stations with the remote control.

'You were a long time, I was nearly coming to look for you,' he said, without looking up.

'I'm bleeding.'

His neck cracked around and his stare was bewildered. Tears welled exquisitely slowly from his eye sockets and moisture bubbled from his nose. I watched him, dispassionate for a moment, before I pulled his head to me and cradled him against my chest. His sobs rushed thick and fast now, snorting howls of anguish.

'We gave it our best shot.' I stroked his hair. 'The odds were against us, we knew that when we started.'

'I really thought it had worked.' His tears were soaking my nightgown. I wondered at so many, when I seemed to have none. 'You were so confident, you had me believing it as well. You said all the pain and distress were front-loaded and we were over the worst.'

'You need to be confident to go through IVF, you have to push the statistics to one side,' I shrugged, uncannily calm. 'It's self-preservation, a willing suspension of disbelief.'

Brendan's tears seemed to be easing. He leaned against me, a crushing weight, but I was glad to carry it.

'We'll do this again as soon as they let us and it will work the next time,' I promised him.

'Do you really believe that?' He gulped back a final, shuddering sob.

'I know it,' I said quietly. I believed it implicitly.

Later hope pulsed again, buoying me up through the inky dark of that long night. I rang the clinic as soon as it opened in the morning, convinced the blood meant I'd miscarried only one of the babies. But surely not all of them? Of course not all of them, I probably still had two or maybe even just one baby left. I couldn't possibly have lost all three of them.

As I dialled the number, I was determined that some positive inference could still be drawn.

'I've started bleeding,' I stammered. 'This doesn't mean I've lost all the babies, does it?'

The voice was detached but sympathetic. 'Unfortunately it does.'

'There's no chance that even one of them might be still alive? I had three embryos returned to me.'

'I'm afraid not.'

'You don't need to test me to check? In case one of the babies has made it? I could come straight in if you like.'

'I'm so sorry, if you're bleeding there's absolutely no chance you're pregnant.'

I hung up as the world buzzed, aloof from me. I could hear the traffic outside the window and the purr of household gadgets, but I seemed removed from them. My eyes followed the intricate Celtic spiral on the black metal of the fireplace, my toes curled into the nap of the claret Turkish rug beneath my feet. The telephone lead coiled against my fingers, animate, waiting to spring. I was aware of these extraneous details but felt separate from them, frozen in a state of suspension.

After a time I phoned Brendan at work and he was unsurprised by my update, for he had not clutched at that bogus hope as I had.

Post fell through the letterbox and dropped on the mat, traffic sounds heightened momentarily by the movement of the flap. At that incursion into my quarantine, the tears bubbled up. I keened for every toe I stubbed, every test I failed, every dress I spoiled, every snub I suffered, every cross word flung at me. I clawed at the air, oxygen supply tapering off, as scalding tears spurted from a bottomless well. I thought they must surely leave ridges on my cheeks, so blistering were they.

It did not stop that day, or the next. Tears were my companion wherever I went. I wept when I was on my own in the house, when I was walking along the street through bustling crowds, when I was in bed at night with Brendan. He tried to comfort me but he couldn't. I allowed him to embrace me but in my heart I rejected him as an inadequate substitute.

I did not want his arms around me, I wanted my own around a baby.

Chapter 13

In this beleaguered state we geared up for a second IVF attempt. Afraid to try again, and even more afraid not to try. We were leaving a three-month gap between cycles – the bare minimum. Now I know it was too short. My topsy-turvy hormones needed time to recover, more breathing space than I was prepared to allow them.

We mourned together over that first failure, Brendan and I. We were puzzled that medical science had disappointed us, because medical science was meant to rescue us, not leave us marooned. We seemed able to produce eggs – was that not supposed to be the hard part? I'd heard other women had trouble in that department but I was a natural-born battery hen. So why wasn't IVF working? But we'd definitely be lucky second time out, we consoled one another. We chattered loudly and insistently about how we were virtually guaranteed a positive result next time. But we never spoke about what was really important: the impact this treatment was having on our marriage, the strains under which our relationship was starting to buckle, and the subtle shifts in our attitudes to one another.

That tendency to jibe at one another, suspended during IVF treatment, resurfaced. As a reprieve from the IVF roller-coaster, we went on holiday for a week to New York between cycles. I discovered there is no break from obsession, though; my thoughts were a monorail. I bought a black embroidered skirt with an elasticated waistband, thinking I'd be able to wear it in the early stages of pregnancy. Then I chose some art deco-style dinner plates in a huge china emporium called Fish's Eddy, still trying to nest. Typical tourists, we visited Central Park, the Empire State Building, Ellis Island, SoHo, Times Square. But all the time I was counting time, wishing my life away.

I sobbed at any setback. When I stepped off a steep footpath to cross a busy road and fell, tearing my new skirt and bloodying my knees. When I lost my sunglasses. When I bought the wrong CD and couldn't find the receipt to change it. I could not distinguish between reasons to cry and reasons to reserve my tears; I was ready to weep for a stranger's misfortune, I was incapable of not weeping at my own.

We flew home again and soon I was back at the HARI unit, IVF cycle number two under way. Some couples left a year's gap between attempts to give their marriages, their lives and their health a fighting chance of recovery. Brendan would have been happier taking a longer break between the first and second IVF sessions, sensible as I could not be, for I was incapable of deferral. I would have started again the next day, never mind three months later, if the doctors had authorized it. I couldn't have put it out of my mind for a year – every month I'd have been angst-ridden over another wasted chance. Pregnancy took so long at nine months – I'd be almost a year older before I was a mother.

'I want to be young enough to pick up this baby and cuddle it,' I insisted to Brendan, when we discussed a delay. I know it sounds ridiculous, now, but I felt ancient. What was that term again for an older woman giving birth for the first time? Elderly primigravida. Imagine seeing that on your medical notes! I believed I didn't have the luxury of time for gaps between IVF cycles, when we could have concentrated on our relationship instead of trying to introduce another component into it. Time was my enemy.

I felt betrayed when Brendan suggested waiting for a few months, although he had our welfare at heart. I dismissed it as procrastination: a woman's chances of the treatment working were improved by youth and I wasn't going to squander what remnants of this precious attribute remained to me. My sense of perspective was so far adrift that a six-month postponement felt as interminable as six years. I was ageing, my womb, ovaries and eggs were ageing, I'd be a haggard biddy among the unlined young mums on the labour ward. That's if I ever reached one. My mother had already produced all of her children by the time she was my age and my granny wasn't far behind. I needed to get cracking.

I read somewhere that the largest increase in the British birth rate was due to women aged thirty-five to thirty-nine but it didn't make a scrap of difference to me. I was suffused with dread about getting too old to accomplish this.

'Six months won't make any difference,' Brendan pointed out.

But as someone on the boundaries of elderly primigravida status, I was convinced I didn't have a day to lose. 'It might make a difference, I can't take that chance,' I explained, borderline tearful, as ever, these days. I turned away so he wouldn't see the moisture in my eyes. I just wanted to be pregnant before it was too late.

Meanwhile everyone around me seemed to be getting pregnant. Everyone. I was surrounded by swollen bellies as far as the eye can see. My covetous nature howled if I had to be in the same room as them, let alone listen to their complaints about varicose veins or back-ache or insomnia. I especially didn't want to hear any complacent 'This is my third' or 'We're hoping for a boy.' Older mothers vexed me because they'd managed to have a career and a family, while younger ones also provoked me because they'd made motherhood a priority. The only pregnant women I could bear in my proximity were those I knew had experienced failure in the past, with previous miscarriages or impediments to conception. Even then my grudging tolerance was less about generosity of spirit, and more about the fluttering hope that if it could work for them it might work for me too.

This warped sensibility turned me into an ogre. I remember listening to a woman at a party chatter about her five children, listing their names, ages and characteristics. She wore a velvet Alice band and I could have torn it cheerfully from her head and twined it round her neck to throttle her. Anything to stop this pleasant, unassuming woman speculating on whether she should try for a sixth baby and what she might call it. I knew she wasn't boasting, yet I was suffused with a murderous spite towards her. Logic, once something I prided myself on, had bypassed me. 'She's hogging all the babies,' I fumed, as though a finite number could be born.

Occasionally I had a blaze of insight and suspected I was turning into one of those cantankerous characters infuriated by everything. But in the main I wallowed. Women breast-feeding were enough to send the self-pity needle quivering off the Richter scale. There's something inherently moving about the synergy between mother and child during it – in the force of their concentration on one another. I'd be trans-fixed with yearning watching them. It could turn me into a blubbering wreck, incapable of moving, or a seething mass of thwarted energy. I'd rush off and vent my spleen on the stair carpet, hauling the vacuum cleaner up and down the stairs and letting it roar on rugs. But nothing could dilute the impression of my nose pressed against the windowpane of a life I seemed disbarred from sharing.

I was determined to move heaven and earth to be part of it all. Cycle number two was under way. Time, now, for the sniffer: in, out, in, out, inhale, exhale. Slowly and deeply does it. Don't start on the second nostril yet, give it a minute to sink in. God, how I anguished over this simple chore. It should have been easier second time around but it wasn't.

The 4 a.m. alarm calls to spray hormone suppressant up my nostrils were a particular worry. I took forever settling back to sleep afterwards. I always woke myself thoroughly before spraying the sniffer, afraid of botching the job if I was half-asleep. I panicked if I even missed the time by fifteen minutes during the day. I was terrified everything would be spoiled.

Brendan would say, 'The sniffer times are only guidelines, don't get so het up about it.' But I'd be distraught if I didn't adhere to the letter of the instructions.

I felt I had my role to play and if I didn't carry it out faultlessly I could jeopardize the entire process. I saw it as carelessness not to be aware of the clock at all times. 'Two and a half hours to my next sniffer,' I'd think. I forgot once and was nearly three-quarters of an hour late – so flustered I could hardly inhale, panting in my agitation, it took half a dozen tries before I was able to believe enough hormone suppressant had been taken into my system.

At night I tried doing it in the dark to avoid disturbing Brendan, who started work early, but I dropped the sniffer a couple of times and was afraid of breaking it. So I began rising and going to the bathroom to snort, and fret, a lonely business in the silence of the night, and my fractured sleep patterns took their toll.

I formed the habit of making wishes during this second attempt: just one baby, I'll die without a baby.

I was compulsive about wishing, I'd do it on anything, from finding a lucky penny to my first glimpse of the full moon.

Just one baby, I'll die without a baby.

It was always the same wish. I'd wish on a coin thrown in a fountain. On a pair of magpies, two for joy. On a shooting star. On the Daedalus statue at the foot of Killiney Hill, because while he fell, he also flew.

Just one baby. I'll die without a baby.

Snorting my sniffer, permanently watching the clock for my next inhalation, and wishing, wishing, wishing. Everyone embarking on fertility treatment is wishing, in truth, however scientific they believe the undertaking to be. Wishing on the magical doctors, the charmed medicine, the miraculous hand of fate.

Just one baby, I'll die without a baby.

I started to wonder at which stage I had become infertile. Exactly when had my fallopian tubes become a maze? Could I have become pregnant if I'd tried a year earlier? Two? Was there a moment as I ate pizza or visited the hairdresser's or washed the dishes or boarded a plane, when my body heaved its last sigh of fertility and became barren? And I never knew it? My body had been shutting down while I, unsuspecting, immersed myself in the minutiae of life, ignorance protecting me. But not indefinitely.

My former happiness seemed to mock me because it was rooted in a lack of foreknowledge. I wished that bodies could semaphore their looming deficiencies to the brain before they became irretrievable. I imagined how, if mine had murmured a tip-off – 'three months left and then you're sterile' – I'd have sprung into action. Instead of continuing to look at menus in restaurants or push supermarket trolleys. But no warning had been delivered, no hint was given of rapids ahead, and I could only construe that my body was no longer on my side. It was a conclusion that shocked me profoundly.

★

Back I went to the HARI unit to keep another appointment. I never saw a flesh-and-blood baby there; not an infant,
not a toddler, not a child of any description. Funny that,
because what we patients all had in common was the desire
to have a child. We were a community of yearning. I guess
the staff realized it might be tactless to allow people to bring
children into the waiting room. They did think about how
we felt, even if it wasn't always immediately apparent.

I could never pretend to be interested in a book or a
magazine while I hovered in the waiting room. I simply
listened for my name to be called, preparing for blood to
be syringed out of my tired veins, to be given another
prescription for drugs. I'd sit there in the tastefully decorated
room with all those tastefully dressed couples. There was no
evidence of poverty or even straitened finances – were we
all middle-class? Were couples on lower incomes not allowed
to be infertile? (The clinic did treat some couples on a pro
bono basis, I later discovered, charging the moneyed a little
extra to cover costs.) I wondered that we never spoke to
each other, puzzling over why the idea of chatting to the
woman next to me should be so daunting. I suspect most
of us were too exhausted for casual conversation.

The old lags were easily spotted, for the air around them
did not quiver with the same degree of tension. They weren't
relaxed, exactly, but they weren't as edgy as the newcomers
seemed to be. Some first-timers verged on overwrought: one
woman with designer sunglasses tangled in curly light brown
hair was there on her own, flicking agitatedly through a
magazine. Slap, slap, slap went the glossy pages. The period-
ical was upside-down. I wondered where her partner was
and wanted her not to be alone there. Such openly displayed
emotion was rare, however, and mostly I was conscious of a
veneer of civilization.

Brendan was less often at the clinic with me during the second IVF cycle. Perhaps he was busy at work. Or perhaps I made him feel excluded. Was I growing self-sufficient? Did he feel increasingly tangential to events? I never thought about how he felt, I just waited. But I tended to feel naked when I attended the clinic without Brendan – I always had a sense that it required a couple to negotiate its detached professionalism. That you needed to have your hand clasped in another's. Consolation received and returned. One and one add up to considerably more than two when you're feeling vulnerable.

On a confident day, I'd look at the clinic's noticeboard, with its photographs of newborn babies, and ask myself how long it would be before our son or daughter joined those infant pin-ups. I never said anything but I must have betrayed my assurance, because sometimes the staff tried to manage my expectations. I didn't want to listen – I was incapable of it. The statistics didn't apply to me.

But those confident days were becoming rarer. I started having other days when the logo on the glass door, which I had once found charming, now caused my pulse to slow. I used to stare at it, willing it to come true for me. Let me share that Mum-Dad-Junior miracle in the heart-shaped emblem. It will happen if I walk home today without stepping on any cracks in the pavement. If I see a bride. A black cat. A rainbow. I'd give blood, let them test my blood pressure, check my weight and any other inspections they needed to carry out on this faulty chassis of mine. Then I'd go to work in the *Irish Independent*, where I was freelancing, or shamble home.

There was a listlessness clinging to me that I couldn't shake off the further into this second tranche of treatment we progressed. It left me limp this time, everything exhausted me. I must have looked as disorientated as I felt because my purse was stolen twice walking home, once on O'Connell Street and once again when I stopped in Moore Street at a vegetable stall. I wasn't safe to be let out on my own.

In the evening Brendan and I would often take the air, because he felt cooped up in his office and needed to stretch his legs. We'd stroll a certain distance and then I wouldn't have the energy to walk back. Lassitude settled on me and I found housework exhausting. I was constantly tired, my head throbbing permanently from the hormone suppressants; but I was afraid to take a pill in case there was an adverse reaction in this body I was attempting to prepare for motherhood. I looked dreadful and friends or relatives who hadn't seen me in a while commented on my appearance: My weight, already slight, dwindled as the pounds fell off: I was thin, wan, limp. I could have explained why but I resisted, unwilling to talk about the IVF, which was a deeply private matter to Brendan and me. A few people knew, of course, including our families, but I didn't want the world to share our secret. It was too private, too painful to talk about.

Brendan's face wore the pinch of nervous tension. Members of his family mentioned he didn't look great to me several times, naturally concerned, but I felt a little defensive, imagining myself criticized. I hardly knew how to explain I was incapable of looking after myself let alone anyone else. With hindsight, I can see that Brendan was feeling the pressure too. Our arguments started sparking more frequently and trailing off unresolved.

Even those we confided in had such odd ideas. They sometimes asked, for instance, if the child would be 'quite, you know, normal'. I suppose it was fair enough to question health problems from children born via IVF. 'Yes, quite normal,' I'd snap. Hadn't these people heard of Caesarean sections? Or did they consider them abnormal too? IVF was a little like a Caesarean section in reverse – doctors were putting in an embryo instead of taking out a baby.

So far there are no medical problems linked with IVF babies and the treatment has been in existence long enough for extensive tests to be carried out – unlike some of the other methods of assisted reproduction.

There were side effects from the fertility drugs used to stimulate egg production, however. Not just the lassitude that afflicted me, during this second shake of the dice, but effects of a more serious nature. A woman needs to be carefully monitored – hence all the clinic visits – to ensure she doesn't develop ovarian hyper-stimulation syndrome, which can mean hospitalization while her over-accelerated ovaries settle down. (Death has occurred in one unfortunate case in Ireland. Medical misadventure was recorded by the coroner in April 2004 in the case of one poor woman, Jacqui Rushton, just thirty-two, who wanted nothing more than to be a mother. Her over-stimulated ovaries produced thirty-three eggs and, following complications, she lost her life.)

There was another reason why this second attempt was fraught: we had been introduced to failure. And we had to be prepared to meet it again. Except, I told myself, we mustn't think about failing, we had to concentrate on succeeding. I forced myself to remember Scotland's historic hero Robert the Bruce and his inspirational spider. The Beirut hostages who never abandoned hope. David and Goliath. The tortoise and the hare. Every triumph-over-adversity story I had ever heard. Quite simply, I felt I had no choice except to press on. I owed it to my husband and to the process I had embraced to do it again, come what may. To call a halt after one strike smacked of defeatism.

In any event it was my only chance of motherhood. By this stage I was starting to feel it was the sole reason I had been put on this earth. I could detect no value in other accomplishments. Honestly. You could have pointed to Mother Teresa of Calcutta and I've had said, 'Yes, she achieved a lot, but what a pity she had no children.' Or to suffragette leader Emmeline Pankhurst, and my first response would have been, 'She had so much to be proud of – five children, wasn't it?' Reproduction was all that signified with me.

As for the occasional woman I met who admitted she didn't want children, I pitied her for what I perceived as her selfishness. Instead of admiring her honesty or even acknowledging her right to choose. 'She'll regret it later,' I thought, with the subtext, 'and it will serve her right.' The more foiled I was in this most natural of desires, the reproductive urge, the more frustrated I grew. Stumped, floundering and hopelessly, pitifully sad.

Wretchedness started to attach itself to me. I wondered if it was visible to others. People don't enjoy being around those who are constantly grieving; you're allowed latitude for a while but then it grates. It's contagious, I suppose. There's always the fear my despondent mood will infect you.

Sadness is tricky to mask, though, it leaks out from behind the eyes and filters through the tonal layers in the voice. Your face in repose betrays you, even if you manage to inject some effort into conversation. 'We thought you were so gloomy,' people who knew me at that time, but were unaware of my circumstances, have said. I was morose, sleepwalking through the motions of everyday life.

Children, even other people's, could galvanize me, however. Heaven help anyone who brought a child to a social event I attended. I hijacked them, joining in their games, helping them colour in pictures or play I Spy. The adults would stand around in one room with their glasses of wine or mugs of coffee, while I'd be in my element in another, reading story books or watching *Postman Pat* videos or admiring dolls. I'd always been interested in observing how children play but now I was besotted.

Babies, in particular, were a source of fascination. I could watch them for hours, noticing how their mouths opened automatically, little baby birds' beaks, before their hands came out to grasp a biscuit.

If I spotted a baby in a pushchair, I morphed into one of those dotty women who walked backwards to look at the child for as long as possible. The day also arrived when I saw a pushchair and loitered in a shop doorway until it was safely past, for fear its gurgling cargo would unpick my precarious composure.

I was consumed by a sense of powerlessness. But I would not surrender to this fate; I would have a child. Maybe, I rationalized, destiny was testing me. Checking how strongly I wanted a baby. But surely, as soon as it became apparent how committed I was to motherhood, fortune would relent? That's how I overcame the misery of a first failed attempt. I accepted my disappointment as a challenge to prove I was worthy. Redemption through suffering. But I'd be given my reward after a second cycle . . . wouldn't I?

My parents were stumped by my infertility, each descended from a long line of profuse families. I have fifty-odd first cousins, so many I've lost track. My sister's infertility didn't count because it was secondary infertility, the result of complications following little Justin's premature birth. I explained about the banjaxed fallopian tubes to them.

'There was never any infertility in my family,' my father remarked to my mother.

'Well, there was never any in mine either,' she responded, indignant.

My father, a believer in the maxim what can't be cured must be endured, never criticized my IVF efforts, although from his strict Catholic perspective – he was a daily communicant – he must have had reservations.

'I'm just trying to make babies,' I explained to him once, 'the Catholic Church approves of that.'

'Well then, I'll pray for you that it works,' he offered, starting a novena to St Gerard Majella, patron saint of mothers.

My father always called them test-tube babies when he mentioned my IVF treatment. In response, I'd crack a threadbare joke about my children being born under the sign of Pyrex.

'It's nothing sinister, Daddy, just a little medical intervention. Modern medicine doing its job,' I'd tease him. 'How are the novenas going? I need the big guns on this one. Is St Gerard Majella able for the job or do we need to upgrade to one of the Blessed Martyrs?'

He'd shake his head and add another novena to his list, this one intended to cure me of leanings towards apostasy.

My sister Tonia and I agreed our genes were just plain clapped out by the time they reached the current generation; the wombs we'd inherited were exhausted from all those vast Irish families that had preceded us. It helped me to laugh about it with my own family. I knew their love for me was unconditional so I didn't feel defensive about my sub-standard fallopian tubes with them.

'Wouldn't it be fabulous if you could return faulty fallopian tubes to the manufacturer,' I sighed to my sister. Then I had a better idea. 'I think they should work on transplanting fallopian tubes, the way they do hearts and livers,' I exclaimed.

'Donor tubes, that's the way forward. You can let me have yours when you're finished with them.'

She was dubious. 'Trust me, you wouldn't want mine. They've had too much abuse.'

'Just like mine, then. Next life around, I'm going to be kinder to my fallopian tubes and take out all my dissatisfactions on my liver or spleen.'

It cheered me up to be flippant about it. But only a little. I never knew why people spoke of the baby blues: my colour palette was unremittingly monotone. A drab shade of grey. So if some banter with my sister lifted the tone from charcoal to dove grey occasionally, I was grateful.

I grew to resent my body. It was slight – only seven stone and 5 foot 1 – and I used to wonder if my frame was too meagre to nurture a child. Occasionally people would comment on my size. 'Oh, you're so lucky, you can wear what you like, you don't need to worry about dieting or what you eat.' I'd purse my lips and wonder if a fuller figure might act in my favour. People didn't refer to buxom shapes as childbearing hips for nothing. I came to despise my body. Even the way I dressed altered: I wrapped myself in a bulky anorak for the first time since the age of nine or ten, bought baggy jeans, flowing skirts, chunky sweaters to disguise my frame. Once I had worn Lycra, clinging jersey, fitted silk – I gave away these clothes or hid them in the back of the wardrobe. I didn't care to look like a slim woman, I wanted to look like a mother. Whatever she looked like. I wasn't 100 per cent certain, I just knew the old me didn't resemble one.

As that second cycle continued, sniffer replaced by injections to kick-start my ovaries again, I stopped wanting to look attractive, even for my husband. I abandoned make-up, washed my hair infrequently, cared less about my appearance. It was only a body and a fallow one at that. I remember noticing, as Brendan came through the door in a suit after work, that he looked exactly how he had in London when I first knew him. And here I was: lank-haired, drowning inside an oversized sweatshirt, not so much as a flick of mascara to enliven my pasty face. I knew I looked like a right mess. And I didn't care.

Sometimes, in the aftermath, I wondered if my festering resentment of my body made it tense and unreceptive during this IVF cycle. *Why should I facilitate her when she's so antagonistic towards me?* I didn't have to be narcissistic but I could have been less hostile. I had this unreasonable conviction that my body was behaving disloyally. Poor old thing. Subjected to those persistent medical procedures, pressurized into a role it was incapable of fulfilling, blamed for everything. Poor little body.

I became fixated on the word barren, that most arid of terms, with its biblical connotations. All those blighted women critically noted in the Old Testament – wives not fulfilling their function. Sarah, Rebecca, Rachel, Hannah, Michal, Samson's mother, who's not even named. Downgraded, and at their wits' end, until God the Baby-Giver (sons please, Yahweh) intervened. Isaac's wife, Sarah, laughed when he passed on God's message that she would have a child in her old age, Genesis tells us. 'Nutty old codger, he's in his dotage,' you can hear her thinking millennia later. Maybe Sarah was laughing with relief, too, with joy, with anticipation: barren no longer.

Barren. I rolled it around on my tongue. I had a barren womb. If the desire to reproduce is natural, then inability to reproduce is unnatural. So I was a barren, unnatural woman. Also a self-pitying one, evidently.

Taking a shortcut through the main building of the

Rotunda Hospital, I often passed teenagers who were anything but barren, defiant bellies poking through dressing gowns as they sucked nicotine into their lungs. I looked at them and looked away. I was afraid if I kept staring, I'd snatch their cigarettes, grind them underfoot, and slap the girls for risking damage to their unborn babies. How many of them truly wanted children right now at this stage of their lives, I wondered? I didn't mean that they wouldn't love them, but how many wouldn't prefer, in their hearts, to live a little first? They were so young, some of these girls. They should be dancing along on tiptoe, not shuffling on the soles of their feet. And yes, I confess it, I questioned the logic that allocated babies to them and denied them to me. 'They'll love their babies,' I thought, 'but not more than I would love mine.'

Brendan and I seemed unable to communicate, probably because he was still functioning rationally while I was operating on tunnel vision. 'If it doesn't work this time we'll take a real break from IVF,' he suggested, halfway through this second cycle.

Rather than consider the merits of his proposal, I felt winded. 'What do you mean if it doesn't work this time?' I spluttered. 'Even if you think it, for God's sake, don't say it!'

The truth was that I was hysterical about any intimation of failure, as though even to whisper it would hex my chances. Any suggestion of it provoked me. Not so much to anger but to flailing panic. It also made me feel isolated, submerged in this difficult undertaking on my own. I cast around for some way of demonstrating my alienation and decided I was going to stop dusting our framed wedding photograph in the sitting room. That would show him!

He looked at me across the rim of his coffee mug and his expression is with me still. I couldn't read it then – to me it was impassive; now I think that, below the deadpan surface, a moment of revelation had just dawned for him. I suspect he had finally grasped that I was not to be reasoned with, that I was mutating into an obsessive. That baby hunger owned me.

In this state of communication meltdown, we spent our last night together before I was due into the clinic for my second egg-harvesting session. We slept with our backs to one another, stiff with misunderstanding, and I touched my bloated ovaries and told myself everything would be back to normal soon. When we were a family.

Chapter 14

Extraction day and it was back to the topsy-turvy dentist. In the car Brendan and I made conciliatory small-talk, trying to paper over the previous night's tension. Then it was on with the silly hospital gown that gives staff an eyeful of your bottom. Has everyone in the room seen it or should I do a lap of honour to hoover up the stragglers?

'Medical people never notice these things,' my sister had claimed, when I had complained the last time, but I didn't believe her. How can someone not notice those naked twin globes if they're waggled in their face?

Feet up in stirrups and time for the egg hunt; I knew the drill. No Professor Harrison this time in the theatre, I observed, and then the anaesthetic pulled me under.

As I recovered outside the theatre, I was fretful that I had only produced ten eggs this time compared with my previous fourteen. 'Ten's very good,' soothed a nurse. 'Some women only manage seven or eight.' That's true, I consoled myself. All I needed was one baby, after all. Brendan didn't express an opinion either way.

I worried more, this time, during the days between harvesting and their return to me, about the destruction of surplus embryos. I felt resigned to it on one level, sad about it on another. I didn't want my embryos trashed — I had gone to hell and back to help create them, after all. But neither could I realistically expect all of them to be implanted in me. I couldn't hope to give birth to quintuplets or sextuplets when producing one baby, unaided, was beyond my capability. I wasn't exactly a natural at this conception caper. So I was pragmatic enough to see that selecting three of the best embryos was the surest path to motherhood. Freezing surplus embryos for future use would have been one solution, but at that time the HARI unit didn't do this.

I feel cross with people who say they're not opposed to IVF so long as there's no destruction of embryos. Recently I read a mother of four express this opinion in a newspaper. As a mother of four she's in a privileged position – I wonder if she'd adopt the same strict ethical stance as a wretched, inconsolable mother of none?

All the same, I'd have liked my surplus embryos to have been donated to a couple with no embryos of their own. Or used for medical experiments if donation was unacceptable. For all I knew, my excess embryos went down a chute. (The clinic later assured me that this definitely didn't happen.) If someone had given them to me I'd have buried them in my garden, but I never heard tell of them again.

I was never worried about the possibility of any eugenics aspect to embryo selection and rejection – tailoring a baby to meet the parents' specifications. There was never the slightest hint of embryo selection on any basis other than choosing the ones most likely to survive.

But when I returned for egg transfer this second time, I raised the subject of my deselected eggs and embryos with one of the nurses. It was the blonde one who had described women undergoing IVF cycles as brave.

'I'd like to donate my surplus eggs or embryos, whatever's needed, to a couple who can't grow their own,' I offered, while we waited for the clinician.

Her jaw plopped open, like a haddock's on the marble slab of a fishmonger's. Then she recovered, the shutters clanged down and she said, 'Donation is illegal in Ireland.'

'I know, but I'm just saying to you here that if the clinic wants them it has my permission to take them. I'd prefer them to be donated but they can also be used for experiments. Someone must have let their embryos be experimented on at some stage or we wouldn't have IVF.'

She didn't respond; I had the impression I'd frightened the life out of the woman.

I hoped they'd take them, though. I hoped she'd report the conversation to someone more senior who'd be prepared to apply the natural law instead of the state law.

Sometimes I fantasize about a young adult coming up to me one day and saying they'd discovered my eggs or embryos had been donated to their parents and I was their biological mother. But I realize it's only a pipe dream. In my heart I know there is no unclaimed child of mine walking about in the world.

And so, as the nurse and I waited for the doctor's arrival, along with the three embryos chosen by the medics to have a chance of locking on to life, I concentrated on them. My three maybe-babies. I had to think about them now instead of dwelling on the other little life forms that wouldn't be returned to my body. It was necessary to prioritize, for the babies' sake.

Into the silence that followed my donation suggestion, the nurse cautiously dropped an ice-breaker. She remarked that I had produced a number of higher-grade eggs. Again that roar of outrage, as before. Imagine my eggs being graded! Judged and given a ranking! I felt protective of the eggs whose scores had been less favourable. 'An A-minus egg might still develop into a Shakespeare or a Picasso,' I wanted to protest. 'I bet they've given me all the beefy jock embryos instead of the weedy creative types.'

But I said nothing. The decision had already been taken, the eggs selected for transfer were waiting.

It was a different doctor returning the embryos to me, a younger woman compared to the first one who'd taken me through this procedure. I was more relaxed because I knew what to expect and decided to indulge in some chit-chat to pass the time.

Ireland is a small country and connections are easily established: after a few minutes' conversation with the clinician, we realized her aunt had taught me at primary school. 'Now that has to be a positive omen,' I thought. Mind you, I'd have found favourable portents anywhere. So we spoke about this energetic nun, long since retired, who'd taught me my first words of Spanish — a Christmas carol — while embryos went whizzing up inside me, one after another, guided by an ultrasound picture.

'Tell Sister Mary I was asking for her,' I said, as she finished and prepared to move on to the next woman due to be reunited with her embryos.

'I can't really — there's confidentiality attached to working here,' she responded.

'I don't mind, I'll release you from it,' I beamed, drunk on hope. Intoxicated by the possibility of life budding within me.

She smiled, non-committal, while I lay there with my legs arranged into that silly frog pose. 'Impersonating a cowboy will be no trouble to me after all this is over,' I thought.

There was twenty minutes of lying absolutely still, dreading an attack of the hiccups and smothering the desire to cough, while Brendan furtively tried not to read his newspaper — although his eyes kept straying towards the headlines — in case he was accused of not being supportive.

All the way home I kept thinking that a constructive attitude was the best way to help our babies. They existed, they were developing inside me, these embryonic babies. I just had to stay quiet, no jiggling about, and absolutely no excitement. I was going to nurture them by being serene, an imperturbable Madonna – nothing would rile me.

Then Brendan accidentally hit a pothole and my head bounced off the roof of the car. 'Brilliant! Superb driving!' I barked. 'The babies have no chance after that. So much for all my efforts.'

I was flushed with fury. And terror. Perhaps I should return to the clinic and ask for another selection of embryos? This trio had no chance, between the lunar landscape of Dublin's roads and my husband's perceived urge to drive straight into the centre of the largest crater. I gnawed my lower lip, convinced everything and everyone was conspiring against me.

I calmed down once I was tucked up in bed again, with the inevitable mug of tea – you don't necessarily want to drink it but it's soothing to cradle – and Brendan convinced me it was safe to start hoping again. Babies were tenacious little creatures and tough as old boots, they had to be to survive. It would take more than a pothole to wipe out our children; we'd memorize its location and make annual pilgrimages to it as a family. I laughed, smitten by the idea of our own panoply of traditions.

I absented myself from work for a fortnight, as before, to lie in bed. The hospital said it wasn't essential but I was prepared to take no chances. I used to notice Brendan giving me sidelong glances sometimes, during that fortnight in bed. He'd sit by the side of it after work and we'd watch television. Just quietly waiting out the two weeks. We were less brash this time around. Not prepared for failure, never prepared for failure, but incapable of the arrogance of absolute belief any more. I'd see Brendan's eyes linger on my face, when they were meant to be looking at the television screen, wanting to read reassurance in my confidence. It was still in place, although not so marked as the first time. But we'd served our time in Purgatory, I reasoned – we deserved a baby now. I could not believe that failure would be visited on us; my heart told me that such cruelty would be unwarranted.

As each day passed, the cloud that had been clogging our relationship started to roll back. Normal service was about to resume, we were on the brink of reverting to the life we'd always planned. And we were happy in one another's company again. Magnanimously, I decided I'd dust our wedding photo as soon as I was on my feet.

That reminded me. I shuffled to the wardrobe, one tentative foot in front of the other, and rooted out a shoebox of old photographs. There was a sun-drenched one of four of us children with our mother, lushly pregnant in a floral dress, picnicking in a patch of meadow near our home. A housing estate occupies our playground now. The field was a riot of buttercups and I had a memory of my sister and me holding them under each other's chin to watch the golden discs of light appear. 'Do you like butter?' we'd chant. I felt a flare of hope, clutching this photograph. That's what I wanted: picnics on a summer's day with buttercups and children's games. It was close enough for me to feel its beguiling breath on the back of my neck.

I visualized our house transformed by a baby. I saw the kitchen cluttered with baby equipment, a sterilizer on the worktop, a high chair by the table. I imagined a pram in the hallway that we'd have to edge past; a swing in the garden, set in concrete to minimize the chance of accidents. Maybe we could build a tree-house in the ash by the back wall if it grew fast enough.

I still had my doll's house from twenty-five years ago,

complete with furniture — a miniature, handmade Belle Époque house with a blossom tree painted on the façade and a red roof with twin chimneys. I had loved that house dearly, it was my best Christmas present, even if it was a shared one with my sister; I decided that as soon as my pregnancy was confirmed I'd have it repainted, to cover rust patches, for my daughter or daughters. I had held on to it for years, moving it from Ireland to London and back to Ireland again, always with the intention that my children should inherit it. Even if I had sons, they might like to play with their mother's old doll's house. That occupied a whole day, visualizing my children with the doll's house.

I wondered if Brendan had any toys from his youth he'd like to pass on to his children. Then I remembered I still had dolls in my parents' house and made a mental note to retrieve them too. There was something captivating about the prospect of my children playing with toys I had loved.

Despite the delight of baby-strewn daydreams, I was fatigued to the bone during this incubation. More exhausted than during the first. I found it odd, for it was summer and energy levels tend to be higher then, but I pushed away such thoughts, loath to reflect on the limits towards which I was pushing my body. 'If I'm tired it's because I'm carrying three babies,' I reminded myself. Between 25 and 30 per cent of couples who have successful IVF cycles produce twins, compared with 1 in 90 of the general population. So I wasn't deluding myself. Not really. I could easily have been carrying triplets. Or twins. Or even just one baby, a singleton.

'I'll save at least one of you babies,' I whispered fiercely.

I didn't name this trio, I don't know why, although I had toyed with names for the first three. But I knew beyond a scintilla of doubt that one of them, at any rate, would live.

I had Brendan believing it too; my willpower was so strong

that he suspended his natural bent towards scepticism. Besides, I would tolerate no caveats: doubt was contagious. There was to be no doubt in the vicinity of our babies.

I felt increasingly optimistic as the days passed; the longer this continued, the more promising the outcome. I'd take a hand-mirror into bed with me – I was nervous of standing for any length of time – and stare at my face to assess if it looked pregnant. Whether a difference was apparent in its dips and curves. Did those shadows under my eyes signify a change in my body? Did the light refracted from my eyes mean an inner glow? Could that suspicion of a double chin indicate the onset of pregnant curves? Did I look more composed, and therefore maternal? Or did I look drained, and consequently an embryonic mother?

I tortured myself about what my eating habits indicated. Did my jaded appetite mean I was in the early stages of pregnancy – or should I be ravenous and eating for two? Or four, in this case? I wished I could flick a switch and discon-nect my brain. It chugged along restlessly, as frenetic as my body was still.

Two nights before I was due into the clinic for my blood test to establish pregnancy, I decided to run a bath. I called to Brendan to push in the plug because I didn't want to bend over in case it caused a strain. My mind was elsewhere as I perched on the side of the bath, waiting for it to fill. I was thinking about what I should wear for my appointment less than forty-eight hours away. How did a mother-to-be with no discernible bump dress?

'Something with an elasticated waistband,' I decided, as I lowered myself into the water.

At that I saw them, first one ruby ribbon and then another. Slivers of crimson matter were floating in my bath. I watched, repulsed, as a few pieces detached themselves from the mass and one of them grew elongated. Shapeless embryonic material: it was all that remained of my babies as they were expelled from my womb. I had lost another three. Incoherent, I scrambled for the plughole, wanting it all sucked away, but as the shape-shifting patches of scarlet tissue were drawn towards the vortex I repented and tried to snatch them back. They eluded me, slipping between my fingers, and vanished. I was left shivering in an empty bath, staring at an empty plughole, with a streak of red on my inner thigh. Alone again.

A buzzing sound whirred inside my skull. It droned, deafening, so that I feared for the bathroom mirror if it escaped from the confines of my brain. I pressed the palms of both hands against my mouth and squeezed shut my eyes to prevent leakage. Once this clamour bled into the room, every surface would be shattered by its force. I hummed along with it, behind the prison of my hands, a tuneless, single-note flow of sound. It blocked out the void inside me.

In the ensuing days I struggled to understand why I had been condemned to fail again. I had made no provision for failure, I didn't know how to accommodate it into my life. If even a wisp of doubt had curled about the possibility of not keeping at least one of these embryos, I had throttled it ruthlessly. I would not allow doubt in my mind because it might contaminate my body, and then what hope for my babies? Nothing that might impinge on their wellbeing could be countenanced.

The trouble with this policy, however, is that when failure happens, slamming into your life with the finesse of a wrecking ball, you are devastated. I had constructed no firewall for myself. Failure wasn't catered for, so when this gate-crasher came it left me inconsolable.

I wanted to stagger into the night, lie doubled up in the

garden and howl to the moon. I wanted to rend my clothes and gouge my face so my anguish was visible. When the tornado subsided, I wanted to find an obscure corner to creep into where I could be left inert, in the peace of the vacuum.

Except you realize you can never know peace again while the hunger gnaws. So you drag yourself out of your suffocating desolation and vow to try again. Knowing, once more, the taste of failure. Realizing it can visit again. Pushing away that understanding, because it will not serve you during your third attempt. Your hollow heart is prodding you forward and you can't let it be held back by whispers of failure.

You must go on.

Chapter 15

I was numb for weeks. Later, as the deadened feeling faded, it was replaced by self-criticism. Was my womb unreceptive? Was I failing to do something? Was I undeserving? The incessant questions left me with thumping headaches. In time, they were replaced by incredulity: how was it possible that my hopes should be thwarted time after time? Finally indignation dawned. It was the first time I had been riled by my infertility but now I felt seriously angry. There was nothing fair about it – this was what exercised me. It was simply unfair, so unfair that I howled with the injustice of it, striking the heels of palms repeatedly against the kitchen counter I leaned over.

'Why do I always fall at the final hurdle?' I interrogated the household appliances. Both times, my period had intervened as I was on the point of going for a pregnancy test. All that effort and it hadn't even been successful. Insult and injury topped off with a squirt of ridicule. Fate smirking at me! Puny human, what makes you imagine you can override your destiny with a syringe and a dollop of hope?

It was going to be backbreaking to pick myself up again and make that leap of faith for the final try. I was quite clear that I had to do it, but I dreaded its impact. I knew I was flaying myself, but I had no choice except to persevere.

When the storm ebbed and I had stopped drumming the worktop surface, I thought of tranquil Eastern religions that advocate detachment from fate's vagaries. If only I could learn such stoicism. But I could not feel soothing indifference;

instead I was incensed by my kismet. This provoked a general restlessness in me, an irritability. The uppermost layer of skin had been seared off and everything stung a little more than it had in the past. There was no tolerance, no generosity in me, just a simmering sense of persecution. I felt more isolated than ever and I had no vocabulary to express it. Not to my husband, who was surely also suffering, nor to friends or family, because an admission of loneliness would smack of disloyalty to Brendan.

I began to wonder, as I had before, if my husband and I even liked one another any more; each of us grated on the other's nerves during the dregs of that summer. We should have been in reasonably high spirits – the evenings were light, there was some heat, still, in the sun, but nothing could please either of us, nor reconcile us to disappointment. Continual failure had soaked up our capacity to grant leeway to one another, trimmed our tolerance for each other's foibles, tarnished our respect for one another. Infertility does not exert this stranglehold on all couples. But I suspect it does it, in part, with many, although most manage to re-group and recoup common ground. The desert can be reclaimed and planted, if the will is there.

On stronger days I chided myself for viewing our marriage as a wilderness. I urged myself to remember our bubbles of happiness. Quick! Pick a bubble. I shut my eyes and effervescence floated in. The two of us smiling promises as we clinked champagne flutes on our wedding day. But even then, on that September afternoon cementing our partnership, I had thought of motherhood. 'The next time we drink champagne,' that bride had imagined, 'will be to celebrate my pregnancy. I'll just be having a few sips, Brendan will be too excited to finish his glass, and we'll laugh at ourselves the next day when we find the nearly full bottle of flat Lanson.'

I opened my eyes: I would not let my fate subjugate me; I would wrest control of it, and of my body into the bargain. I would have a baby.

I always referred to them as miscarriages when each attempt failed, but they were actually heavy periods. The embryos had died some days earlier, maybe almost as soon as they'd reached my womb. They were probably dead even as I sang lullabies and bargained with them to cling to life. They were dead all along and I hadn't known it. How could I fail to pick up on that? So much for mother's intuition. Had I ever been pregnant, even for a day, an hour? I'll never know. The only pregnancy I was certain of was the one that almost killed me, my ectopic pregnancy.

I pondered increasingly on that little boy, my finger-joint-sized son, in the aftermath of the second failed attempt. It's impossible to rank one loss above another, but I mourned that baby in a different way to the others. I wished, again, we could have survived or been doomed together, that fleck of life and I.

We had that second failure shortly before Princess Diana's death. I was swathed in fold upon fold of defeated sorrow, and this concurrent loss, that affected people so powerfully, even in Ireland, seemed entirely appropriate to my mood. There was mourning in the air. While I felt no one else could understand my personal sense of emptiness, there was consolation in the general aura of bewildered loss.

That Sunday morning, 31 August 1997, we rose early to drive to Belfast for a christening in Brendan's family. I really did not want to attend it, for I was still too raw, too uncertain of my ability to maintain composure. We listened to news bulletins about the princess along the way, the car crash in Paris dominating all the stations, and I was mesmerized, associating the tragic waste of her death with my own failed hopes.

The nearer we drew to the city, the more I chafed at the duty that lay ahead. I dreaded that christening, so soon after the loss of my embryonic babies. I did not want to be in the vicinity of a new baby, with its downy cap and rosebud mouth. I did not begrudge its parents the joy it would bring them, for I liked that couple very much, but I did not see how I could join in the celebration. It was a burden I would have preferred not to carry. I tried to explain this to Brendan but was inarticulate, while he felt blood loyalty meant it was important that we attend. The couple had waited some time for that little boy, their second child, and they deserved our help in marking the occasion. This was true, and I was honestly glad for them. But a self-preservation instinct urged me against attending, emotionally and physically brittle as I was.

Brendan was keen that we go, however, and in this he was motivated by an understandable allegiance towards his family, who were very decent people. I felt an obligation not to disappoint anyone. I was withdrawn during the day, however, and acutely conscious of the baby I had to psych myself up to admire.

As for the christening ceremony, I blanked it out. I stood and sat, as directed, in a haze, all the time wanting to flee. At the party afterwards I swallowed the first glass of white wine I was offered as greedily as a drowning man gulps water. My teeth were chattering, although it was warm, and I had to sit in a corner for a time. I think I remember babbling inanely to other guests later, scarcely conscious of what I was saying.

We were both out of sorts, perhaps because the baby reminded us of what was missing from our lives. I felt we did not present a united front and that other eyes beside my own had noticed this. It occurred to me, as we drove home, that other people detected the cracks too. This was an uncomfortable possibility and I decided, fairly belatedly, that we needed to concentrate on our relationship.

Even I, solipsistic though I was, realized the folly of a third IVF attempt in a marriage that was increasingly shaky. Still, I consoled myself, it's only natural that a couple who've had their hopes of parenthood impeded should drift apart.

What we needed was some effort and my solution was quality time. A double-edged sword if ever there was one, but it was all my atrophied brain could devise. I remembered our first Christmas together as newly-weds and how snug we'd been. We'd drunk champagne as we'd opened our presents and I had been thrilled by Brendan's gift, a gorgeous oval Art Deco mirror that was hanging over the fireplace in our Ranelagh home. I hoped to replicate the harmony of those early days by spending another Christmas together on our own. It would be the first time we'd done this since our return to Ireland. Yes, quality time would salve the friction in our relationship.

Brendan was dubious, because he said his mother loved gathering the family around her, and I hesitated to disappoint this undemanding, kindly lady. However I theorized it was for the best. My husband and I would regain our former intimacy and we'd start the New Year on a firmer footing, well-placed to embark on our third and final IVF cycle.

But it wouldn't matter that it was our last try because this time it would succeed. We'd be rewarded for our perseverance and then former animosities would be washed away. There was absolutely no way we'd fail a third time. Such cruelty would be unconscionable and was not even worth consideration.

This Christmas would be a redemptive one, I believed, as

I decorated the tree to the strains of Wizzard's 'I Wish It Could Be Christmas Every Day', shopped for presents, stamped and addressed cards. Brendan asked for suggestions about what he should buy me and I came up with a croquet set, imagining family games on our back lawn. My future was such an idyllic one in the accommodating frame of my imagination. It was shot through with sun-drenched days, jugs of home-made lemonade and the laughter of children playing croquet.

I was back at work, freelancing for the *Irish Independent*, and it was busy there because the prelude to Christmas is frenzied in newspaper offices with extra pages to fill and early deadlines. Scarcely anyone knew of my fertility treatment and it wasn't a subject to raise casually around the water cooler. Sometimes I locked myself into a cubicle in the Ladies to cry, despising my tears but incapable of staunching them. 'How have I turned into one of those weak women who snivel continually?' I hissed at myself. But still the tears seeped out.

Yet I looked forward to this Christmas as a bonding time with Brendan, realizing how the wedge between us was driving us further apart every day. If we could regain some of our former familiarity, it might ease us into that third IVF cycle, which I'd be ready to embark on in February. I didn't want to undertake it with a husband who had started looking at me the way Brendan did, even if I deserved it.

Christmas Day dawned damp and squally. We ate breakfast, made family phone calls and exchanged presents, looking at what we had bought each other without much evidence of enthusiasm. Our re-connecting Christmas wasn't off to a promising start. Maybe this was about what I wanted and not what we wanted as a couple – which I'd somehow persuaded myself were interchangeable. Possibly my husband would have preferred a family Christmas. And there was something else I'd noticed lately: that smile of his, which had first attracted me to him, no longer reached his eyes when he directed it at me.

We gathered up discarded wrapping paper, saving other gifts to open until later, for Brendan was now anxious to take a walk along the canal. He was always keen on going outdoors. The rain was relentless but he was dogged, so we ended up driving the short distance to the Grand Canal, where ducks and sometimes a pair of imperious swans sailed by. I brought bread to feed them, hoping they would be there, for I'd always loved the legend of the Children of Lir. It never struck me as such an ill-starred fate, to be transformed into swans by a wicked stepmother. But the rain continued torrential, horizontal stripes across the windscreen – even the ducks were taking shelter. We sat together in the car barely able to see through the windows. Finally I suggested that we go home.

Back at the house we started preparing the traditional Christmas dinner. I'd only cooked it once before, years earlier, and wasn't over-confident about my abilities. Still, I reasoned, we'd muddle through together. His mother had given us one of her homemade plum puddings so at least I didn't have dessert to worry about. For a while we chopped and peeled, until we had words over some minor detail, and at that I couldn't carry on. I left the kitchen, closed the door carefully behind me and sank onto a sofa in the sitting room. Then I let my face droop into my hands and the tears oozed out. Not sobbing howls, just silent tears of hopelessness. Later I felt weary, ineffably weary, as I sat at the festively festooned table.

No doubt I was sullen and uncommunicative that

Christmas evening. My mind was troubled. 'Are other people's marriages like this?' I wondered. 'Perhaps it's normal.'

But deep down I knew it wasn't.

We called into a neighbour's house for drinks on Christmas night, where it was a relief not to be dependent on one another for company. The bonding exercise had been an abysmal flop.

I suspect both of us were thinking the hackneyed death chant of beleaguered couples everywhere, *This can't go on.*

You accept you're on a slippery slope when you resort to cliché and mean it, and it's as relevant to you as though you've just coined the phrase.

We're tearing each other apart.

I can't bear this any longer.

And most insidious of all, still potent because I would not surrender it: *a baby will solve all our problems.*

I could see that as time passed the friction between us had grown, not incrementally, but in leaps and bounds. I have no doubt that I, too, exploded over minor infractions. Our marriage was disintegrating at such a rate that it felt as if there was nothing I could do to save it. Except have a baby. I had unswerving faith in a baby's magical properties. I knew people always warned that children can't shore up a marriage but it would be different with us.

A few years later I read a newspaper article about Christmas stresses on relationships. I suspected the counsellor quoted in it had been loitering behind the fir tree at our last Christmas. He admitted he couldn't describe the secret of a happy marriage, but he could offer one of the main reasons for an unhappy union: negative behaviour. He said that in such couples, partners criticized and belittled one another, wouldn't listen and projected blame onto one another. Both partners did this but only saw the other's behaviour. Men experienced this conduct as faultfinding and women found it insulting.

I had a moment of self-recognition. I was spellbound by the article's inventory of main causes of marital breakdown, ticking off five out of the eight, including poor communication and failed expectations. The 'failed expectations' reason made me pause and study the configuration of letters for a time. Failed expectations. It covers a multitude of sins. Including being deprived of parenthood. Being two instead of three or more.

When a relationship is buoyant, any difficulty can be transcended. Even infertility. But when the relationship is limping along, problems become insoluble. Even relatively minor ones become insurmountable impediments to happiness if the relationship is starved enough and two people start regarding their lives together as a punishment instead of a gift.

Chapter 16

It was February 1998 and time for IVF attempt number three. How casually I write it. Time for IVF attempt number three, as though it was on a par with hair appointment number three or job interview number three. What I put my body through – I wonder we're still on amicable terms.

Brendan and I should have had holidays after each failure, to remind ourselves of what was worthwhile between us and to ease the sting of setbacks. New York was the only holiday, after the first cycle, then they tailed off. Money was tight, needed for more IVF. The thought of delaying another cycle by even a few months to raise the cash for a jaunt was abhorrent to me. I couldn't see that it was expedient for us as a couple, to help us reunify. My emphasis was exclusively on baby production.

We had scrabbled together the common sense to agree a short break in the New Year, catching a ferry and driving to my sister's house in Oxford. Tonia and her husband Tom had a year-old baby daughter, Aoife, as well as Justin – the toddler I had taken Brendan to meet when we were courting. Perhaps it was unwise to go where there were children, but in Irish families children are always part of the equation. And staying with relatives was the only holiday we could afford. But it was not a success and Brendan and I circled one another, querulous. I thought about asking my sister whether couples grew hostile amid the stresses of IVF treatment, but raising the subject would reveal our own strains. Even with family, I didn't want to admit that Brendan and I were in difficulty.

During that break I broke my own rule and sidled off to buy baby clothes for the first time. I had a christening robe already, but it was an inherited garment; now I wandered through shops and touched whisper-soft clothes in pastel shades to cover the tiniest of limbs: an apricot sleep suit with a rabbit on the breast, a pair of embroidered dungarees, a mint green velour top with rainbow-striped sleeves were purchased and secreted in my luggage, to be ogled at my pleasure. I was trying to give substance to my baby – preparing its clothes to pave the way for it – but I dreaded Brendan finding these treasures for I realized they might make me look . . . desperate. I didn't want to look that way, although it's a fair description of my state of mind.

On the way home we stopped off in Chester overnight, where our differences intensified. Stupidities sparked arguments, such as Brendan's reluctance to reserve a hotel room in advance, and my petulance about arriving in a strange town and having to spend an hour or two looking for somewhere to stay. All we could turn up was a noisy, cramped room above a pub. I left him to it and went off for a sulky walk on my own, crushed by the burden of being expected to enjoy myself on holiday.

We hardly exchanged two words during dinner, as I fumed over previous holiday disagreements about not booking accommodation, incidents magnified to neon-lit signs of utter incompatibility. There was a sense that this fractious version of life we had stumbled into, and from which we were unable to reverse, couldn't continue.

Still, we both wanted to go ahead with the third IVF attempt, and we were only tetchy with each other because of this blight on our hopes of parenthood. At least that's what I persuaded myself.

Nevertheless, in the months that had elapsed since the

second failed IVF cycle, there was an incipient realization between Brendan and me that we were teetering as a couple. It was nebulous, this recognition, and it shrouded our life together. Our sorrows were separate. Lack of communication was the fundamental problem: we didn't talk about what was really bothering us, so it was easy to misconstrue each other's responses. I think perhaps, in our heightened emotional states, we may have been inclined to ascribe more negative motives to one another than was the case. But grief is enervating, so even when I became aware of subterranean reefs I was incapable of altering course to avoid them.

I awarded myself the right to inhabit my sorrow, to withdraw from social duties when I found them onerous. I think – although I'm only surmising, from his behaviour – that Brendan believed it was important to show a brave face. He disliked it when my spirit wilted and seemed impatient of it. This made me feel isolated and defensive. Maybe I imagined it. But I did not imagine the lack of affection between us. The times when our backs were turned to one another in bed. The distance that can yawn across a double mattress.

I used to fantasize about us falling into each other's arms saying: 'At least we have each other. Even if we never have children, that'll be enough for us.' But neither of us ever said it. I was unambiguous that the marriage needed children. You see, I was convinced I could make our relationship gel if we had a child. It would bring out the best in us and help us to work as a team, a skill we lacked. I believed that if I could overturn childlessness, saving my marriage would be a piece of cake by comparison.

One hinged on the other, however, a dangerous juxtaposition. Even I recognized that – yet still I had faith that I could accomplish it all. Slot the first piece of the jigsaw into place and the others would follow.

But driving to the clinic for my first appointment, at the start of that third cycle, a ridiculous spat flared. The argument culminated outside the Rotunda with my shouting at Brendan, 'Get away from me!' and he obliged.

Sitting there in the clinic my faith began to shrink. Not just in my prospects of motherhood but in the roadworthiness of the marriage. So I caught faith by the scruff of the neck: I wouldn't let it dodge me, faith and hope were going to keep this venture afloat.

'What about love?' whispered a traitor voice.

I ignored it. I was determined to kiss and make up as soon as I returned home to Brendan in Ranelagh, no grudges, because I knew we couldn't proceed on sour terms.

As I trekked down O'Connell Street, traffic thundering past me, trying not to look at the bleeding foetus photographs on the anti-abortion placards outside the General Post Office, I was grappling with a puzzle at the prospect of kissing and making up. When was the last time Brendan and I had kissed as lovers? Mouth urgent against mouth, lingering kisses? I reflected. I'd spotted before that the kissing was tailing off. I'd noticed its absence that day when I'd collected exam papers in the Coombe, more than a year before. But I hadn't done anything about it. Kisses had been the first casualty as our marriage had floundered, as each of us had discovered that marriage can be a savage, forlorn place. I counted back. It was February. By the time our third wedding anniversary had rolled around five months earlier, I realized I had totally forgotten that couples made love for pleasure. The only pleasure I was interested in revolved around a doctor's surgery and the words, 'Congratulations, you're going to be a mother.' I don't suppose that would ever have made it into the final edit of the Karma Sutra.

Something insidious happens to couples when the prospect

of infertility enters their lives, it happened to us. We forgot about making love for fun, or in response to the gush of desire. Passion became sublimated by need, not for each other, but for the child that would complete our lives.

But I would not let our relationship falter any longer – I would save my marriage with our IVF babies. I pasted on a smile as I turned the key in our green front door, stroking one of the nasturtium glass panels for luck.

Brendan was sitting on the sofa reading the newspaper. We regarded each other warily.

'I'll put the kettle on,' he said.

No kiss. But at least no hostilities.

Sometimes during those fraught days of our third IVF cycle, I'd study our wedding photograph, baffled. It was framed in silver, but no frame could contain its image of a laughing woman, flowers in her hair, and a man in morning suit radiating pride. I'd frown as I stared at the couple, whichever task I'd been engaged on suspended, willing myself to recapture that manifest joy. Happiness couldn't evaporate so rapidly. It had been only three years and five months since I'd picked my way along the gusty seafront, holding the hem of my ivory silk dress out of the dirt, my sister and twin nieces, Michelle and Louise, tripping along beside me. My father bringing up the rear – saddled with the communal make-up purse but good-natured about it. We couldn't have mislaid that day's glow so soon. Were we really so profligate?

I loaded up the fridge with drugs, pushing aside cheese and butter-substitute spreads, and started sniffing, pummelling my hormones into submission. Apprehensive about the future, even as I tried to shape it. A memory of a visit to a fortune-teller surfaced to reassure me. I had forgotten about it but now the incident replayed in my mind. When I lived in England I had consulted a woman with a reputation to match the Oracle at Delphi's, an outing arranged by some friends from work. Four of us drove to her small terraced house in a County Durham pit village to find her minding her granddaughter, a solid, fair girl in teddy-bear pyjamas. The child sat placidly with us in the living room while we waited our turn to go into the kitchen and have our palms read.

During that phase of my life I wanted to hear about exciting career opportunities, the promise that I'd make my mark in journalism, but the woman mentioned nothing in that line. All she told me was that I'd wear two men's wedding rings and there'd be a delay before I'd have children. But I shouldn't despair because she saw two small boys playing in the garden of my house. I was disconcerted by the mention of twin marriages and, even then, by the paucity of only two sons. And what about my career? The grandmother's work-gnarled hands touched the deck of cards I had shuffled but she could foresee nothing more.

I remembered the fortune-teller now, as I desperately tried to convince myself that my happily ever after was delayed, not derailed. I saw again the woman's lined face, eyes narrowed against a plume of cigarette smoke, and seized on the certainty in her voice. She'd been right about two wedding rings, she could be right about two small boys playing in the garden of my house. These little fellows bolstered my hopes during that last IVF attempt.

In all the time I spent at the HARI unit I met only one person who chatted freely to me. A bubbly, dark-haired woman in her early thirties, crimson slashes of lipstick a bulwark against the grey day. She admitted she was twanging with nerves because it was her first day there.

'You look the youngest in the room,' she added, 'so I thought I'd risk talking to you. What are they like in this place, are they decent? I don't care, I'm glad to be here. I only live around the corner, near my mother. All my brothers and sisters have children, I'm the odd one out.' She gabbled as she spoke, fingers tapping the packet of cigarettes she wasn't allowed to smoke.

She was the only woman I met whose treatment was covered by the medical card so she didn't have to pay. 'I wouldn't be in a position to do this otherwise.' She was candid. 'I'd never be able to find the money. My fellow's not mad keen on the idea but he's humouring me this once. Only because it's free, mind.'

After a momentary silence she started again. She was obviously dying to talk and, leaning in towards me, she pitched her voice slightly lower. 'Actually the reason we can't have kids is because of me. The first fellow I ever slept with gave me chlamydia and I didn't know. Not until years later when all the damage was done. I can barely even remember being sick, but it damaged my insides and I know that's why my husband's so annoyed about things. He's your average man – won't come right out and say anything – but I'm sure he thinks it's all my fault. I wouldn't mind, only it's not as if I had a lot of boyfriends or that either of us pretended we were virgins getting married.

'Typical, isn't it? There was me being sensible, romantic even, waiting to have sex with someone I loved. I was twenty and my first boyfriend was a really nice fellow. I was with him for a few years and I'm still fond of him. Me and my friends thought it was great that we could go on the pill – not like our mothers who couldn't get their hands on it, and would have been too scared to take it even if they could – and we didn't have to mess around with condoms. But no one ever tells you that you don't have to be sleeping around to catch something.

'Anyway, I hope to God this works because I'll be broken-hearted if we can't have kids.'

She sat back and let out a sigh, as if a weight was off her mind. I didn't think she needed me to say anything. All she wanted was someone, preferably a stranger, to listen. I speculated, fleetingly, on how many other women there were in this waiting room whose husbands or partners weren't mad keen on the idea of them going through treatment, or who blamed them as the infertile ones. Imagine the horror of being unable to have the baby you so desire, and also having to deal with your husband or partner regarding you with a critical eye, thinking that your sexual history has brought you both to this.

Then her name was called.

'Wish me luck,' she smiled.

I showed her my two hands, each forefinger and middle digit twined.

I watched out for her, from time to time after that encounter, but I never spotted her again. I still wonder today whether she was lucky. A one-in-five statistic.

By the time a couple embarks on fertility treatment they're desperate. The IVF process is only likely to exaggerate those frantic feelings. There's a lull before the storm, prior to the first cycle, when you're convinced it's only a matter of time until you're pregnant – and you mean weeks, not months, so inflated with confidence are you. You haven't the sense to manage your expectations and prepare for failure. By the second cycle doubt has set in, but still you buoy yourself. Well, of course it was a little presumptuous to anticipate a result first time out. By the second outing you've learned it's not as straightforward as you'd imagined. But the lesson hasn't really penetrated because naturally it will work this time. What could possibly stop you from having a baby if the obstruction preventing sperm from reaching egg is circumvented?

IVF was invented for people such as me – I was ideal for it. Relatively young, ovulating, healthy, moderate in everything (except baby hunger), and with a husband whose sperm had a sense of direction – not as commonplace as it sounds.

If I thought I was on familiar terms with desperation before, I was fooling myself. I didn't know the meaning of it until starting that third IVF cycle. My last try, we'd decided, Brendan and I. Its outcome would determine the course of my life. Motherhood or – blankness.

Desperation? I thought that summed up my attitude towards the close of our perplexing first year of trying and falling short. I thought I was desperate as I lay in a hospital bed and mourned my ectopic baby. I thought I was desperate after the first failed IVF cycle, and again after the second. How mistaken I was. Now I understood desperation. And as the drugs pulverized me, I raged and wept.

I'd sit in the waiting room, eyes drinking in the collage of baby photos from grateful patients who'd succeeded in having a child, and I felt superannuated. I rebuked myself for having procrastinated until this advanced stage in my life. I couldn't imagine what I'd been thinking of; such gross irresponsibility – my timing was askew. Imagine believing I had as long as I liked. Imagine laughing, in the past, about coming from a long line of hyper-fertile women. (My maternal grandmother had had eleven children.) Imagine waiting until I had a husband, a house and enough years of work under my belt to feel comfortable about a career-break. Imagine fantasizing that I could control this aspect of my life. Imagine being so elderly. And I was growing more ancient by the day. Just because the face in my mirror was relatively line-free didn't exonerate me. I was aghast at my foolishness in waiting until my thirtieth birthday had passed before acknowledging the biological clock.

I started to develop a phobia about my age. I imagined the clinic staff were profoundly disapproving when they looked at my records and saw my date of birth. 'Reckless deferral,' they'd mutter. 'What was that woman thinking?' I was probably one of the younger patients in the clinic but still I slated myself.

'Why me?' my interminable self-interrogation badgered. I'd be a much better mother than those women I saw dragging their screaming youngsters along by the hand, cramming them with cavity-inducing sweets, buying them burgers and chips instead of cooking wholesome meals, abandoning them to videos instead of reading to them. If they were mine I'd read them *The Borrowers*, *The Secret Garden*, all the Dr Seuss books especially *There's a Wocket in My Pocket*.

I'm embarrassed for that self-righteous person, looking back. For that woman convinced she'd make a superior mother to some others she observed, with no consideration for their circumstances. But I was telling myself what I needed to hear at the time in order to survive. Fate, which had de-selected me, was mistaken, and I had to look no further than the evidence of my eyes in every McDonald's in town.

One day I saw a small boy of about eight, fringe in his eyes, puff a furtive cigarette while he guarded his brother in the pushchair outside a shop. I was rooted to the spot when I saw him raise the cigarette to the Cupid's bow of his lips. As he inhaled a second time, I was galvanized into action. Nauseous, seething, scandalized, I pushed inside the shop and glared into the face of each woman I met. Are you the unfit mother? Is it you? I thought her guilt would be apparent in her countenance. Yet they all seemed normal. As I searched the shop, my passion was diverted from the woman, whoever she might be, towards Nature. How could she be so dense as to give that woman two children and leave me with none? Suddenly I realized my self-control was so precarious that I was not in a position to tackle anyone. I retreated, but for days afterwards I was anxious about that boy.

Having a baby, I thought, straggling homewards after a check-up on my hormone levels at the clinic, had become a life-and-death matter for me. I was amazed that the grief of continued childlessness didn't bring my heartbeat to a standstill, arrest the pumping of my blood, shut me down. I didn't know how I could be alive, still, with this abyss inside.

Another day, cutting through St Stephen's Green, I paused, enthralled by a pair of toddlers, a boy and a girl who were holding hands as they waddled about on the grass while their mothers gossiped on a bench. Why should that stir me so much? It's the stuff of greeting cards, scenes deliberately contrived to foster a sentimental reaction. But the sight of a couple of tots with their podgy hands linked made me catch my breath and blink back tears.

Baby seats in cars fascinated me, even unoccupied. I couldn't pass them by: I'd hover by parked cars peering in, noting little circles of crumbs around the seat where the baby had dismembered a biscuit, or a sticky patch where a drink had been splashed. There might be a soft toy discarded nearby, flung aside with an infant's trademark despotism. My eyes would linger on the Baby On Board sticker, craving one for our car.

Baby slings were another source of fascination. I studied them all: the vibrant lengths of material African women used with innate grace, the slings from Mothercare that were almost seats in their own right. 'You'll get back-ache carrying a child in that,' warned an inner voice. 'Bring it on,' I replied.

Baby socks with lace pelmets were my downfall. They sent my pulse racing, turned my insides to mush and my knees to jelly – effortlessly managing all the chemical reactions that heroes spark in heroines in romances. Two strips of cotton edged with a ruffle of lace. Meltdown.

All through that third IVF cycle I grieved for the children I had already let slip through my fingers, even as I prepared to welcome others into my life. Seven were gone so far, more were gestating as my turbo-charged ovaries pumped out eggs for conversion to embryos. How could I entice this batch to take a chance on me? I had to make absolutely certain they knew how dearly they were wanted. There must be no room for confusion.

I chose a set of names for my babies, while I was still injecting myself to help them grow from eggs in my ovaries. I was unwilling to pass on the names chosen for their earlier siblings, fearing it might nullify those precursors. I would not erase their identities by replicating their names. These three had separate identities for me, they were my last chance and they deserved to be distinguished from the earlier children. Rory, Molly and Finbarr were blooming, now, in the egg farm that geared up for harvest.

As I plunged into this third attempt, I fretted about the random nature of what lay ahead. Having a baby via fertility treatment hinged on luck, everyone was agreed on that. But luck was a commodity no one could rely on. What if, I worried, everyone was allocated a certain amount of luck during their lifetime and I'd used up all mine? Anxiously, I scanned my history. Nothing much to blight it. No bereavements, no disasters, no traumas; I could honestly say that life had handled me with kid gloves. So did this mean I was due a kick in the teeth? Or could I count the infertility, the ectopic, the two failed attempts, as payback time for an unruffled passage until I'd tried to introduce motherhood into the equation?

The notion of luck and how arbitrary it was haunted me as I injected myself to stimulate my ovaries, an old hand at it now, so blasé I was able to nip into the Ladies in a café or shop to do it. During prior attempts I'd take a day off or not go into work until after the injection.

On the brink of yet another crack at this near-impossible business of pregnancy, I wished there was some way to store up luck until you definitely-positively-absolutely needed it. A nugget of luck you could squirrel away: in case of emergency, break glass.

I grew preoccupied by whether my being lucky precluded someone else from achieving a similar result. If I won a baby in this lottery, might it diminish someone else's chances? During the first two attempts I had been blind to other women's pain; but now I started to consider this band of thwarted mothers, each of us with the same hollowed-out hearts. Triumph for one woman meant catastrophe for at least four others, that's how we fared under the statistics. You'd never begrudge that one woman her baby, you appreciated what she had endured to produce her child, but the selection process was haphazard. Winners and losers. That left me ill at ease: realizing that if I were to become a winner I'd have to outstrip a batch of losers.

What made me more uncomfortable again, however, was the knowledge that I was still grittily set on being the one in five on the winner's podium at the end of the treatment. I fancied I deserved it most.

Chapter 17

During the third cycle Brendan and I found ourselves in a situation where everything about the other irked us. Perhaps we really were ill-matched. Or maybe we were displacing our frustration at failure, becoming disproportionately incensed by vocal tics or petty grievances. Yet we pressed ahead with IVF.

We were not, by this stage, operating as a team. However we both still wanted a child and by unspoken agreement we decided to try and shake off our differences to see out this third and final attempt. Quarrels would be suspended while the common goal was pursued. Sometimes I wished for more affection and compatibility between us while we chased this mutual objective. Indeed, I wondered what was worthwhile about us as a couple beyond the imperative of our common goal. But such a thought opened up perspectives that panicked me.

Still, as I made my way to the HARI clinic, I often felt alone. I expect Brendan felt alone too, during his working day. Our paths were diverging and I think we both had a sense that only a successful outcome to this last cycle could stop them sundering. Occasionally I wondered, during that third cycle, if Brendan felt excluded. My body, my treatment, my fixation. Could he have thought I was doing it for me and not us? Yet Brendan wanted us to have a baby too. These thoughts nagged at my composure, until I pushed them away: they were a distraction from the main event.

★

In the US now, fertility experts recommend that couples initiating treatment attend counselling for stress-lowering strategies. Not only does this help them deal with the process, but the chances of success are increased.

Baking helped me to pass the time. I had a powerful nesting instinct during those yearning years and was forever poring over cake recipes. Anyone who knows me now would probably laugh at this unlikely vision of domesticity: me in an apron, up to my elbows in flour. Brendan would come home to racks of fragrant home baking, which I'd flourish as a badge of merit. I used to bake several times a week – scones, apple tarts, cherry cake and gingerbread, as well as my grandmother's bread recipes passed on to me by my mother. I was practising to become a mum, somehow convinced that if I played the part, it was only a matter of time before act became fact. My mother and her mother had baked, so I'd bake. As I made dough and rolled it, lulled by the repetition, I imagined a day when I'd be making Rice Crispie cakes with my children. Or drawing smiley faces with pastry on individual apple tarts for them. 'Perhaps,' I thought, growing ambitious, 'I'll learn to bake birthday cakes shaped like their favourite cartoon characters.'

I haven't baked once since those days. I gave away my cake tins.

While the dough rose and turned golden, I'd ring my mother to hear stories about myself as a child. How, as a toddler, I buried my silver christening bangle in the back garden and although she dug everywhere for it the bracelet could never be found. How I loved a pair of red and white cowboy wellies and wore them summer and winter, howling at attempts to strap me into more appropriate footwear. How I'd watch for my father returning from work, racing out to him and stretching my arms to be lifted – reaching instantly into his breast pocket for the bar of chocolate he'd have waiting there. Unremarkable stories such as any family could recount. But which were remarkable to me.

I adored hearing my mother repeat them, even though I was word-perfect on each tumble, each lost milk tooth, each mispronounced word, and Bridie humoured me. They gave me hope, when hope was growing harder to find, that I could have a child too. It was such a mundane event, after all, having a child. People did it all the time. My mother did it seven times in rapid sequence – I could do it too.

'Tell me about the cowboy wellies again, Mammy. Did I want to wear them to school?'

By this third attempt it must have been like marriage to an IVF handbook for Brendan. I had committed to memory every stage of it, each step we had to take. The only possibility I didn't provide for was an unsuccessful outcome. The drugs seemed to affect me more deeply this time – possibly the cumulative effect of successive treatments close together – and I was continually weepy, inclined to over-react, easily unbalanced from my tentative equilibrium. Come to think of it, I lacked anything remotely resembling equilibrium.

'You're in a bad way,' Brendan said to me in the kitchen one day, after I had flared up and then dissolved into tears over some imagined provocation.

I looked at him and knew it was true, but I also knew I had no choice but to persist. It was either kill or cure: I had a glimmering that I either had a baby and saved our marriage, or I failed abysmally and lost everything.

I didn't care how antiseptic conception was or how many medics had to intervene to help my eggs and Brendan's sperm coalesce as embryos. I didn't care how often I was prodded around or how many people saw me nude from the waist down – they could sell tickets for the spectacle for all I cared. I didn't care if Brendan felt like a walking sperm bank whose only function was to make deposits. Unromantic? I didn't care if we never had sex again, let alone a candle-lit dinner.

Our existence was coloured by absence. I couldn't enjoy what we had for imagining life with what we hadn't. A walk on the beach sent me fantasizing about a little creature toddling in our wake, pausing to poke at stones with a stick and collect flotsam treasures. Brunch in a coffee shop had me scanning the premises for high chairs and watching parents juggle reading the Sunday newspapers with popping morsels into their baby's mouth. I didn't even care, towards the end of our three IVF cycles, if my marriage was a casualty in my drive to reproduce. I don't mean that I wanted a baby without my husband – I always felt a child was entitled to two parents – it was just that this quest I had embarked on skewed my perspective.

Let it name its price: I'd pay it.

I wasn't using the sniffer in the bathroom this time, for I was bone-tired from successive treatments and preferred to stay in bed. Rather than wake up Brendan, I moved into the spare room. He didn't invite me back to our room so I stayed away. Childish of us both, really. Despite our good intentions, petty disputes flared between us as my ovaries swelled, my stomach grew distended and the waistband of my trousers pinched. I knew, from experience, that I'd be ready for egg extraction in a couple of days.

When the time came, however, it was as though the arguments of the preceding weeks had never happened. I told him I was booked in for extraction in a couple of days' time and he immediately responded that he'd arrange for the day off work to bring me to the clinic. I felt a wave of love for him – or perhaps it was gratitude washed through with relief.

This could work, I thought, and moved back into our bedroom: our babies couldn't have parents who slept in separate rooms.

The anaesthetist had crinkly eyes that smiled at me above his green surgical mask as he tapped my hand repeatedly, waiting for a vein to pop up. I smiled back at him, reassured. He was the only person in the theatre I didn't know. The doctor and nurse at the bottom of the table were both familiar from previous appointments at the clinic. I was flat on my back, legs in stirrups, but the medics had a routine that steadied me. What had seemed outlandish was becoming commonplace.

The anaesthetist had located my vein and now he was stroking my wrist, as though sensing I needed to be soothed. Inordinately moved by this act of kindness from a stranger, I felt indebted to him – but I also wished that Brendan could be the one stroking me. Those crinkly eyes, such a long way above me, were the wrong colour.

It felt like seconds later when I was back with my husband, drinking a cup of sugary tea. 'I like this, put more sugar in it,' I said muzzily. In the cubicle next to us I heard a man dress a woman, I knew it was the woman who had been first into the operating theatre today for extraction, at the topsy-turvy dentist's. The couple were preparing to leave. Rustle rustle, mumble, mumble. The man finished every sentence with 'darling'. Longing penetrated the fog in my brain: *I want to be called darling.*

Brendan was talking about something though; he seemed downcast. 'They extracted seven eggs,' he said.

Seven? Warning klaxons sent the fog scurrying. Only seven! That's half of what they harvested from me the first time. My fertility levels were in free-fall. I was devastated and started to whimper, convinced our chances of parenthood were negligible.

'I've no chance,' I blubbered, 'I'm not producing enough eggs.'

A door opened and the anaesthetist left the operating theatre. While he moved down the corridor, he looked across at us, drawn by my sobs. Then his crinkly eyes slid away and he continued walking. My husband was embarrassed. I was indifferent who saw me cry – it seemed so unimportant. I wept the tears of the cheated as Brendan shushed me, trying to drag clothes onto my limp body. Floppy from the anaesthetic, I was no help to him as he pulled on socks and shoes.

We retreated home to wait for fertilization. Only now, during this third IVF attempt, did an axiomatic fact occur to me: my eggs and my husband's sperm would connect when we weren't even in the same room, let alone the same building. It was the post-biblical version of the Virgin Birth. I remembered the prayer card given to me by the nun in hospital after my ectopic pregnancy – was it really only a year and a few months ago? It had shown the Virgin Mary, impregnated by the Holy Spirit. Lucky, lucky woman. She was celebrated in the Rosary as a vessel, I wanted to be a vessel too. Spiritual vessel, vessel of honour, vessel of singular devotion. What use was a womb except as a receptacle for a child?

The hours turned into days and passed excruciatingly slowly, while I rested in preparation for the eggs' restoration to me – to the return, too, of my vessel status. Provided the eggs fertilized. For the first time, I wasn't confident they would. 'Only seven,' I mumbled to myself, dismayed. Yet because I now had so few, compared with fourteen eggs during my first cycle, these seven seemed infinitely precious to me.

In that hiatus between extraction and replacement, my mind circled relentlessly. I found myself fretting, once again, about what would happen to the surplus eggs. If they couldn't be used for research or donation, I wished they could be frozen. But I knew this still wasn't an option – a doctor I spoke to compared the embryo defrosting process to removing a bag of peas from the freezer, remarking that they couldn't be treated as analogous procedures. 'We have no idea how the thawing out process may affect the integrity of the embryo,' he said.

By the end of my third cycle, however, the idea of not having to undergo the entire treatment each time was appealing. Imagine having a pool of eggs ready to draw upon, just one egg at a time, month after month. It struck me as substantially less stressful – and for me, stress was always the crux of my problem. I knew embryo freezing wouldn't help me at this stage: this was my last shot. But I thought it might be useful for other women.

For two and a half days I thought about nothing but eggs until I realized that I was weary of eggs. Sick and tired of worrying about them, agonizing over whether we had managed to produce enough and if any of them had fertilized. 'All I want to have to think about eggs is whether I fancy them scrambled or poached,' I blurted out. But I doubted if I could ever eat another. Egg and chips were off the menu in our house.

On the day designated for egg replacement the wonderfully nurturing neighbour who had sat with me, quilting for her daughter, gave me a reiki session. This is a form of healing that uses the hands to remove blockages and restore the flow of energy to the body. I wasn't convinced alternative remedies were useful beyond acting as another aid to relaxation, but I had nothing to lose. And the benign nature

– the sisterhood – of the gesture appealed to me. In any case, a woman who wore green clothes because she hoped they might enhance her fertility and burned her wish in the flame of a red candle was in no position to raise an eyebrow about alternative remedies.

By this stage I had read up on the psychology of superstition and discovered that when people feel they have lost control of events, they suspend their belief in the rational and turn to a world where rules seem more flexible. Superstitious tics help them regain a sense of control, even if it's illusory. So my red candle, my avoiding the cracks in the pavement, my wishing on rainbows may have been something the experts call cognitive shortcuts – but they certainly kept me hoping.

Anyway, the reiki was restful and refreshing, just as my neighbour had intended. Then Brendan arrived home from work to collect me and we set off on the last leg of this long-shot journey. Leaving the house, I paused to touch the glass nasturtiums for luck. Shoots of spring-fresh optimism sprang up in me, beckoning with all the promise of the first time.

My serenity lasted less than an hour. Just long enough for Brendan to drop me at the Rotunda and drive off in search of a parking space. He seemed to take an age finding one and my name was called twice but still he hadn't arrived. I couldn't progress to the next stage without him. I was becoming increasingly agitated, convinced I was going to miss my turn and that my embryos wouldn't be implanted. 'It's like the stacking system for planes taking off – lose your slot and you go to the back of the queue,' I wailed to myself. I was certain that all the return slots for eggs would be filled that day, while mine would be retired to the laboratory until the next time a session was scheduled. By which stage the embryos might have shrivelled up and died. This was irrational but the maternal compulsion is not grounded in logic.

As the minutes ticked I grew convinced it had all been in vain and the clinic would cancel the transfer. It looked as though we were too casual about it. Finally, Brendan strolled in with a newspaper under his arm and – poor man – I was incandescent. It seemed to me that if he'd taken time to go in search of a newsagent then he wasn't treating this most crucial final stage of the treatment with the urgency it deserved. This was unfair of me, but I had no sense of proportion and I felt betrayed. All Brendan could see was a woman throwing a tantrum over a newspaper.

This heightened feeling of being alone left me silent as three embryos were returned to me. Usually I felt chatty – indeed, exuberant – during the procedure but the incident had distressed me. However, I lay there quietly, following instructions, and three more embryos had their homecoming.

'Two As and a B,' said the nurse.

I sighed, lacking the energy to worry about the B. I couldn't even rally myself that Toulouse-Lautrec was probably a B.

Afterwards, I procrastinated about going into our house. I stood on the pavement, looking at the tree in the front garden in honour of our lost embryos, and I hardly dared to walk through the gate. Subconsciously I wanted to stay in limbo. I knew we could manage this part: we could grow eggs and convert them into embryos, but I couldn't seem to carry the embryos long enough for them to become babies. We were reaching the point where I always stumbled.

'Come on,' said Brendan, who had been fetching something from the car. 'You shouldn't be standing around, let's get you inside to rest.'

Chapter 18

This was my happiest incubation period. Despite the pressure of it being the third and final try, despite the tremors in my marriage, despite the isolation I had felt as my embryos were replaced, I was more positive than ever before. With my trio inside me, safe and sound, I was euphoric. I roosted there, singing lullabies to my babies, calling them by name – Finbarr, Molly and Rory – chattering as though there were four of us tucked up in bed together. 'There goes the phone. I bet it's Daddy checking to see how we all are.'

For fifteen days I chirruped, each day more elated than the previous one. I stroked the baby clothes I had stashed in the back of my wardrobe, I gazed, awestruck, at the christening robe, imagining it swelled by an infant's body. Of course, I'd need to buy or borrow two more robes. I sketched out the enchanted story of our life together as a family: the trips to the pantomime, the sandcastle holidays, the helium balloon-filled perfection of it all. I told them about their cousins, a raft of small boys and girls who would be their playmates and share their toys.

'There's Justin and Aoife, Christopher and Clodagh, they'll play with you. Then there's the older ones, Francis and John, Stephen and Ciaran – they'll be too old to play with but they might show you how to play computer games or help with your homework. Whoops, maybe I shouldn't mention homework. And there's Michelle and Louise, they'll babysit for you.'

Chatter, chatter. I didn't need television or radio to keep me company, I had my babies.

'Wait till you try out a bouncy castle, you're in for a treat. And learn to ride a bike. Taste your first ice-cream. Find your grandad's toffee-jar. Wait till you discover pocket money. Toyshops. Disneyworld. Midnight feasts. Pick 'n' mix.'

My trio may have been a long way from viable life – not even foetuses, at an elemental stage of their development – but I knew no distinction. They were simply my babies.

I was a ball of concentrated willpower. Nothing could insinuate itself between me and motherhood: the role for which I had been born was ready for me. It was the most joyful period of my life.

I was still daringly blissful, that night before I was due back at the clinic for a pregnancy test. Still daringly blissful as I tottered cautiously along the landing towards the bathroom, the strains of *Coronation Street* drifting after me. Still daringly blissful, for a heartbeat or two, as I stared at the pink streaks through my urine in the porcelain bowl and denied the evidence of my eyes. The bliss seeped away as I touched myself, doubting Thomas fashion, and my fingers were daubed with blood. The bliss was extinguished as comprehensively as if it had never been when I called to Brendan and extended my hand with its telltale smears.

'I've lost them. Our babies are gone.'

It was springtime when my hopes of pregnancy bled from me for the final time. The month of March. The opening, the ancient Greeks called this season. And indeed, the earth was waking up after winter – daffodils poking through the soil, dim days yielding to tentative sunshine. Our tree had leaves of the palest green trembling on its branches. All around me Mother Nature's fertility asserted itself.

I was beyond emptiness.

★

That last night, after I had visited the bathroom and touched the blood that signalled defeat, I lay awake and listened to the creaks an old house makes, floorboards and pipes groaning, while my husband slept beside me. I wondered at his ability to slip away from consciousness. My babies, I realized, had never been real – except in my heart, which had welcomed and named them. Planned their futures. Cherished them. These words trickled through my mind.

You have taken the east from me; you have taken the west from me;
You have taken what is before me and what is behind me;
You have taken the moon, you have taken the sun from me,
And my fear is great that you have taken my God from me!

The lines come from an eighth-century Gaelic lament, in which the speaker mourns her absconding lover, but they seemed specifically designed to express my grief for our unborn children. I wallowed in heartache that night. If there is such a concept as distilled misery, then I experienced it during those lonely hours. I had reached the end of the road in my quest for motherhood.

I had no tears after this third failed attempt. Not because it mattered less, but because it mattered too much to cry. I'd sobbed before, never realizing I was wasting my tears on trivia – on disappointments I could not even recall. Now weeping, which had been an adequate means of venting my emotions before, struck me as woefully insufficient. How could I cry over a pain in my leg one day and a pain in my heart another? So many pointless tears shed already in my lifetime; if I'd known what was looming, I'd have stored them up to cry them, now, when they finally meant something.

I was seduced by mourning. It encased me in a rind no one could penetrate. Not my husband, not my family. Queen

Victoria's lifetime-long welter of bereavement for Prince Albert wasn't a patch on mine. I grieved over the loss of motherhood and the uncertainty of a future for which I no longer had an atlas; the maps I had been consulting were obsolete. I grieved for my unborn babies but for myself too. For the realization I was to be refused this gift I had set my heart on. Motherhood denied. I grieved at the brutality of failure and its finality. I was stupefied that so many momentous events could have happened in such a narrow band of time. Our years together were not great in quantity – only in experiences; Brendan and I had already spent a lifetime together.

My life was a void. Un-life. Voices reached me across a yawning distance and scarcely registered. I was neither conscious nor unconscious but floating between the two states. My reality was my three unborn babies. Finbarr, Rory, Molly. Daily life – the one with bills to pay, supermarket visits to make, dental appointments to keep – meant nothing to my babies and consequently it meant nothing to me any longer. I was an automaton, and incapable of calling for help.

As the weeks passed, Brendan was taciturn in his disappointment and sorrow, while my desolation showed no sign of waning. Tellingly, I remember no discussion of holidays to cheer us. Perhaps in time we might have considered adoption. But a glass wall reared between my husband and me; each of us was seared by pain but neither shared it with the other. Neither one reaching out or comforting the other. We shared a house but were no longer a pair. We seemed to ricochet off one another, connecting for an instant and then rebounding.

I suspect that when my husband looked at me he saw the pain and misery, and yes, the anger and incomprehension of infertility. When I looked at him, I saw the same. And we veered away from one another; from the sorrow and failure each of us represented.

Sometimes I tortured myself by wondering if my children hadn't wanted to be born. If the embryos returned to my womb had simply let go. Assessed the lie of the land and thought, 'No thanks, this isn't for us.' I never believed it was me per se they were rejecting, just everything that came with me. Life at the rump end of the twentieth century. The greed, the injustice, the violence, the alienation.

'But there'd be candles on birthday cakes, snowmen in our back garden, stories at bedtime,' I had reassured them. Or maybe I had entreated them. Except I was having the conversation with embryos that had already eluded me. They had slipped from my body and were never going to become children.

Brendan made one final effort to reach me; he said something that left me wailing like a banshee.

'I think we should try again.'

It was less than two months after the third attempt failed and I was scraped raw. I said no. I didn't just say no, I hollered it. He was being pragmatic, as men often are, but some kernel of the survival instinct whispered that IVF was killing me.

It was death by despair.

Emotionally, spiritually and physically I was on a knife-edge. I could no longer bear the cycle of false hope and disappointment. I could stomach no more drugs in my body, no more bloodlettings, no more anaesthetics. I needed space and peace to mourn, to come to terms with a different version of my life to the one I had attempted to fashion.

'A fourth attempt?' I yowled. 'And if that fails do we have a fifth?'

He nodded. 'If that's what it takes.'

I screeched . . . God knows what I screeched. All I can remember is the bile that rose. He paled, shocked by the vehemence of my response. I left the room and in that moment our faltering relationship began to surrender its battle for life.

Now, perhaps for the first time since we'd embarked on our quest for a child, we had to consider our marriage. Except we attempted nothing as sane or practical as sitting down and discussing it. Instead we did what wounded couples do: we attacked one another. The marriage imploded.

We returned to that insidious habit of no longer sharing a bedroom. One of the benefits of a four-bedroom house, when a marriage is failing, is that you have a choice of rooms. It's one of the drawbacks too. Sleeping apart cements the differences. Bodies cannot comfort each other in the anonymity of the night; mumbled confidences can't be exchanged, nor tentative gestures made towards reconciliation.

I knew, as he did, that the situation between us couldn't continue. That house was saturated in misery: it oozed through floorboards, slipped out from under skirting boards, penetrated keyholes. I could envisage no way to repel the sorrow and reclaim our happy home.

Yet I loved the house too, in a perverse way: I had come as close as I ever would to being a mother inside it. I had lost all my IVF embryos on our upper floor. My babies' tree was growing in the garden. One baby's stained-glass memorial flanked the front door.

I took to watching our wedding video, searching for something I couldn't define. An indication that the couple whispering in each other's ears as they danced to 'Love Is All Around' knew there might be rapids ahead. Portents.

Premonitions. Where are the harbingers of doom when you need them? You won't spot them in wedding videos. What you will find is confidence that your life together is going to be as enchanted as the wedding day. You're intoxicated by the fantasy made flesh, by the groundswell of goodwill from family and friends.

Children cropped up in the marriage service.

'Are you ready to accept, with love, the children that God may send you?' asked the priest.

'We are,' Brendan and I replied in unison.

You know, I never heard the word 'may' during the service. It only penetrated then, three years and a half later. Until that day I believed I'd vowed to accept with love the children that God would send me, with no prevaricating tenses.

I gazed on the scenes played out in a Sligo seaside village framed by Ben Bulben. Still my favourite mountain. Fast-forwarding through, I giggled, charmed, by the warm-hearted German guest who erupted spontaneously into song as the meal drew to a close. It was a Marlene Dietrich number about a prostitute under a street-light, and the priest and the Mammies tapped their feet to keep time. I paused the video, too, for my nephew, Justin, just two, sitting on my knee and inspired by the German lady to sing 'Incey Wincey Spider'. He nearly remembered all the words! My sister and I exchanged glances of pride. Justin was the baby who had attached a loudhailer to the tick of my biological clock.

It struck me how a disproportionate number of the guests were children; my nieces and nephews, as well as Brendan's, and the children of our friends. It was the most child-centric wedding I have ever attended. In virtually every shot there are tumbling youngsters – inquisitive babies, excitable toddlers, self-conscious pre-teens. See the twin flower-girls swinging their joined hands and warbling along to 'Sonny Don't Go Away', played at their request; listen to the quartet of junior rappers borrowing the microphone to perform on the dance floor. I was reminded of why it seemed normal to Brendan and me to want children – we both belonged to overflowing Irish families.

He held my hand so tightly during the wedding service – I'd forgotten that but the video hadn't. He reached out his warm hand and gripped mine. The sight made me feel sentimental. I was entranced, look, he's stroking it gently. Studying that pair in their wedding finery, as certain about their future as it's possible for any couple to be, I didn't know whether to sympathize with them for their future misfortune, or dislike them for their inability to cope with it. I did both.

Sometimes I rewound the tape to scrutinize the expression on my soon-to-be-husband's face as he turned from the top pew to watch me walk up the aisle towards him on my father's arm. His look conveyed overwhelming love. He flashed me a beacon of a smile before turning back towards the altar.

'See?' I'd tell the television set, freeze-framing the video. 'We started with the best of intentions.'

I didn't yet know that my marriage was in its death throes, when I stormed out of the room after Brendan suggested a fourth IVF attempt. But I suspected it as the arguments blistered, and I knew it as I saw that my husband's eyes were glacial, now, when they rested on my face. They were not the eyes of that bridegroom at the top of the aisle. But threadbare though it was, I did not want my marriage to unravel. I believed my husband and I would mutilate each other further if we stayed together, yet I lacked the courage to strike out on my own. I longed to cling to familiar objects, to shelter in the cave I knew – frightened by the dragons outside.

I was in torment at the time, and no doubt impossible to live with. Looking back, it's obvious I would have benefited from professional expertise, but nobody from the clinic suggested counselling and it was not routine. (I understand that now there is a facility available.) All I could think, obsessively, was that I was a failure. I believed I had failed both as a mother and as a wife. Two of the pivotal roles in that array of functions a woman adopts during her life, and I could sustain neither.

The relationship seemed beyond repair. I dreaded the scratch of his key in the lock, I imagine he shuddered at the sound of mine. Both of us realized the marriage was too damaged and damaging to continue with. But if I'm honest, I'd known when embarking on the third IVF attempt that its result would make or break the relationship. Except I believed it would make it.

I reminded myself the fertility treatment had been a process initiated in love, even if that emotion had become swamped by myriad others. But now, for the first time, I wondered at the authenticity of our love. Could the membrane between love and indifference – or worse – be so thin? Animosity shuddered between us and it seemed to challenge the integrity of my IVF cycles, so that I was haunted by one thought: 'That's why we failed.' I whispered it to myself. 'The love was flawed.'

There's always a specific moment when a splintering relationship snaps asunder. Ours was trite, as they often are; it's straws that break a marriage's back. It was soon after Brendan's suggestion of a fourth IVF attempt, when I had rounded on him, incensed. A week or so later I wanted to throw something on a skip further along our road – I can't even remember what it was now but he was opposed to it.

'Come on, Brendan, what's the big deal? Everyone does it.'

'It's theft. You're stealing space in someone's skip.'

'Don't be silly, we've done it before. And when we had skips we accepted other people's rubbish would be pitched into them, we didn't mind.'

'You can do it if you like, Martina, but I'm not going to be party to it.'

'Right, I will.'

I stepped outside and he followed me into the front garden, where something seemed to fracture inside him and public shouting followed. Aghast, I dropped what I was holding, retreating into the house – and in that instant I knew, beyond any doubt, that the marriage could not be salvaged. It was a husk. Brendan must have realized it too. He came back indoors and yelled the words I'd been waiting for subconsciously. 'I want a divorce.' Shaken, I ran upstairs and silently prepared for bed. I kept dropping my toothbrush, my hand was trembling so much.

My mind was in a tumult. Through it, one thought kept surfacing: if divorce was the answer after three bouts of IVF, we must have asked ourselves the wrong questions.

Even when it was clear that this marriage was doomed, I still resisted the inevitable. Coming from a traditional Catholic background, it had been a difficult step divorcing my first husband – at that time there had been only one divorce in our entire extended family. In the wake of my divorce I had been granted an annulment by the Catholic Church – in its eyes the first marriage had never existed. This meant when

I met Brendan, I could have the church wedding that was important to parents on both sides. It was a second chance, and I felt blessed to have been given it. When it became apparent I had another failed marriage on my hands, I was shredded with shame.

Imagine being thirtysomething and having two failed marriages already behind me. I thought of Oscar Wilde's Lady Bracknell and how she'd intone: 'To lose one husband, Ms Devlin, may be regarded as a misfortune; to lose both looks like carelessness.'

That first marriage had been one of those spontaneous impulses. We were barely out of our teens and couldn't bear to be apart: we fell in love at first sight and were engaged eighteen days later. We had a calendar on which we marked off the days until our wedding day, a matter of just months after our first date. I thought he was the handsomest man I'd ever seen, with his curly hair and ski-slope cheekbones: I couldn't believe he was interested in me. But he was. He sent me yellow rosebuds from his tiny trainee's salary and bought me my first diamond. He was one of the kindest, most honourable and gentlemanly men I was to meet in life. I still retain the strongest ties of affection for him and remain in contact with his family.

But . . . we grew up and grew apart, divorcing and then going through an annulment. We separated amicably, with frequent lunches to check the other was well and happy. I went to his housewarming party in his new flat in Soho after we split up. There was goodwill between us and I trust that will always be the case.

My first husband and I weren't an important part of one another's lives by the time I married Brendan. Indeed, I sometimes found it a struggle to remember I had been married before. It all seemed so long ago, as though it had happened to someone else. To some other carefree girl who'd just arrived in England and felt destabilized because she was no longer surrounded by her close family, and who had responded to an engaging young man's offer of a substitute family, via his own affectionate, welcoming group of relatives.

When I think of him, it's with the tenderness you might reserve for a brother. We'd been so young that by the time I met Brendan, I tended not to think of us as having been husband and wife but as boyfriend and girlfriend playing house together. The irony isn't lost on me that if I'd tried to become pregnant while married to my first husband, there is a strong chance I would be a mother now. But I was young and eager for a career, I imagined I had all the time in the world.

Now that I look back I'm not certain I was capable of making a slice of toast let alone a decision, but I realized that standing still was not an option. Brendan and I agreed we no longer wanted to be together. Appalling though separation was to contemplate, I had to consider it. We both shared the view that the marriage had no future, although I was frightened to leave it.

During those final months, as I gathered my resources to leave, blazing rows were commonplace. I contributed to them, by sulking even more than by yelling.

'Why does there always have to be shouting? Can we just stop shouting?' I said once.

Brendan shrugged. 'Shouting gets your anger out of your system, it's healthy.'

But I needed to be free from this inner turbulence. I craved peace, silence, solitude. I still wasn't well – it had only been two months since my body had been pumped full of hormones – and I didn't know how I would start over. I longed to stop wanting so desperately: babies, to be a family, a happy marriage . . . not to feel like a failure, not to have this ache inside me. I'd settle for nothingness – just let me feel nothingness.

There was some discussion about marriage guidance counselling but we could not agree to it. In May, a little over two months after that final IVF attempt, Brendan and I decided to part.

Waiting for the end was excruciating, as the lawyers thrashed out a settlement. Because of our various financial and property circumstances Brendan and I agreed that he would buy out my interest in the Ranelagh house and I would buy another one. Still there were so many uncertainties. My one certainty was that Dublin was my only option if I were to remain in Ireland and earn a living. While I was going through the IVF treatment, freelance journalism had suited me because I could just vanish when I needed to, but this meant that my income had been erratic. I needed to establish a consistent flow of earnings.

I started scanning the 'to let' ads, trying not to remember the cheerful circumstances under which I had last been hunting for a home, the euphoria of our reunions as I'd flown in from London for the weekend and we'd pored over maps of Dublin. I found somewhere suitable, a landlord specifying a single female who was a non-smoker, and was told I could move into the flat in October.

Even when you realize the end is in sight, you try to defer it. I bought a shed for the back garden shortly before I left, knowing I wouldn't be using it. Not wanting it to be so. I thought of the stained glass panels in the door I had designed to commemorate my ectopic pregnancy, I looked at the tree in the front garden we had planted for one of our IVF attempts. Hoping, still, that some miracle might intervene to save us. But there was no miracle. The chairs we sat on, the plates we ate off, the mirrors we looked into became 'mine' and 'his', not ours.

Brendan was away the day I moved out. Three women friends arrived in their cars to help me move my possessions, transforming what could have been an austere episode into a jolly one. It was a sweet moment, for I realized I could still count on friendship. The loyalty of women has been a constant in my life.

The flat in Rathmines seemed tiny after our house. I used to lie in bed, boxes from my Ranelagh life piled around the room, staring at the lampshade. I needed to keep the light on at night, I don't know why. Echoes of childhood, perhaps. One restless night I rose and sat there looking at the keys to the Ranelagh house. They no longer fitted the front door. But then, Brendan and I no longer fitted each other either.

Chapter 19

By Christmas 1998, I was a formally separated woman. It all happened at dizzying speed: only the previous year – our 'quality time' Christmas that went awry – we had still intended to turn ourselves into a family. I could never have imagined that it would turn out to be our last Christmas together, or that within a matter of months the civilized veneer would crumble. The official separation documents were signed on 21 December, the year's shortest day. Long enough for us to sign off on our marriage, though. Merry Christmas.

It's an uneasy state initially, separation. How long before you remove the gold band, tick Ms instead of Mrs on forms, train yourself to stop saying 'my husband', throw away the wedding album?

Each milestone precipitated soul-searching. I could slide off my wedding ring but it still left an indentation on my skin, I might not want to look at our wedding photographs but I hadn't the heart to destroy them. The last time I sneaked a peek, I was struck by how the woman no longer resembles me. There she is, pinned-up hair and dangling Victorian pearl earrings bought by her husband as a wedding present, and she's a version of me, I can't deny it. But she's the pre-IVF version. I pity her, ignorant of what lies ahead, but I'm proud of her too, for surviving.

That woman's ivory silk wedding dress with its fishtail train is kept in a black bin-bag at the back of a cupboard in my spare room. The dressmaker's name was Mairéad. A warm-hearted woman with a houseful of children; she hugged me as she handed over the gown on the night before my wedding. I tried to give away the dress once, offering it to a friend's daughter for her dressing-up box, but it boomeranged back a few weeks later. My friend felt uncomfortable about her having it. So now I'm resigned to holding on to the dress. I have my wedding band too. I offered Brendan the glorious diamond he had bought me at a Sotheby's auction, but he declined it. Then I offered it to my mother. 'Thanks, angel, that's really generous of you, but I could never wear it. It wouldn't be right.' I sold it at another Sotheby's auction and donated the money to a children's charity. I'd have flogged the wedding band if I could, for the same cause, but if used engagement rings are out of favour, second-hand wedding rings are even more unpopular: people are superstitious about attracting bad luck. It sits in my jewellery box, that band of gold, looking rather smug. *I'm not so easy to get rid of, am I?*

As I settled into the flat I'd rented, in the run-up to that first Christmas of my new life, I puzzled over why we had never discussed adoption at any length. Why IVF, instead of adoption, had been our super-highway to parenthood. It was too late then, of course, but I was indulging in one of those why-oh-why sessions that were meat and drink to me at the time.

Initially there had been an unspoken agreement between Brendan and me that adoption would be explored when other avenues were exhausted, when a child composed of our DNA was no longer a possibility. It wasn't that we would have loved an adoptive child less, that we were obsessed with reproducing from our own gene pool. I had no burning urge to see the same dimple that indented my chin, or observe my husband's gift for charming people repeated in our child. Baby hunger was never about replication, it was about someone to love. (Yet when my sister said of Aoife, her infant daughter, 'She has your nose,' I felt immeasurably moved. It wasn't my nose alone, but my father's, my aunt's, my grand-mother's. There was a sudden rush of atavistic joy: something of me would survive, after all.) It was simply that the waiting list for adoption was two years long and our need for a child had been so pressing that the delay seemed unbearably protracted.

So here's the conclusion we had arrived at, and it's one I consistently marvel at: it was easier to have IVF treatment than to apply to the health board for an adoption assessment.

I was never tempted, in that final cycle of fertility treat-ment, to apply to adopt. It had struck me as profoundly immoral – as selfish as it was wrong in our unhappy circum-stances. You could argue that trying to have an IVF baby in our circumstances had been wrong too, and I'm not sure I could offer much of a defence. But my convoluted emotional intelligence reasoned that the rancour between Brendan and me would be re-routed with a baby to divert it.

Blind? Of course I was. I look back at that woman and cringe at her stupidity, but I also want to hug her because she hadn't given up hope yet. Hope for the particular version of happily ever after she craved that simply wasn't in the script.

After the IVF failed, in that two-month intermission before Brendan and I had broached the possibility of separating, I had known in my heart it would be wrong to register our names as adoptive parents. We were not a stable unit. We could not be loving parents towards any child because we were barely capable of speaking to one another with civility. Often I slumped on a sofa and wallowed, while he walked off his misery and loneliness outside. This wasn't normal, I knew that much. But I had floundered over how to regain what passed for normality.

Once I was no longer in the grip of an IVF cycle or preparing for a new one, I had recognized that no child was capable of healing our divisions. I believed it would be wrong to adopt and lay that expectation on its tiny shoulders. A child was entitled to a set of loving parents, not a mother and father who would use it as ammunition in their war of attrition, as I feared we would have done. I believed it would be a sin to seek out a child, to bring it from China or India or South America, and transplant it to our house. We had no home, it was a battlefield.

Pick a man and make it work.

The phrase floated across the years, sailed over the Irish Sea and landed noiselessly in my mind one day in that little Rathmines flat, separated by perhaps a quarter of an hour's walk from my old home. Although distance can't be measured, always, in metres or minutes. What would the coterie back in Covent Garden make of it all now? Most of them were married and rearing their families. Making it work. But doing that had been tougher than either Brendan or I had anticipated, once we discovered we could not inhabit the life we had mapped out. What had happened to all those vows about for better or for worse, in sickness and in health? We'd made them, and we'd meant them at the time. But keeping that bargain had been beyond us.

I wished I had known in advance how IVF treatment has the capacity to rip, tear and lacerate, how it can eat you alive, organ by organ. How it isolates: a woman from other women, a wife from her husband. Forearmed, I might have been prepared for what was to follow. It might have helped Brendan and me to be more compassionate to one another – to appreciate the enormity of what we were embarking on and to make allowances. Counselling is essential in advance, and would be beneficial during a cycle, but ours was cursory. A meeting with a specialist before being accepted for treatment – concerned primarily with the physical rather than the emotional – and an hour with a counsellor between the first and second cycles. It was a perfunctory encounter and she made no effort to persuade us to open up about how we felt; we were guarded, going through the motions, afraid to say anything negative in case it torpedoed our chances of staying on the programme.

Couples need to be warned about how the drugs might affect them – exaggerating the impact of this rollercoaster they've climbed aboard so optimistically. We paid our money for the ride thinking we'd be taking a spin on a carousel, but it turned into a loop-the-loop and we'd no idea how to cope. We were being flung all over the place but we couldn't ask for the ride to be stopped – we'd miss out on the prize.

In the middle of this maelstrom is a woman, ranting and seething, or weeping uncontrollably, or slumped in dejection, or maybe all three in rapid succession. The original hormonal harpy. And there's a man who's staring at the woman, unnerved or bewildered or excluded, or maybe all three in rapid succession.

Different women have different experiences, of course, with everything from life history to emotional stability to the nature of their relationship with their partner contributing to the outcome. Every IVF cycle is influenced by previous ones, so no two cycles are identical. Some responses are universal, however, and the desire for comfort during this emotionally desolate time has to be one of them.

Strange, how the bond between a couple can be powerful enough to prompt them to marry, but not to allow them weather their storms. Ours had arrived thick and fast, and we had hoarded too few happy memories to tide us over. The relationship never matured, I suppose. We had been able to play the falling in love part to perfection, right down to a marriage proposal in Prague and a Victorian engagement ring, a breathtaking chunk of diamond that could dazzle at twenty paces. But we teetered when conditions grew choppy.

I was naïve within the marriage, no better prepared for it because it was my second. I had been fortunate or cosseted – depending on your perspective – in previous relationships. I thought to find myself petted and consoled, indulged, a little, when our hopes were dashed. I expected this, regardless of how tetchy, temperamental or just plain unbearable to live with the drugs left me. That was unreasonable because I was married to a man, not Sir Galahad, and I wasn't the only one with dashed hopes.

I certainly wasn't the bride who had walked up the aisle, worried that her twenty-minute delay might have caused her husband-to-be anxiety. I grew self-absorbed during the marriage. My craving for a child was a voracious affliction that had eradicated my ability to consider anyone's needs apart from my own. There was no parity of suffering, only mine.

Some couples find strength in adversity – they cling to one another when life throws them one of its curved balls. We lacked that grace; we retreated inward with our regret and our grief, each of us excluding the other. We did not create a common bond from our setbacks, but reconfigured them as a landslide of defeats. Suffering individually, not together.

Clearly both Brendan and myself had been irredeemably

affected by the stresses of IVF treatment. We had endured too much too quickly and could tolerate no more. It had been a graceless finale to our marriage and there is much about that ending I regretted then and still regret. The reproaches. The misunderstandings.

We had been lacking in compassion towards one another in those final, chaotic days and it troubled me. I wished I could turn back the clock for just a few seconds to wish Brendan well, as I do now. Why couldn't we have hugged each other one last time and said 'Good luck'? I've whispered it countless times in my imagination. But I can't change what happened between us, for all my wishing, and so I try to remember that I loved Brendan once. I cared enough to marry him and do my utmost to have his babies. Those nine embryos, that ectopic baby no bigger than a finger-joint, were his as much as mine.

As we prepared to part, Brendan had said I should remember he had been deprived of the chance of parenthood too.

'It might still happen for you,' I countered. 'You could meet someone.'

'Unlikely,' he shrugged, downcast, as you are when the world as you recognize it is shifting its contours, and you're so inured to misery that the prospect of happiness seems like a fairytale.

I felt a pang of sorrow for him.

I never said sorry to my husband. *But I am sorry, Brendan, that I couldn't have children for you. I'm sorry that my past intruded on our marriage and dealt it the death blow. I'm sorry if the relatively normal woman you married mutated into a harridan. I hope you know contentment now.*

Even during the dying days, in the midst of the acrimony, part of me wished for him then what I wish for him now, with all my heart. Fatherhood. I always believed he'd make a fine father. I hope he might, after all, have met someone he can have children with – if that's what he still wants.

Auden said, 'Love each other or perish.' We perished as a couple because we forgot to love each other, because we didn't know how to do it in the active sense instead of in the passive. Marriage tests a person. You learn about yourself and how you respond under pressure, and you don't always like what you discover. You are less tolerant, less accommodating, less compassionate than you imagined.

Although I am at peace with the life I have fashioned for myself, I still feel ambivalence about the decay of the marriage. Sometimes it seems a betrayal of our embryos. But I doubt if we could ever have been happy together again. The landscape we shared was too – here's that word again – barren.

As I write this, it occurs to me how much easier it would be if it were fiction because then I could tweak it for the outcome that best pleases me. I could re-write those final scenes, allowing fate to smile on that couple, Brendan and Martina, so they wind up with their heart's desire. Maybe I'd let them be lucky on their third IVF attempt. Perhaps I'd bring meaning to their lives with an adopted child. Except I'm not sure I ought to tinker with the ending – I'm not convinced either scenario is the right outcome for those characters. I think a couple who could not weather their vicissitudes or accept their limitations are better apart, for they were never truly a partnership. It takes more than swapping wedding rings to make a couple man and wife.

One day I noticed the wedding video sticking out of a box I hadn't yet unpacked. 'I'll throw it away one of these days,' I told myself, but I never did. It's the only film we have of my dead father talking, smiling, linking arms with me, and I cherish it for that. I can listen to his voice on it, when its timbre and nuances threaten to elude my memory. It's wonderful to see him able to dance and joke, because our last memories centre on a poor, dear, exhausted invalid's body. Yet there was a time when he waltzed in tails, with a rosebud in his lapel.

It's not the only reason I retain the wedding video. I keep it because my second marriage is a part of my life and I can't deny its relevance. The person I am today was shaped by what happened during that marriage and its aftermath. Consigning a video to the rubbish bin won't change anything.

Our love appeared to require children for ratification. Neither of us seemed to realize that love alone was the prize and anything else was a dividend. We expected children, we thought we were entitled to them, we felt discriminated against when they didn't arrive to order. Without children, our love contracted.

To go from love to attempted parenthood to separation – communication restricted to letters via lawyers – in the space of a handful of years; that's not the person I am.

Except it is.

'Don't do it!' I feel like shrieking at the couple in the wedding video. 'Look behind you!' But the freeze-frame unclicks, the tape starts rolling again and the gracious bride-groom pays tribute to his glowing bride. Then the singer calls them to the floor for their first dance as man and wife.

Nothing can save them.

Chapter 20

Reconstruction work on my life was under way. I had an apartment, now I had to start earning the rent. It was time to resuscitate my career, although since I had married and moved to Ireland work had played second fiddle to imminent motherhood. The woman who had spent her twenties in London pursuing a Fleet Street career was long gone. I regarded the snippets of journalism I did as a way of earning money to pay for IVF treatment, they had no intrinsic value for me. A considerate colleague who was a senior staffer on the *Irish Independent* once took the trouble to advise me.

'You're selling yourself short, writing the odd piece here and the odd piece there whenever you're asked, on any subject they suggest. You're wasting your talents. Just write one article a week and make it a brilliant one,' she said.

Although it was obvious she was a person who thought deeply about issues and was well-disposed towards me, I couldn't bring myself to confide that journalism was no more than a means to an end, at this stage.

'The sums don't add up,' I shrugged.

I could not admit why I badly needed to earn money; I felt ashamed of my incompetent body.

I did have one asset: ranged foursquare behind me was a loving family who made it plain they valued me. It was only a matter of time before I would rally, provided there were no more blows for a while.

There was something else, too, a blessing gradually revealing itself to me. During those months priming myself to move out of the house in Ranelagh, I had started to write a novel. Halfway through I realized that it was maudlin rubbish with death, obsession and denial at its nucleus. (No surprises there.) So it never saw the light of day. But that aborted novel taught me fiction could be used as an escape. If reality was unbearable and everything seemed beyond my control, maybe I could invent my own version of reality and direct the events unfolding there.

In my Rathmines apartment I began another novel, a more upbeat one, although I did sneak in a stillborn infant because it takes time to give obsession the slip. I'd tap away at my computer keyboard and keep the pinched quality of daily life at bay. The hours would pass and sometimes I could put in sixty minutes at a time without thinking about my babies. 'Yes,' I thought, 'maybe I can manage this eventually.'

Inevitably, however, some nights I'd lie awake torturing myself. 'Maybe if I'd had a fourth attempt, maybe if I'd tried a different clinic, maybe if we'd loved each other more . . .'

Still, I was on the slow road to recovery when New Year's Eve 1998 rolled around. 'Well,' I said, sharing a drink with a group of friends at midnight, 'at least all the bad luck is out of the way. Next year has to be a better one.'

Even as I spoke I remembered a saying of the neighbours who'd helped me through IVF treatment. 'Good luck, bad luck, who knows?' she'd shrug. Meaning it was impossible to assess the repercussions of anything. And didn't that uncertainty make life interesting, she'd imply, counselling me in her discreet way.

Still, I imagined life would be plain sailing for a time. It had to be someone else's turn for fire and pestilence.

Thirty-six hours later, I came within a hair's-breadth of dying in a car crash.

★

On a clear, bright Saturday morning, on 2 January 1999, I was driving to Omagh to take my twin nieces to a Boyzone concert. I never got there. Instead I was caught up in a three-car pile-up on the N2 between Slane and Collon in Co. Meath. It all happened so fast: we were on a straight stretch of road when I saw the driver ahead of me slump over the wheel of her car and shoot across into the path of an oncoming vehicle. The impact sent her car careering back to strike mine. The front bonnet of my Volkswagen Polo folded in, accordion-fashion, around me, while I sat in a daze with my foot rammed on the brake pedal. Two people were killed, four of us were injured and I was the sole driver left alive, with my car a write-off.

An ambulance rushed me to Our Lady of Lourdes Hospital in Drogheda, along with a teenager on a stretcher who screamed constantly during the journey – he had plenty to shriek about, poor lad. He had been on his way to Dublin Airport, to go on a skiing holiday; now his father was dead, his mother and sister were injured and it looked as though he was seriously hurt.

But my fortunes weren't on a rising tide either. After several hours lolling on a chair in Accident and Emergency, I was diagnosed with a broken sternum and prescribed bed rest.

'Not more bed rest,' I thought. It reminded me of the last time I had spent a prolonged period beneath the duvet, hatching my babies.

I had taken the brunt of the impact across my chest, so there were concerns about possible heart problems, but these proved unfounded. I also had a gash on the forehead that was unsightly, required stitches and would leave a scar. However I had grown accustomed to scars and was indifferent to it. (More than a year later, during a routine eye test, I discovered further complications. That blow to my forehead, when I had struck my head against the windscreen before the seatbelt had pulled me back, had caused my right retina to start detaching. It had been deteriorating since then and was caught at the eleventh hour. Even after major surgery my eye has only limited vision now, although fortunately my left eye compensates. In my right eye I have a sort of tunnel vision. As if there hadn't been enough tunnel vision in the preceding years. I laugh about it sometimes. Only sometimes.)

I was faced with frighteningly steep hospital bills from the accident – and the broken sternum meant I couldn't work for two months. I had no private medical insurance. My husband had been on a free work-related policy, and I had been entitled to cover as his spouse. The separation agreement had been signed just before the Christmas and New Year holidays – twelve days previously – and I hadn't got around to organizing alternative cover. Dealing with all these issues was a reminder that I was on my own now.

Chinks of light penetrated, all the same: I was alive and that had to be worth something. In any disaster when some are spared and others taken, neither rhyme nor reason can explain why. Nevertheless I puzzled over why my life was salvaged from this car crash. 'I should be dead too,' I thought.

But I wasn't.

A few days later my father, Frank, and brother, Celsus, collected me from hospital to bring me home. We stopped off at the garage where the remains of my little green Polo had been towed.

'That car saved your life,' said the garage-owner. 'Anything less sturdy and the metal would have ripped through you like a knife.'

'Well, well, well,' I thought, 'so green really is a lucky colour.'

I had paused, setting off on that journey from Dublin a few days earlier, to buy my mother some flame-bright tulips, audacious fireballs catching my eye. The tulips were lying on the floor of the car and, amazingly, although droopy they were still living. We brought home the blooms to my mother and she revived them for a day or two. She kept them in a Belleek china vase on her coffee table long after their petals had started shedding and they should have been consigned to the dustbin. A sentimental attachment, one the would-be mother in me appreciated. Initially I was inspired by the resilience of the tulips – but soon my euphoria evaporated and I wished I could simply fade away, like them. It looked as though I had suffered one setback too many.

My family wanted to keep me in Omagh to recuperate, but I persuaded a brother to drive me back to the little flat in Rathmines. It was Celsus, the brother whose former girl-friend had ended my impasse over the consultant's letter. My parents were dubious but I was insistent. In my willing embrace of victimhood, I wanted to retreat to dulled mollusc state. I planned to spend the time in a state of muffled consciousness – not through writing, my intention in pre-car crash days – but with Mogadon, prescribed to dull the pain from my sternum that kept me awake at night.

I had sleeping pills from the hospital dispensary, more from the health centre in Omagh, and when I arrived in Dublin I registered immediately with a new GP in Rathmines and asked for another batch: I was determined to stockpile them. They were my best insulation against feeling. With feeling came self-pity, and occasionally self-loathing; I preferred chemical sedation.

At times I woke in the night, confused, and swallowed another tablet, forgetting – or uncaring – that I had already taken one. The following day would pass in a sluggish blur and I welcomed that. I felt my body, which had betrayed me repeatedly by not reproducing, even when the heavy-hitters had waded in, was deceiving me yet again when it nudged me towards lucidity.

Once or twice I considered swallowing my supply, one after another, until they were all gone. Nothingness. How sweet, I imagined. I weighed the temptation and it was compelling, but my love for my family was more compelling again and I could not deliberately cause them pain. So I set aside the thought. It slithered out from time to time but I contained it. It was never that I wanted to commit suicide, particularly, that was too pro-active; I simply didn't want the trouble of breathing any longer. Of thinking and feeling and hurting.

The sleeping pills were my crutch. They kept flashbacks at bay: the screaming boy, a car sliced open by firemen, a young girl's solitary trainer near the wreckage, my own puniness and impotence. I shuffled these scenes of death and destruction, equated them with my babies, also dead to me, and reached for the Mogadon. My store was depleting, however, and I returned to my GP for more, trembling when he seemed reluctant to prescribe them. In an effort to persuade him, I told him about the timing of this accident, hot on the heels of three failed IVF attempts. He allowed me one further prescription of pills but referred me to a psychiatrist.

I was diagnosed as 'emotionally fragile' after one session but I never returned to him. My faith in doctors was shaky. The medics had supplied me with caveats before I started IVF treatment but their admonitions had not prepared me for failure. I saw only the promises in their statistics; yet I had empty arms. What use was a one in five success rate if I wasn't the one? Happy outcomes for others were inconsequential to me, I could take no pleasure in their triumph over the odds. I was the person supposed to beat the statistics. I didn't care to be a graceful loser, I wanted to be the winner.

Once I believed in doctors the way our ancestors believed in their druids. But doctors can't perform miracles any more than priests. There was one service doctors could definitely supply: oblivion. They could write prescriptions. I trailed back to my GP for yet more sleeping pills, which he refused to prescribe.

'He must imagine I'm addicted.' I shook my head over his ill-informed presumption. Just because I needed them and wanted them didn't mean I was hooked on them. I found another GP who supplied me with a prescription, lumbered home and retired to bed with my trusty Mogadon.

Eventually, I hoped, when the storm passed I'd feel . . . resignation. It was the best I could anticipate, I certainly didn't think I could manage anything as submissive as acceptance.

'Still, though,' a voice echoed in my brain, 'why was I created with a womb – and then had the entrance blocked up?' I looked at other women and wondered why their bodies could nurture life and not mine. I was haunted by the regret that I had never looked into any of my babies' eyes or held them in my arms. I would have liked to carry that memory with me through life.

I punched one of the sleeping pills through its foil casing – 'too easy to take if all you have to do is tip a bottle upside down,' the doctor had explained. What did he know? He thought I needed these tablets. Of course I didn't need them, I just liked them. What I needed was to regain my equilibrium. Perhaps if I could start writing again? I switched on my computer and the screen wheezed into life, letters ghosting in front of me. It was useless, my imagination was as barren as my body. I could concentrate on nothing other than survival.

Weeks passed. I used to float towards wakefulness in the morning and then, just as consciousness struck, try to submerge myself in sleep again. I didn't want to face the day, for no good could come of it. It would be yet another child-less one. Insulated by the remnants of sleep, brain not yet functioning on all cylinders, at least my pain was blunted and I didn't need to accept that I had tried my utmost, wished intensely, and the level of effort had made not the slightest jot of difference. I had failed as conclusively as if I had been half-hearted about IVF, approaching it as casually as you'd try out the latest beauty fad.

Sometimes, while I lay in bed waiting for my sternum to knit back, for the Mogadon to kick in, for my life to re-ignite, I excavated my past for clues – for sins to justify this litany of punishments. I had to find a reason, you see; it struck me as incredible, as immoral, as downright impossible that there could be no reason. That random chance alone had left me infertile, then given me a ruptured ectopic preg-nancy, three failed IVF cycles and a near-fatal accident. Again and again I returned to that first failed marriage. I convinced myself I had been profligate in allowing it to end, instead of working at preserving it. No wonder my luck had turned – natural justice was intervening.

I felt trapped. Not just by the accident, which required bed rest, but by the belief that nobody else could under-stand how I felt about a childless fate. There was a cavern at my centre that nothing could fill except a baby. It didn't have to be a child of my own, any baby I folded into my arms, inhaling its scented softness, satisfied that need. Except

I knew I'd have to hand back the baby that didn't belong to me.

Sometimes, too, I wondered what was so terribly wrong with me that the template had to become obsolete. I had an image of God or Nature or whoever decides these matters, scratching their heads and saying: 'Whoops, dud model, don't know how she sneaked through quality control but we'll see to it she's the last in that line.' I'd envisage scenarios where I was phased out of production because all my children would have been born with incurable diseases and suffer excruciating pain during their brief lives, say. Or I'd have had a baby that would grow up to become a serial killer. 'All right,' I'd think, 'I can handle infertility in those circumstances.' I was clutching at straws, because the truth was unpalatable. My infertility was down to blind chance.

Finally the day came when I knew I had to ease out of this trough. I psyched myself up to perform one final assignment on behalf of my babies. It was February again, 1999, six weeks after the accident. A year had passed since I had embarked on that final IVF cycle. I had accepted that I would never be a mother, and no amount of wishing for the impossible would change that. But I was treading water in this new, misshapen phase of my life. My fractured breastbone was still tender as I lugged a basket of scented soaps past the amusement arcades on O'Connell Street, the jangle of gambling machines pursuing me.

I was en route to the fertility clinic at the Rotunda Hospital. 'The futility clinic,' I called it to myself. I wanted to give a gift to the staff, in acknowledgement of their kindness – I could not manage a more lavish gesture, for I was still not working after my car accident. I suspected they were probably awash with chocolates, like my nurses at the Meath Hospital, but everyone liked scented soaps. I bought an assortment of thirty.

I had to pep-talk myself for a week until I drummed up the nerve to return to the HARI unit. My heart plummeted, tripping my ankles, as I walked towards the building in which I'd invested so much hope. I averted my eyes from the heart-shaped motif on the glass door, with its mother-father-baby trinity, and reminded myself to stay well clear of the notice-board. Photographs of infants sent in by grateful patients would unstitch me.

'You can do this,' I told myself.

It was unfinished business and it was time I dealt with it.

I wasn't even sure if the staff would remember me, since so many desperate women turn to them. They must blank us out after a while, for how else could they cope with so much undiluted yearning?

As I entered the reception area I wanted to turn tail. To stiffen myself, I imagined I wasn't just one woman doing this. I was a representative of every infertile woman – each one of us who undergoes a cycle of IVF treatment, reaching for the moon, and comes to terms with the realization that she can't quite stretch out her hands far enough. In my insignificant way, with nothing more valuable to offer than a basket of soaps, I wanted to pay tribute to the clinic for bringing the moon a little closer for some of us.

There were three couples and two single women in reception waiting for appointments. I looked at them, tense with expectation as they listened for their names to be called, eyes turned aside from one another as mine had been in similar circumstances. I envied those women before me who had not yet emptied their hearts of hope. But I also knew I could never be one of them again.

I recognized the nurse behind the desk, a silent, black-haired woman in her forties with – was that a Tipperary accent? – whom I had grown to like. I used to cringe when the nurses approached me with needles but it had never hurt as much when she had taken blood. She had a careful way about her.

'Can I help you?' She raised dark eyes to mine.

I knew there was no recall in them. 'I had . . . treatment here.' I passed over my basket. 'I wanted to say thank you. Could you maybe leave this in the staff room so people can help themselves?'

The nurse blazed one of her rare smiles, teeth white against olive skin, and thanked me. 'What did you have, a boy or a girl?'

'I – I didn't have anything,' I stumbled. 'I wasn't lucky.' Despite my best efforts, I could feel my eyes moisten and my nostrils prickle. I clamped cautionary teeth against my lower lip, determined to see this through.

The nurse's smile evaporated but her eyes were kind. 'You did your best.'

At this simple expression of compassion my tear ducts welled and I fled. I ran through the hospital grounds as though my life depended on it. Ran so that my teeth clattered inside my mouth and the ground reached through my shoes to judder my kneecaps. Ran so that my fractured sternum, slowly fusing together again, threatened to fragment. I courted the pain, hoping physical distress could take the place of emotional.

On the street outside the Rotunda, I slumped on the kerb.

A woman touched me on the shoulder. 'Are you all right, dear?'

'I'm fine,' I lied automatically, eyes swimming.

'Why don't you go home and have a nice cup of tea. It won't seem so bad. There's a taxi rank,' she pointed.

I stood up and limped off in the direction she indicated. But I had spent all my cash on the soaps. So I kept walking along O'Connell Street, up Westmoreland Street and along Dame Street, careless of the curious glances my blotchy face was attracting. I placed one leg in front of the other until finally I was back at my apartment in Rathmines. Then I climbed into bed, fully clothed, curled into the foetal crouch and pulled the duvet over my head.

I had never been a woman who cried much, before the days when I had started hankering after a baby, but now I seemed unable to do anything else. Later the nurse's words returned to me and the torrent abated. *You did your best.* That was worth something.

There's an O. Henry short story called 'Roads of Destiny' that has always fascinated me, about the different directions a life might take. It follows a French poet bent on making his mark on the world. He sets off on his journey but falters when the road branches and he has a choice of routes. 'Three leagues, then, the road ran, and turned into a puzzle. It joined with another and a larger road at right angles. David stood, uncertain, for a while, and then took the road to the left.' The narrative reports his fortunes on first one road, then scrolls back to the crossroads and sends him down the other path. In the final segment the young bard is sent home to his village, following a change of heart about venturing into the world. Each direction leads him to the identical end – a bullet in his heart from the same pistol.

You didn't need to be a literary critic to grasp O. Henry's message: our fortune is our fortune and a predestined finale awaits us, irrespective of our adventures along the way. I read it first as a teenager and it stayed with me. When I no longer had any hope of motherhood, I hunted out 'Roads of Destiny' and read it again, mulling it over. Had I been wasting my time all along? Despite all that energy and endeavour, storing hope in a sieve, I had nothing to show for my repeated efforts to become pregnant. Would I have done better to concede gracefully, at the first hurdle, instead of flapping my arms in agitation – and still winding up childless? Single and childless, in this case.

No, I decided – at least I knew I'd given it my best shot. *You did your best*. It's not an enormous comfort, to be honest, but it is consolation of sorts.

Although I didn't know it in the bedroom of that Rathmines flat, with its damp-carpet smell caused by an over-head leak; although I thought my life was beyond endurance, nothing was ever as grim again after that last visit to the IVF clinic. I may have huddled in bed whimpering. But when I climbed back out several hours later, for something as mundane as boiling the kettle for tea, I was ready to continue. I had passed a watershed.

Chapter 21

For a long while I missed the house in Ranelagh – it was one change too many in my life. But perhaps it was better for me to start afresh, that could have been a stroke of luck in disguise. (Good luck, bad luck, who knows?) It's easier to stay than to go but the short-term wrench might have produced long-term benefits. 'Count yourself lucky,' I used to lecture myself. 'In some cultures you'd have been an object of scorn or pity. The shame of infertility would have killed you.'

It was March and I was trying to steel myself for my first Mother's Day since the collapse of my prospects of motherhood. I had no car – my little green Polo had to be sold for scrap after the crash – so I was intending to catch the bus to Omagh with a present of make-up for my mother. Bridie has always had a weakness for Christian Dior lipsticks.

However, I was finding the prospect an ordeal. I hadn't anticipated that – to most people it's just a day when they take their mum out for a meal or buy her a bouquet of flowers. But when you want to be the recipient rather than the donor, your outlook changes dramatically. It wasn't that I hankered after lavish display or a huge fuss made of me – a bockety card with paint splotches all over it and a laboriously executed signature would have thrilled me. Or a little pink and gilt plastic heart with Mum doodled across it, such as the one I'd admired on a stylish woman in a designer suit. Anything at all to admit me to the motherhood club.

That Mother's Day in 1999 I sat across the table from the woman who had given birth to me, my sternum battered and heart behind it in worse condition again. I wondered if she could possibly appreciate the magnitude of the gift bestowed on her. In her day it meant hard toil with few labour-saving devices, any aspirations for her own life left on hold for decades. My version of motherhood was infinitely more privileged. Still, I envied her.

'Have you any idea how fortunate you are?' I asked my mother. Demanded of her.

She looked at me uncertainly, not wanting to give the wrong answer. 'I feel lucky now,' she admitted. 'But I didn't always feel that way when you were all small. It was a lot of work.'

I'm not sure that anyone can appreciate fully what comes readily. I didn't doubt for a second that my mother loved us, but I did speculate about whether she valued motherhood for its own sake. Seven children in less than ten years of marriage: that's an abundance some women might shrink from, especially on a limited income such as my parents', with my mother working in the home and my father driving for Ulsterbus. (Years after he retired, he used senior citizen pester power to persuade the company to install a bus stop near our house to save my mother's legs. I chuckle when I pass it, celebrating Daddy's persistence. I wonder if all Ulsterbus's retired drivers imagine they're entitled to their own personal bus stops!)

My mother could argue that I glorified motherhood and exalted what was denied me. Except she wouldn't, of course, in case that upset me. I might argue that at least Bridie had the choice. But she didn't. She had even less choice about her fertility than I did, because contraception was unavailable to Catholics of her generation. In this, I come slap-bang against the contrariness of fate. My mother had children because she had no option and I didn't have children because

I had no option. She wouldn't have chosen to have so many, but loved all of us anyway because of the mothering instinct. None of my children lasted more than a few weeks in the womb, but I loved all of them anyway because of the mothering instinct. Its power and tenacity are awesome.

Part of the reason I wanted children was a selfish one: someone there for me in old age. Someone to kiss my wrinkled cheek, stroke my thinning hair. There are no guarantees but parenthood remains the closest to a warranty of some attention in old age. That's why elderly people feel cheated if their children ignore them – the contract isn't being honoured. I envisaged an empty old age with no children or grandchildren. So I also mourned for my lonely elderly unloved self, facing into extinction with nobody of my own blood following after. Oh, I turned brooding into an Olympic sport.

However blighted by fate it pleased me to imagine myself, my life seemed to take matters into its own hands and kick-started again. The sleeping pills were becoming troublesome to lay my hands on, plus I found – to my surprise – that I didn't want to be mummified in cotton wool all the time. Sometimes I enjoyed the sensation of the breeze ruffling my hair, or watching yellow crocus buds measure their height against a garden wall.

One morning, after a night when I had taken a sleeping tablet as usual, I stepped in front of a car that screeched to a halt with millimetres to spare. The driver was too shaken to protest. We regarded one another through his windscreen and I thought, 'I don't want to die this way, splattered over the road.' I returned home and threw away my sleeping tablets. Later I reconsidered, reclaimed the packet from the kitchen bin, and finally threw them into a communal bin outside the apartment block from which I could not retrieve them. Tried to anyway, but couldn't find them under someone else's household waste.

When I moved from our house in Ranelagh I was a freelance journalist, just starting out on the Irish scene after my study break – although I did have a great deal of experience in Britain. Self-esteem is porous for most of us and I was no exception. Mine had evaporated after the marriage collapsed and then I had had the accident, failure mounting on failure. So I never thought to advertise my seven years' experience with the Press Association in London. I just turned up at the *Irish Independent* and wrote freelance features, receiving payment if they were published. Piece rate.

But I was lucky. Within six months of moving out of the family home that had no family to fill it, just after my sternum fused together, I was given a staff job in the paper's newsroom. Suddenly I dared to hope that my life might no longer be on a trajectory towards rock bottom. Indeed, a new life seemed to be taking shape.

I was often sent to Belfast to report from Stormont, in the wake of the Good Friday Agreement, and I'll never forget a Sinn Féin party worker making conversation with me while I waited for a few words with Gerry Adams. I'd already spoken to the Democratic Unionist Party so I was aiming for a little balance.

'You're having a baby?' asked the Sinn Féin member.

Except I mistook the question for a statement and was dumbfounded. 'If the Shinners can promise babies they win my vote,' I thought.

'A baby?' I mumbled.

Unfortunately she immediately backtracked. 'Sorry, it's just the angle I was looking at you. I thought for a minute you were pregnant.'

At that, Gerry Adams was free and she pushed me towards him. I was too preoccupied to ask him a single thorny question.

The permanent job meant I could look for a new home, because it allowed me to apply for a mortgage. My income had been too patchy to do that before. Rathmines was dangerously close to Ranelagh – I needed to move away from the area where Brendan and I had been living, for it pierced me every time I had to pass the house with the nasturtium stained-glass panels and the tree that beckoned to me in the front garden. It wouldn't matter, I promised myself, that I'd no longer see these memento mori. I carried my babies inside my heart.

With the sleeping pills more or less gone – I had weakened and procured more, but the times when I needed to take them were growing infrequent – I returned to writing fiction. I dusted down that novel I'd made a start on and finished it, devising an adaptation of reality to superimpose on the one I still found austere.

Slowly and surely, however, I was starting over. My spirits fluffed themselves out and climbed a few tentative rungs. I went on a date – I left after an hour, despondent at the effort of trying again, but at least the ice had been broken. I managed to buy a house in the suburbs, near the coast, and moved in and painted my living room. I had seagulls to look at now, instead of telegraph wires. My brothers and sister pitched up to visit me, bringing their children, and I smiled to see them gather the apples that fell from the tree in my garden, race each other along the length of my hallway and slip into my bed at night for stories and midnight feasts.

Babies continued to be born to other people, to friends and relatives, and I would buy them gifts. Blankets or jewellery, books or photo frames – but never clothes. I could not bear to walk into a shop and handle diminutive ruched frocks or fleecy pyjamas with teddy bears printed on the material. (I still can't, all these years later. I avert my eyes and scurry past if I glimpse them in a department store. Who would believe how the sight of a minuscule baby sock, a ruffle of lace at its cuff, could shred your composure?)

I had good days and bad days. I learned how depression can swamp a person, descending in a heavy blanket that suffocates. You're prone beneath it, winded by the pain of it. But it's unlike a physical pain in a leg or the stomach that can be isolated and contained – this pain is crushing your entire body. I tried to keep busy. Sometimes I felt angry. Or self-pitying. Or victimized. There were times I wanted to scream aloud – when elderly relations would say, 'If a baby never makes you laugh, it will never make you cry either.' They meant well, but it was a struggle not to round on them. 'I'd risk the tears,' I wanted to tell them, 'I'd take my chances.'

I never did.

I seemed to function adequately, going to work and coming home again, but I knew periods of suffocating desolation even two years later. Once I finished a shift at the *Irish Independent* and was on the DART commuter train home. It was about 10.30 p.m. Instead of disembarking at the Salthill and Monkstown stop, near where I lived, I felt a compulsion to stay on until the end of the line and spend the night in the carriage. Perhaps if I curled myself into a corner railway staff wouldn't notice me. I lacked the emotional resilience to walk home to my empty house and eat a solitary supper. But I hurled myself out at the stop after mine because – far gone as I was – I could still recognize despair and where it might lead, unchecked.

I remembered family birthdays, made cinema visits with friends, had the appearance of someone putting the past behind them. But I wasn't engaging with life – my heart remained hollow.

For a long time, I felt I was being swept about on a current. Finally it dawned on me that it's not what an indifferent fate lobs your way that matters, but how you respond to it. That's all you can control. It was up to me whether I sank or swam, whether I judged life worth living or not. I could embrace a childless existence but it did not have to be a child-free one.

And then something magical happened: I had my first book published. *Three Wise Men* appeared in bookshops in December 2000, two years after my separation agreement was signed. I walked into a shop and stood there, gazing at my novel with its red and gold cover on the bestseller shelves, where it spent nine weeks, and I felt something shift inside my chest. It was a sensation so alien it took me a while to decipher it. This was an emotion I never expected to experience again. It was joy.

Chapter 22

I started writing fiction as a diversion, hiding inside imaginary worlds. But what was envisaged as an escape developed into an end in itself. My books helped me re-engage with life. However, grateful though I was for the consolation of fiction – the distraction of it, the semblance of a purpose it lent me – I was dogged by a conundrum for which I had no answer. What was my function in life if not to reproduce?

People with children don't have to field questions about how they fill their days and whether such activity is meaningful, they're too busy raising their babies. Teaching them how to crawl, speak, behave. I watched my sister-in-law, Julie, encouraging her five-month-old daughter, Sophie, to roll over from her back onto her tummy, and marvelled at the spectacle. Such a fantastic gift, it must be, to show another human being how to do absolutely everything. How to put one foot in front of the other so they're walking. How to press their lips against each other so the word Mama emerges. How to kick their arms and legs and swim.

'Show your aunt how you can clap your hands,' Julie exhorted her baby a couple of months later. For a while Sophie baited us, pretending impassivity. 'If you're happy and you know it clap your hands,' we sang, trying to persuade her to perform – and then unexpectedly she did it, crowing over her achievement. See? I've learned coordination!

In the aftermath of my acceptance of infertility – no, not acceptance, that didn't come for years. In the aftermath of my resignation about infertility, I pondered how to pass my time. This commodity, which is in short supply for parents, especially of young children, gaped towards infinity for me. How would I while away the hours? Where would I find zest or pleasure in anything again?

There'd be work, of course. I knew I could never become a workaholic, though, even in the interests of withdrawal from life. So after work, what then? What of the evenings and weekends and holidays? Well, then I'd write, and maybe some of what I scribbled would see the light of day in more books.

It seemed impossible to me that I'd ever be with another man. I prepared myself to become a spinster such as those that have all but died out now, who lost their sweetheart in the First World War, remaining true to his sepia-tinted memory. I felt they had made a better bargain than me, for theirs was love interrupted, not love cancelled. Yes, I'd be a spinster. Except, and my melodrama was pierced by a stray giggle, could a woman who'd worked her way through a brace of husbands ever define herself as a spinster?

It seemed that my babies were to be my nieces and nephews and the children of friends. And so it has turned out. I'm fortunate in the generosity of the women in my circle, who let me share their wee ones. I was there the first time Christopher dressed up for Hallowe'en as some gruesome shlock-horror serial killer and Clodagh went to the pantomime – like all the other little girls, she had to have a light-up wand and tiara in the interval. I held Sarah's baby Amy-Rose when she'd barely left the birthing pool, and Imelda's daughter Derinn when she measured her age in single hours. Suzanne let me be godmother to copper-haired Matthew. I was there to see my youngest niece Sophie, the baby of the family, assess the feeling of wind on her cheeks, the first time she was pushed in a baby swing in the park. I watched her weigh up this unfamiliar sensation and then laugh, tickled by it. I looked on as she considered the ritual whereby her mother held her at the top of a slide and skimmed her down to the bottom. She puckered her lips, gauging this strange activity, and finally smiled, sanctioning it.

I feel grateful that I can enjoy Sophie and other babies now. Sophie, who opens her mouth for the chocolate buttons I pop in, squawking complaints, peacock imperious, at any delay; who wriggles in my arms if I hold her too close; who clings to my forefingers like a limpet to lever herself to her feet; who abandons me without scruple when her Daddy comes home from work, as is his due.

Once the pleasure was conditional. I remember driving to a hospital with a present for a friend who had just given birth and sitting in the car park for half an hour, watching raindrops detonate against my windscreen. Pretending to be engrossed by them. Anything to deflect the moment when I'd have to go inside the labour ward and admire eight pounds of perfection, smiling until my jaw throbbed. But she was my friend and I knew I couldn't cloud her hour of maternal triumph with grudging admiration. Nor could I make her feel guilty that she'd been chosen and I hadn't.

So I smiled and asked how long she'd spent in labour, how much the baby weighed and what she was to be called; sparring manoeuvres, until finally I'd danced around on the sidelines long enough and could bring myself to lean into the scrunched-up face in the crook of her arm, eyes fastening onto that yawning, burping vision of paradise ungained.

Those days are gone. It's unadulterated pleasure, now, to hold someone's milk-breathed infant.

Mostly they're enough for me, these other children linked to me by blood or friendship. Mostly, but not always. For a long time I thought I was well provided for and fancied I had finally come to terms with my childlessness. Recently, however, I found myself fluctuating. Was it too late to have another crack at IVF? Could I bear to undergo it again? Was I strong enough, either emotionally or physically? How would it affect my reconstructed life if it failed?

What sparked my reconsideration was spending time with Sophie. My heart sang when she burrowed into my shoulder with a spontaneous hug one day and her mother said, 'Sophie's only done that for her mum and dad before.' Being with Sophie was the silver lining lightening a clouded time. I was staying with her parents, my brother, Conor, and his wife, Julie, as the family converged on Omagh to help care for my father, Frank, during his last months of life. Although a lifelong non-smoker, he was sinking into a lingering death from fibroids on the lungs, which meant he hacked and toiled for every breath.

It was a bleak time for the family, trying to make our father as comfortable as possible and nursing him at home where he wanted to be. But Sophie made it bearable for me. I'd carry her into Daddy's room, lilt a fairy reel and she'd jiggle on the duvet and we'd all say, 'She's doing her Irish dancing for her grandad.' We knew – as he did – that he wouldn't live to see her walk, let alone dance, but he enjoyed her in a *carpe diem* spirit. A baby's smile can keep death at bay for a time and Sophie was not a child who rationed them out or had to be cajoled to part with one.

I cuddled her warm, soft body, loath to set her down, and her mother had to prise her off me. Each week I noticed how she was growing heavier and her body longer, so that odd limbs spilled from my arms. I was always suggesting Julie should go off shopping while I minded Sophie, or recommending her and Conor to have a night out – I did it so regularly that they joked about me kidnapping their daughter. Once I dreamed they went to the cinema and just never came back so I kept her. Nothing terrible happened, there was no accident or anything, they just . . . ceased to exist. I was riddled with shame when I woke up, but baby hunger is merciless.

Sometimes I'd creep into Sophie's room at night and listen to her breathing. I'd watch her sleep, two hands clutching each another as though she nodded off in an act of imprecation, teething spots of pink on her cheeks, like a china doll. And I was awed by her. She'd smile when she saw me in the morning. Once, after I'd been away for a week and returned, she held out her arms to me. Imagine having that every day. Do mothers ever grow blasé about it?

In her grandma's house I push forward the hands on the cuckoo clock, although I know I shouldn't because it might break the mechanism, so the bird will strike the hour. Then Sophie's round, wondering face registers delight. She's fascinated by the clock, brought by me from Munich a quarter of a century ago, and stares at it long after the mechanical bird has retreated. It's the first object her eyes seek out every time she's carried into this room. I whisper into her rosy eardrum that I'll buy her one for a wedding present.

One evening I was balanced on the saddle-board of her bedroom door watching her, when she woke. I raced in, ostensibly so she wouldn't disturb my brother, who was having an early night, but really so that I could be the first to hold her. My arms yearned to carry her. I sang her the lullaby I used to sing to my unborn babies.

> *Hush little baby, don't say a word,*
> *Papa's going to buy you a mocking bird,*
> *And if that mocking bird won't sing,*
> *Papa's going to buy you a diamond ring.*

I'd last crooned it for those babies I hadn't manage to keep alive inside my body, but was glad to have the chance to do it again anyway. I paced the nursery as Sophie struggled against sleep, her eyelids closing and then inching open, and I felt at one with mothers everywhere. Even though I knew I was on borrowed time. There was a pain in my lower back from Sophie's weight and I revelled in it. The following day I wanted to go about telling people, 'I have a dreadful back-ache from nursing Sophie, she just wouldn't go back to sleep last night.' I'd shake my head indulgently about it, the way I'd seen mothers do.

So it was Sophie who set me thinking, six years after my last IVF cycle, could I risk it again? Should I even dare the attempt?

Part of me weighed the consequences of success: I might never write another book, as I conducted a love affair with my baby. (I no longer imagined I'd produce two or three children. One would be a treasure trove.) 'Agreed,' I thought, 'even if there are no more books, it will be a fair trade.'

Suddenly I realized I was presuming success again. The Achilles' heel that had left me exposed before: my inability to countenance failure.

But failure would have to be factored into the equation if I undertook it. I turned to the Internet and read that delivery rates per IVF cycle are only 15 per cent as a woman's fortieth birthday approaches, never mind when it's past. I paused: so my chances were in freefall. But it does work: I know someone who gave birth to a gorgeous son in her early forties after sustained, courageous attempts. He illuminates her life.

Just when you think it's safe to go back in the water . . . just when you imagine you're over the baby hunger, it nibbles again.

But it was more manageable now. I shared some sense of Sophie's parents' worry when she was unwell, but didn't experience their atavistic fear. I was better at joining them in their gratification: look how strong she is, she hauled herself onto her feet; look how cultured she is, she's keeping time to the music; look how determined she is, she almost managed to wriggle out of her baby seat; look how clever she is, she threw away her bread stick when she saw chocolate. I revelled in every tooth she cut, every ounce she gained, every obstacle she overcame in her infant's exploration of this vast, peculiar world, as though she were my daughter. Well, almost. 'That's worth something,' I reminded myself. 'Many childless women don't have as much.'

But was it enough? I assessed the risks of taking another chance on the IVF lottery. I hesitated. You see, I was afraid. Afraid of failure, naturally, but afraid, too, of the way it might destabilize my painstakingly renovated life. I didn't know if I had the internal resources to manage another recovery, I suspected I might fold and submit to my former bedfellow, despair. So I dithered for a time.

I had a lovely, supportive boyfriend – the decision to embrace spinsterhood hadn't lasted, nor had the subsequent urge to hie me to a nunnery (not that they'd have wanted me) – and I spoke to him about it.

'How would you feel if I had another cycle of IVF?' I scrutinized his expression to gauge his response. Not just the words but the emotions underpinning them.

He didn't hesitate. 'I'd be worried for you but if it's what you really want, then I'll support you all the way.'

It was exactly the right answer. But it didn't help me to reach a decision.

I considered adoption too. The world was full of unwanted babies, why didn't I find one and offer it a loving home?

Wouldn't that be a better use of my time and effort than embarking on another cycle of IVF? Questions battered my brain but I had no answers.

There is a fault line at infertility's core whereby a rift can develop between men and women. With a man the possibility of a child is cerebral, but with a woman it's both physical and emotional. Her heart yokes itself to the idea – even when the baby is no more than an aspiration, it has the capacity to rule her life. It occupies no basis in fact for a man until it cries and he can carry it in his arms, but it is real to a woman from the moment she attempts to conceive. My babies were always real to me. I could smell them, hear them, all but touch them.

Someone said to me once about IVF, 'What an odd way to try to have a child.' I never felt that, I was simply relieved it existed as an option. I was determined not to accept my infertility docilely. I didn't regard it as medical science usurping God's role, as some critics do, I didn't see it as unnatural. It was as natural as the doctors could make it. Granted, most couples who decide to have a baby probably go out for dinner and then take a crack at it, or open a bottle of wine to facilitate relaxation. It's true that there's nothing natural about sperm and egg being introduced by a third party inside a surgical dish, instead of chancing upon one another within a woman's body. With IVF, those have-a-go-heroes are led by the hand to the woman's eggs, just as I once fantasized. But as soon as embryos are formed they're returned to the womb. The men and women in white coats step aside. The integrity of the procedure remains intact; it still hinges on the synthesis between a woman's egg and a man's sperm, not genetic engineering. And then the doctors let nature take its course.

A pattern of failed IVF cycles hacks lumps out of a woman's emotional stability, her ability to rationalize, her peace of mind. Years later I grasped why I had instinctively resisted the idea of continuing to have IVF treatment. Why I had said no to a fourth cycle with Brendan and why I was irresolute when the idea occurred to me to attempt another. IVF exacted an exorbitant price, in my case. It borrowed my soul and I had to fight tooth and nail to reclaim it.

If a couple have a child already they can teach themselves survival for its sake. But surviving for your own sake alone requires a degree of self-love, and your store of it has been ground into dust. You despise your puny body and your punier ability to control your insistent need. You view yourself as worthless – if you had any intrinsic value, you would not have racked up one failure after another.

It can take the longest time to realize that failing doesn't make you a failure. It makes you someone who cared enough to try.

Did I have the courage to try again? Maybe, older though I was – definitely an elderly primigravida this time – I had mastered the serenity thing. Or was I fooling myself, telling my heart what it wanted to hear . . . ? Suddenly newspapers seemed to be full of advertisements for fertility clinics. I tore out one for a clinic in Barbados and left it on my bedside table, looking at it each morning, wondering if a sunny climate would plump out my spirits and enhance my chances. I allowed the question of whether to risk IVF again to lodge in my heart and carried it about with me for a time.

Then one morning I awoke and the answer was there. No lightning bolt, no burning bush, no Damascene intervention. I simply knew it for certain and the knowledge welled through me.

There was no going back.

Once I had been fired up by a passion so overwhelming that it threatened to define me. But I didn't feel the need to be a mother any longer in that former, compulsive way – there were flashes of it but they didn't consume me. It was an echo from the past, one that still had the power to stir me, to cause me to re-evaluate my life and wonder if it was enough.

Was it? I didn't know for sure. But this much I did know. Tilting at windmills was part of what life was about but so, too, was acceptance. Not acquiescence, never acquiescence, but bowing to forces that could not be changed. I'd served my time tilting at windmills, at least this version. So now I was hoping for acceptance – and the regular loan of my nieces and nephews. Especially the babies with their starfish hands.

Chapter 23

My greatest regret . . . I know we're not supposed to have regrets – we lionize people who dispense with them, but this one I do feel. My greatest regret is that the marriage disintegrated so utterly that there is no relationship between Brendan and me today. It makes limited sense from the perspective of the immediate aftermath, when we were both hurting intensely. But I would have liked us to reach a civilized plateau in time. We endured a lot together and, although we failed, it was a joint failure.

Four years after we formally separated, it was possible for us to divorce under Irish law and proceedings took their course. Even after all the time that had elapsed, I found it sad that the adventure we had embarked on so joyously was reduced to exchanges of letters between lawyers. Yet, I wondered, what could it matter: by now we were severed irrevocably and it was sensible to finalize the ending of our relationship. What really bruised, it eventually dawned on me, was the sense that by taking this final step to close the book on our shared history, we were also turning our backs on those embryo babies that were the closest we came to having the family we wanted so much.

I had thought of Brendan sporadically in the intervening years and had trusted, simply, that life was treating him with kindness. I didn't imagine we could ever be friends, but I felt no ill-will towards him – quite the reverse – and I hoped he wished me well too. The period of marriage break-up is inevitably tumultuous but in the aftermath comes the calm of reflection, when I had started to feel sympathy for his plight – and hoped he might have experienced something similar for me.

I had seen him only three times since the separation agreement had been signed. Once when I had called to the house to collect a few items of furniture left there, an exercise that had ended badly, as it was almost guaranteed to do; once more, some months later, at a colleague's leaving do in a pub, when we had nodded at each other in a distant manner. I had set down my drink and had left immediately afterwards, feeling uncomfortable.

Years later, shortly before Christmas, I was in the city centre laden down with shopping bags, and I glanced across to the other side of the street. A familiar man was standing there. Brendan looked the same, apart from a little more grey in his hair. I hesitated, wondering whether I should go across. 'If he looks up I'll do it,' I decided. 'Just to wish him season's greetings.' But he extracted a mobile phone from his pocket and, engrossed in making a call, didn't notice me. I took it as a sign. 'Merry Christmas, Brendan,' I murmured, and went on my way.

It would be another year before the divorce was granted, in January 2004. Just over nine years since our wedding day and five and a half years since the marriage had imploded.

It brought back memories, naturally. Why had Brendan chosen me, all those years previously, and why had I chosen him? Struggling to recall the pair that had been us in the days before infertility, I rang a friend who had known us both – one of the Covent Garden set. 'He was besotted by you,' she reminisced. 'He was single-minded about pursuing you.'

I wondered at this. Then I summoned up one of our early days together, when we were still at the falling in love stage. It was a Sunday afternoon and we happened upon an Italian festival in north London, where a statue of the Virgin Mary was carried on a float and exuberant Italians pressed glasses of *vino rosso* on us. *Joie de vivre* laced the air, strangers laughed and included us in their celebration, and I looked at Brendan and thought, 'This could work between us.' As the divorce approached I tried to evoke that day, instead of those other ones peppered with arguments or sullen silences. When marriages curdle, the glad times become obscured – it helps to remember they existed.

My solicitor told me I didn't need to be present for the divorce but I debated going anyway, feeling it might be my last chance to salvage some remnant of the common purpose that had once united us. I could walk up to Brendan at the end of the court proceedings and shake his hand, for the sake of those ten babies who didn't survive. 'The best of luck to you,' I'd say, looking him in the eye, and leave it at that.

In the end the decision was taken out of my hands, as so many of the momentous ones often are. I wasn't in Dublin that day, I had to be in Omagh. My father had only a few weeks left to live and we were waiting for the inevitable. I sat on the edge of his bed reading the newspaper to him ('How about some sports news now, instead of all that world news. Any GAA fixtures?' he asked). But my mind was more than a hundred miles away in a courtroom.

Later that Friday afternoon my solicitor telephoned to tell me I was divorced. I felt no rush of celebration, just a sense of termination. And then something else: a faint undercurrent of bamboozlement that my marriage had failed. Even so many years later, I was conscious of promise squandered. 'Throw a divorce party,' urged friends, but I could not bring myself to do that. I understand why some people might, but with me it struck a triumphalist and therefore jarring note. There is nothing to fete in the confirmation of failure.

I'd anticipated the divorce for some time, yet when the day dawned it brought a sense of anti-climax with it. A divorce is sad as well as liberating. The granting of a decree absolute occupies an uneasy place at the interface between life as a separated woman and life as a divorcée. Even when you want to be divorced, you are obliged to acknowledge the sour aroma of failure – and your own contribution to it. Celebrate such a state of affairs? I think not. The only cause for celebration was our survival. It came at a price, of course, and that price was the marriage.

But I had regained my equilibrium. Life reclaimed me.

My little niece Aoife goes around broadcasting, 'My Mum shares us with my aunt because she can't have children.'

At first I was disconcerted at this public statement, delivered in her piping tones, but then I thought, 'She's right. I am allowed to share children: not just her and her brother Justin, but all my other nieces and nephews. The offer is there, from their parents – it's down to me how far I want to avail myself of it.'

So I learned to share other people's children. Sharing them is second-best, of course, but it's worthwhile still, believe me.

I try to remember that parenthood is a gift, not a right. I had to teach myself to understand that I had no automatic claim on motherhood. I could wish for it, as I might long for Slavic cheekbones or a facility with languages, but I could not demand it. This was a lesson that took time to penetrate, for it relies on logic outweighing the clamour of emotion. Babies demand an emotional response. With their Buddha eyes and accordion chins, they bypass every intellectual response and squeeze your heart, enslaving you with a flirtatious look.

They drool on your silk shirt and you beam your indulgence. They chew your hair, blow raspberries, scratch your face with their needle-point nails and defecate lustily, to the accompaniment of unmistakable facial expressions. And what do you do? Press your lips against the satin of their skin and murmur endearments. Babies have power over people; God knows, they have power over me. I suspect they always will.

People ask me sometimes, 'Is it all right now? Are you over it?' They want me to say I've conquered the baby hunger. But there's no antidote except time – even then, it's a palliative as opposed to a remedy. The truth is that it can never be eradicated. I'll never be over it. I don't think I even want to be, because that might mean I am no longer moved by the curve of a cheek nestled against its mother's shoulder. Or by ten teeny toes that have never been crammed into shoes. Or by a podgy hand clinging to my shirt or hair, its atavistic urge to hold on to me just as mine is to hold on to it. I'm lucky, I can still bear to be around babies. At times it aches – but it aches more not to be near them. So I'll take the rush of joy when a baby unleashes its gummy smile on me, even if, occasionally, it's the forerunner to a stab of loss. You cannot allow disappointment to taint your life. That landscape of failure has to be left behind, whether you run from it, walk from it, crawl from it.

My nieces and nephews helped nudge me from mine. Also my life took an unexpected detour and books occupy the space where children might have been. As compensations go, they rank as special; I'm grateful to say they are a consolation. There are days when I continue to regard myself as defective, although I know it is self-indulgent and leads to self-pity. But such times are increasingly rare.

Family groups continue to mesmerize me. I watch them in all their glorious ordinariness: the straggling youngsters poking sticks at excitingly mysterious objects, the harassed mothers trying to have eyes in the backs of their heads, the laden-down fathers with buggies and baby slings and discarded coats. My eyes dart between mother and father: do they exist as separate entities for each other, I ponder, or have they become Mammy and Daddy? I glimpse a tiny female forehead reproduced from a large male one, or see a mother's caramel curls on her infant son's head, and I marvel how anyone can ever tire of observing themselves reproduced in and on another human being.

I mentioned how I thought I would explode with gratitude when my sister, Tonia, commented, quite casually, 'Aoife has your nose.' Perhaps I wasn't facing extinction after all. If my nose could survive, maybe something else will too. This nose that mirrors mine required no skill or virtue on my part, it was an arbitrary quirk of genetic fingerprinting. Yet how reassuring to know it's out there.

How can parents, I deliberated, not bear to stare fixedly at the results of their handiwork – this unsystematic *mélange* of their features and characteristics? Then I noticed how my brother gazed at his baby daughter, Sophie, how he and his wife hung over her crib to tuck her in at night, and I realized, 'That's what new parents do. They gape at the mind-boggling miracle of being able to produce life, and at this scrap of insistent demands that has turned them from a couple into a family.'

I can never be the mother figure in one of those family groups but I remind myself that I feature in other versions of the family. I am a daughter, a sister, an aunt, a niece, a godmother. Family eddies around me – I am not at the epicentre of it, as I would be if I were a mother, but I have a place in the unit. Families need sisters and aunts and all those other permutations of relationships. They were never intended to function as self-contained units, but were designed for inclusiveness.

'Aoife's getting the hang of reading at last,' my sister tells me, eager to share her pride.

'Aoife's getting the hang of reading at last,' I tell my boyfriend David, eager to share my pride.

'I knew she would, she's bright as a button,' David replies, sharing my pride.

See how families absorb anyone who's willing to participate in them?

There's something else about Aoife, though; she's an IVF baby. So it does work sometimes, this long-shot treatment – she's the living proof. We tend to forget about it in the family, we don't look at her and say, 'There's our miracle baby.' She's just a normal little girl who holds her nose when she lifts her older brother's trainers, believes I have fairies in my garden (she leaves them letters and I write back), is thrilled at losing her milk teeth, executes heart-stopping tumbles on the playground climbing frame and thinks she might like to be my housekeeper when she's quite a big girl, maybe eleven or twelve. But without IVF we wouldn't have Aoife – without IVF many families would lack their Aoifes. Random it may be, but in its absence there'd be more hollow hearts than mine.

I was not meant to be a mother – finally I can accept that. I don't know why it should be so and I have no expectations, as I once did, that I'll unravel the mystery some day. Still, I have understood the lesson that wanting is no guarantee of success, regardless of how ardent the longing might be. It was the last message that penetrated, in the wake of my obsession, and it was the one that took the longest to sink in. I thought if I wanted something desperately enough, pursued it doggedly, sooner or later it would be mine. How wrong I was.

Was it ever a trace of vanity that set me on this path, I quizzed myself? Vanity would be a reason for failure – setting my heart on a mini-me. But it was about need, primeval, insistent need. I've come close to appreciating what prompts women to snatch babies. Lowering your face to the infant's, inserting an index finger into that minute fist and watching its prehensile instinct to latch on, realizing you could make this baby yours simply by feeding and caring for it, knowing it would love you like a mother because it would have the habit of it.

I contemplate my IVF babies from time to time. The one I dwell on most is my finger-joint child. That little boy, as my fancy dubs him, who was trapped inside a fallopian tube and had to be cut out. I estimate his age, each summer, when he would have celebrated his birthday. This year he'd be turning eight. Probably starting to be dubious about Santa Claus's existence, maybe reaching up to my shoulder, no doubt surgically attached to his Gameboy. I can chart his stages by mentally positioning him between my nephew, Christopher, and my niece, Clodagh. I measure him against them and think, 'Oh, so now he'd be riding a bicycle without stabilizers.'

Oh yes, I can understand the instinct to lift a baby into your arms and start walking. Morality? It doesn't enter the equation when this dependent being nestles against you. A child in your arms is the only morality in the grip of baby hunger. The overwhelming majority of us don't do this, of course, and the reason is simple. We know if we can feel a sudden upsurge of emotion for a stranger, then its mother must love it a hundred thousand times more. And so we give back the baby, avert our eyes from its siren gaze, withdraw from that scent of powdered warmth. 'He's lovely,' we mumble, and force ourselves to turn away.

★

For several years I had a tendency to search for meaning, to ask myself 'Why am I being punished?' as though someone made a deliberate decision to leave me childless. Instead of it being a random act. My infertility was medically explicable but emotionally inexplicable and it shredded me. I wanted a reason. Then I read this: Love the life you have, not the life you think you should have. And I felt an eruption of relief because it made such perfect sense. So I try to do that. It's one of my favourite nuggets of advice. I copied it out in giant letters and pinned it to my notice-board. It doesn't mean I've completely abandoned the 'if-only' gripe – I'm still susceptible to it; sometimes it rears up at me when I least expect it. But it happens less often.

Occasionally I look at children in the street holding their parents' hands, chattering excitedly, and wonder, 'Is that what my son or daughter would have looked like? Could I have had a little girl with a ponytail poking up from the top of her head like Pebbles from the Flintstones? Or a toddler with that John Wayne walk all tots seem to have? Or a small boy leaping from rock to rock along the seafront, turning to me for praise when he manages a clear run?' But sometimes, too, I consider the harassed expressions on parents' faces – especially in supermarkets when they're distracted from shopping lists by a child's whine – and I realize there are advantages to being childless. There's freedom in it. Not everyone has to have children – some choose not to, it doesn't suit everybody. It's just that I never had the choice.

There's a question I'm sometimes asked: would I still undergo IVF, knowing what I know now? That it would make a wasteland of my life and there would be times when I did not see how I could possibly survive the grief? The answer is yes, because I believe it's crucial to try. Misery alone does not kill us, although we imagine it can. It's essential to pursue what we want, regardless of the odds stacked against us. To dare, because at least by daring we have a chance of winning. The only obstacle is our own lack of hope.

Life experiences change a person. I don't think anyone needs pain in their life to make them a more rounded individual, but it can mould them into a more empathic one. So perhaps my baby wilderness has offered me that gift. And I might not now have this writer's life, which I'm grateful for, if I had a child. My financial freedom to choose such a way of living may have been compromised with a child to support. Other women manage to combine both – I've always loved author Nuala O'Faolain's description of Mary Lavin's *modus operandi*, writing in bed early in the morning, leaning her pages on a breadboard, while her children slept – but I may not be one of those women who can juggle. Perhaps children would sap any shoots of creativity I have, although I suspect I'd surrender them voluntarily. Preferring to bake fairy cakes with my little ones than to toil over a sentence. As compensations go, books with my name on their spine rank as special. But would I swap them for a baby?

In a heartbeat.

There's an African fertility doll who watches me in the study where I work. She delights me, when I pause to catch her eye, with her bulging stomach and prominent bosoms; her hair in corn rows and a necklace dangling from her neck. I bought her after my marriage break-up, while visiting my sister and her family in The Gambia – she came from the kiln of my nephew Justin's pottery teacher, a genial man with a smile that could power an electricity generator.

At this stage I realized I would never become a mother, but nevertheless I found myself drawn to the fertility doll.

'There's more than one kind of fertility,' said the potter, flashing those binary tiers of ivory at me.

'He's right,' I thought, and rooted out my purse.

Even if I was succumbing to a sales pitch, I decided it could not override the intrinsic truth of his remark. So she travelled back to Dublin in my hand luggage with me. I call her Bella, and I stroke her head when I start a new piece of work. For luck, and for a share of her bountiful fecundity in the creative process. There's more than one kind of fertility.

Looking back, it's tempting to dissociate myself from the narrative of my own life and to think that all this happened to a different person. And perhaps it did, in some measure, because I was a different person then. I was the pre-disappointment Martina Devlin. Now I know life can proffer wonderful gifts but withhold others, and you can't choose which to receive and which will pass you by. That pre-disappointment version of me was sunnier than the present-day one, more optimistic that she could formulate a life plan and it would unfold as she specified.

She was weaker, however. She had no experience of adversity and didn't know whether she was capable of withstanding it; and, even if she could, whether self-pitying bitterness would accompany survival. She was less kind, too, for unhappiness teaches the value of compassion.

At least I still have my scars, even if they've paled to silver. My body wears the proof of what it tried to do. I gaze at them in the bath, tracing their indentations: the laparoscopy jags, the ectopic slash. My attitude to them has softened over the years – once I cringed from them but now I see them as badges, not of honour, exactly, but of trying. They've been through a lot with me. I've earned them and we're indivisible now, my scars and me.

After a time I realized something that seemed to ease the shadows. I discovered that shade allows you to appreciate the light and the experience of pain helps you value joy. So my years of searching for motherhood have been enlightening. I tell myself, hoping to convince – from repetition, if nothing else – that no lesson worth learning in life comes easy. We remember best the messages accompanied by bruises. Misfortune can be arbitrary, but so can good fortune, as random as infertility. Bruises heal eventually, even emotional ones. My heart did, so did my self-esteem. When my life plan didn't work out I drew up a new one – not better, just different.

Sometimes happiness catches me unawares and, when it sneaks up on me, I no longer take it for granted as I once did.

Once, minding my niece Aoife, then five, she said, 'You'd make a lovely kind Mum.'

I bathed in the glow for a few moments, then replied, 'Can't I make a lovely kind aunt instead?'

'Oh yes,' she agreed hurriedly, 'I like you better as an aunt. Mums have to be cross sometimes but aunts don't. Can I stay up really, really late tonight?'

I laughed and conceded an extended bedtime, but afterwards I mulled over our conversation.

It's true that I can never be a mother. But I can be an aunt, a godmother, a friend to children. I slip their nicknames and birthdays into my novels, their pets, dolls, habits and sayings. We giggle together about it afterwards. 'There's a baby called Clodagh in my aunt's new book, she's only ten months old and she can't walk yet.' My young niece Clodagh preened a little in front of her teacher.

I have another home now, nearer the sea, filled with framed

photographs of people who love me, and whom I love in turn; I have a spare room that's often occupied by members of my family; I have a life that pleases me in more ways than I ever envisaged; I have learned to love the life I have, not the life I think I should have. Hollow hearts can plump up again. Mine did.

Bodies never cease to amaze me. I find it odd that I still feel occasional twinges on the missing tube side of my body, the place where my ectopic baby lived for a few moments in time. The finger-joint baby I think of whenever I see nasturtiums.

I always liked nasturtiums, but I resisted growing any after the Ranelagh days because their resonance was bitter-sweet. Last autumn I finally decided the time had come to plant some in the garden of my new house. I gathered the seeds from my parents' garden in Omagh and brought them to Dublin, digging them into the moist, crumbly soil. Then quite recently, as I tapped at my computer keyboard, eyes straying towards the greenery beyond the window facing me, I remembered something. Something that made my breath catch and my fingers mis-type. The flowers in Omagh were grown from seeds produced by nasturtiums that had bloomed in the Ranelagh house. The cycle of life had returned them to me. These new nasturtiums loop back to a crop that lived where and when my ectopic baby lived, the small boy I mourned most, of all my unborn children. It felt like a gift from my baby. Emotion welled through me at the notion – not the pain of loss, as so often in the past, but gratitude.

Some day I'd like to take a stab at writing a children's book. For the ones I never gave birth to, for the ten embryos I loved – still love, can't forget and don't want to – and for those other children who flit in and out of my life. That's a worthwhile ambition. You see, little by little I've learned to do something regarded as old-fashioned now: I listened to my mother. I looked at my life and tallied up the positives – I am an aunt and a godmother, my friends have babies who wander through my house, there are ways to have children in your life if you choose to accept that consolation.

So I count my blessings, as my wise, loving mother advised, and in enumerating them I am struck by this. Their quantity.

Epilogue

I had many reservations about laying bare my IVF history. Among them was the instinct towards privacy; a reluctance to analyse and dissect the past; my fear of always being tarred as the woman who can't have children. Indeed, that hesitation has been realized. At a literary conference, when the topic for discussion was the influence of childhood places on the geography of fiction, a man approached me afterwards.

'You're that girl who can't have children, aren't you?' he observed. I nodded, at a loss for words. It's true, I am that person. But that's only one constituent in my parts, other experiences have shaped me too.

I imagined I could speak about infertility and IVF for a day or two and then drop the subject. But I've been astonished by the response to the truncated version of my story that's been revealed, prior to writing this book. By the confidences it has elicited. A former neighbour turned up on my doorstep and poured out his own tale of disappointment that he and his wife had not been blessed with children. People assumed they were too beguiled by their foreign holidays and new cars to make space for babies in their lives. These material compensations were simply substitutes, however. And relatively inadequate ones. I was the first person, apart from his wife, to whom he'd opened up about it, and he described it as a relief.

I made the decision to speak about my infertility because I was concerned that IVF is perceived as the universal panacea. We have blind faith in modern medicine dispelling all woes. I know I had. We expect this every time we place ourselves in the hands of those all-singing, all-dancing miracle-workers, the doctors. I heard women talk about leaving childbearing until later in life, after their careers were established and suitable homes bought, joking about fertility treatment picking up the slack. Women tend to regard fertility treatment as their safety net. But it doesn't matter how high your financial or emotional investment in it, how much angst you go through or how desperately you want a baby, it's still a lottery. It works for some women, I'm glad to say, but they're in the minority.

Couples should understand that two people pursue IVF: the one undergoing treatment and the one at his partner's side, perhaps promising her happily ever afters, even if he believes he's lying through his teeth. It doesn't have to be true: *just say the words and ease me past the next injection.*

Every couple has its own way of communicating, of dealing with difficulties, but I think the key for those undergoing IVF is to try and remember the love that united them in the first place. The treatment is demanding and exhausting, and all you can do is to keep telling one another how deeply you care about each other, how much you mean to each other, and how you would change nothing about each other – least of all the imperfection that has brought you to this crossroads. Sometimes it's not easy to be with a woman undergoing IVF. Her pumped-up hormone levels mean her emotions can be volatile. It's a challenging time for a relationship and couples considering IVF need to realize that even a woman who was previously a rock of sense may become temperamental and unreasonable, while her partner may feel utterly helpless or frustrated in the face of that. All you can do is remember the love. If you manage that, then you'll make it through the IVF minefield – irrespective of the outcome.

A man told me recently, while he and his wife were preparing for IVF, that these were the words he intended to use to help her through. 'It's only a body,' he'd say, 'don't get upset if it isn't doing what you want it to – that's unimportant. You're what's important. Our love for each other is what's important.' I could have hugged him for working out this deceptively simple formula. It's such a healthy attitude, the sort of stance every couple embarking on IVF should strive towards.

I could think of dozens of reasons not to write this book when I was first approached to do it, and just one to persevere. But that single reason was so compelling that it overrode my vacillation. I hoped my story might reach out to other couples grappling with the incomprehension and loneliness that is infertility. It's a condition that leaves couples, but particularly women, isolated. Everywhere, every day they are confronted by pregnant bellies and baby buggies; they convince themselves nobody can understand their sense of loss. Often they don't even discuss it with their partners, they just bury their grief. Except it never quite fades.

There is a sense in which the infertile are disenfranchised – we mourn the loss of something we've never had, and other people can be dismissive of such a concept. But it is possible to feel the absence of something from your life, to miss it as poignantly as if it were a presence snatched from you. To those of you without children who feel empty or sad, blighted or victimized, ground down or hopeless, I want to say this: your grief is legitimate. But don't let it colonize your life. Acknowledge your loss and then focus on what you have, not what you lack.

★

I bought a bicycle because of you.

A woman sent me this message through a mutual friend.

I was intrigued. She'd heard me on the radio talking about life after childlessness and had realized that wheels keep turning, whether or not she could be a mother again for a second time. So to celebrate, she'd bought a bicycle because she'd always wanted one but had been putting her life on hold. Now she was exploring Dublin on it with her son on the back. I'm smiling to think of it; that was a grand result.

Such incidents made me hope that maybe my story could help people make sense of their own. Or am I back there, trying to find reasons to explain those IVF failures again? It was never intended in that spirit, but perhaps in the process this book has become a way of salvaging something from the wilderness years. Certainly, the hope that my experience might help other people kept me motivated while I wrestled with the pain of remembering, as I committed my history to print. Even if it comforts only one other person with a hollow heart, I'll be satisfied.

Nearly everyone I meet has an IVF connection – a relative, friend or neighbour who has been through it or is about to chance their luck. I'm always struck by how much more frank people are about it now, even in the space of a handful of years. When I was immersed in the treatment there was a feeling that it shouldn't be referred to openly. That it wasn't quite seemly. Shame seemed to be infertility's corollary, an additional burden. Now some people are able to discuss it with their friends and family, which must be a relief, although for others it will always remain an essentially private sorrow.

When an acquaintance volunteers the information that they know someone who's been though IVF, I always pose the same question: were they lucky? Most times the answer is no. Which tends to act as a conversation stopper. There's a shuddering undertone of 'There but for the grace of God go I' from the speaker. Recognition of an epidemic that blights some and spares others – and nobody knows why one was chosen and another passed over. That biblical reverberation again. 'Maybe they'll be lucky next time,' I generally say.

I always trust they might be, although I know how the odds stack up.

I take a moment when I'm alone later to think of that anonymous couple and send them a shower of good wishes. It can't do any harm. At least I'm not advising them to walk barefoot through a dandelion patch in the moonlight (although I still think green is a lucky colour, I can't help it). I'd like everyone who undergoes fertility treatment to have a baby to show for it – they deserve it after handing over their bodies to the doctors. Their hopes, too. They invest everything in the attempt. Of course the miracle doesn't happen for everyone – miracles, by their nature, are rare.

But sometimes some of us get lucky.

Acknowledgements

I was always a science dunce and this is high-tech territory I'm dealing with. So while I've taken pains to make sure all the medical terms and descriptions are accurate, any mistakes that may have sneaked in are entirely my own. I apologize for them.

I would like to thank Professor Robbie Harrison for taking the time to read my manuscript and for his useful pointers. He has recently retired from the HARI unit at the Rotunda Hospital in Dublin and I wish him a long and happy retirement. Actually, while I'm at the gratitude part, I should thank him for having tried to help me have a baby in the first place.

Also due thanks are my sister Tonia Blanchard and her husband Dr Tom Blanchard, for their generosity in giving me permission to refer to their IVF experience.

I'm grateful to Patricia Deevy, my editor, whose marvellously ruthless advice to purge adjectives helped make this a better book. And thanks to all the Penguin Ireland team for their wholehearted support, especially Michael McLoughlin.

I shouldn't forget David Murphy, who listened patiently while I whined about writing it.

As for my mother, Bridie Devlin – she's always self-deprecating about her brain-power, but she's the wise woman who advised me to count my blessings. And wasn't she right?

Thanks to my agent Stephanie Cabot of the Gernert Company, who was so supportive while I wrote *The Hollow Heart*. As was her assistant Jamison Stoltz.

The birth notices on pages 118–19 and 120 are modelled on those in the *Irish Times*'s Saturday column, but they are fictitious. Finally, in order to protect a couple of people who feature in the book, including my former husband, I have changed their names and some identifying details. However the events and individuals are as true to life as I could make them.